Armin Lange

Computer Aided Text-Reconstruction and Transcription

Armin Lange

Computer Aided Text-Reconstruction and Transcription

CATT-Manual

with an Introduction
by
Hermann Lichtenberger

and an Appendix
by
Timothy Doherty

J. C. B. Mohr (Paul Siebeck) Tübingen

Gedruckt mit Unterstützung der Fördergesellschaft der westfälischen Wilhelms-Universität Münster

Die Deutsche Bibliothek – CIP-Einheitsaufnahme

Lange, Armin:
Computer aided text-reconstruction and transcription: CATT-manual / Armin Lange. With an introd. by Hermann Lichtenberger and an app. by Timothy Doherty. – Tübingen: Mohr 1993
ISBN 3-16-146149-5

Typeset by T. Doherty in Münster/Westf.; printed by Gulde-Druck in Tübingen; acid-free paper by Bohnenberger & Cie in Niefern; sewn binding by Heinr. Koch in Tübingen.

Leo Baeck

May 23rd, 1873 – February 2nd, 1956

Acknowledgments

This manual has been made possible only by the help of many many friends, scholars, hard- and software corporations, and institutions whom I would like to take this opportunity to thank.

First of all the software corporations Aldus, Logitech, and Micrografx should be named for providing me with the latest versions of PhotoStyler, FotoTouch, and Picture Publisher. In this context, special thanks must be given to Mr. S. Horst and Mr. R. Zacherl of Aldus Germany for their help. Mr. F. Goeddeker and Mr. F.-J. Plaßmann of the Goeddeker Computer und Zubehör GmbH have always had an open ear for me when information about particular hardware was needed. Scanning of photographs has only been possible due to the kind help of the Computer Center of the Westfälische Wilhelms-Universtät, Münster, especially Dr. H. Pudlatz should be named here. For help in computers, I am also indebted to Prof. Dr. A. Suhl, the computer coordinator of the Faculty of Protestant Theology of the University of Münster.

The editor in chief of the Dead Sea Scrolls, Prof. Dr. E. Tov, has made it possible to check first results of CATT back on the Scrolls themselves, and has given methodological aid in the reconstruction of damaged manuscripts. For further methodological aid in the reconstruction of the Dead Sea Scrolls, thanks must especially be given to Prof. Dr. Dr. H. Stegemann. In this context Prof. Dr. B. Aland and Mr. K. Witte must also be named for helping me in testing the method on fragments of New Testament manuscripts.

The curator of the Shrine of the Book, Prof. Dr. M. Broshi, and Mrs. S. Durocher of the Israel Antiquities Authority gave the permission to publish the photographs of the Dead Sea Scrolls found in this book. Prof. Dr. G. Brooke, Dr. P. Pilhofer, and Dr. A. Steudel tested the manual prior to its publication.

For financial aid, I am indebted to the Gesellschaft zur Förderung der Westfälischen Wilhelms-Universität Münster: it funded a journey to Jerusalem for Prof. Dr. H. Lichtenberger and myself to check the results of CATT back on the original fragments of the Dead Sea Scrolls, and it paid for the typesetting of this book.

Last but not least, all members of the Institutum Judaicum Delitzschianum of the University of Münster must be mentioned: first and foremost its former director Prof. Dr. H. Lichtenberger who helped me in all the ups and downs of the computer aided work on the scrolls and who made this book possible. Mrs. E. Reimann and Mr. Kai Süchting may be mentioned here for all other members of the institute.

As the typesetting and printing of a book are the last steps in the long way of producing books, Mr. Timothy Doherty must be thanked at the end of this long list of helpful people for his everlasting patience in correcting my broken English and his tremendous work in typesetting this book, and Mr. Georg Siebeck of the J. C. B. Mohr Company must be thanked for publishing the book.

There are more people and friends whom I would like to thank, but this list would be endless if all were to be named.

The book is dedicated to Leo Baeck whose fate should not be forgotten, especially in the time of renewing German racism and faschism.

Armin Lange, Münster, June 8th, 1993

Contents

Introduction

In a class on newly published Dead Sea Scrolls, which I held in the winter semester 1991/92 at the University of Münster, Mr. Armin Lange, who is working on his doctoral thesis on the Dead Sea Scrolls, surprised me with a convincing reading of a nearly undecipherable word. Asked how, he showed me the word in question on the screen of his personal computer, using a digitalized photo of the fragment in question. He regulated the brightness of the photo until the word was displayed in good contrast and was relatively easy to read.

Lectures given by Mr. Lange in Paris and Jerusalem on the subject met with a general interest of scholars working on the Dead Sea Scrolls and caused several questions for help in the decipherment of damaged words and characters. This manual has been written to enable its reader to use Mr. Lange's method of Computer Aided Text-Reconstruction and Transcription (CATT) with his own personal computer.

For the developement of the method, no new program had to be written: presently available image editing software had only to be adapted. The method itself has been developed on the Dead Sea Scrolls, but can be used for the decipherment of any damaged manuscript, inscription, or print. Because every damaged text has its own specific problems, the manual regards itself as an introduction into the method and as a framework which can be adapted to the requirements of the text to be read.

The method has been developed on IBM compatible computers and only programs written for this system are described, although the operations of CATT can be performed with any system for which the necessary image editing software is available.

The manual is structured in three main chapters. In the first chapter, different kinds of text damage are described and an introduction into CATT is given. In the second chapter, the hard- and software requirements are described and an introduction into DOS and the graphical user interface Windows is given. The third chapter represents the main part of the book. Here Mr. Lange explains how to decipher and reconstruct damaged texts with four image editing programs: FotoTouch 2.1, PhotoStyler 1.1, PhotoStyler 2.0,[1] and Picture Publisher 3.1. Each program has its own section. The sections of the programs are structured according to the problems caused by damaged texts: i. e. „Magnification," „Darkened or Faded Texts," „Comparision and Joining of Fragments," „Mirrorwriting," „Character-Fragments," „ Comparison of Characters," „Reconstruction of Textgaps."

The „Fördergesellschaft der Westfälischen Wilhelms-Universität Münster" has funded the typesetting of the book and a research journey to Jerusalem. The English of the manuscript has been corrected and improved by Mr. Timothy Doherty, who also typeset the book. Mr. Georg Siebeck accepted and realized the manual with great interest. With the method documented here, Armin Lange has created a useful tool for working with damaged antique manuscripts. All may be cordially thanked.

Münster, March 31, 1993

Hermann Lichtenberger
Institutum Judaicum
Delitzschianum

[1] The Aldus Corporation made an early beta version of this program available for us so that not only PhotoStyler 1.1, which may be still in use in many institutes und universities, but also PhotoStyler 2.0 can be explained here.

Chapter 1

CATT – Purpose and Operation

1.1 Damaged Manuscripts and Inscriptions

Antique or medieval manuscripts and even early prints often confront their readers with an – in many ways – deteriorated text.[1] Therefore one of the most difficult tasks for a scholar is the reconstruction and transcription of such damaged texts. Often interpretation and reconstruction go hand in hand – especially if there are text gaps to be reconstructed. The scholar is usually confronted with techniques and technical problems which are far out of his field.[2]

In addition to damages done by men to scrolls, codices, and inscriptions (e. g. fire), many texts are seriously damaged simply by their old age: the stone of inscriptions disintegrates in the course of time, papyrus and parchment crumble or rot because they absorb humidity – sometimes the ink is even washed out. The different types of damages done to manuscripts and inscriptions are numerous, but may be classified roughly in five groups.

- Scrolls, codices, and inscriptions are broken and crumbled to numerous – and usually disconnected – fragments; in cave four of Qumran, for instance, thousands of fragments have been found which belong to only about 600 former scrolls.

1 CATT has also been tested on cuneiform writings, but the enormous amount of different cuneiform characters as well as the different shapes of each cuneiform character even in one text make the operations of CATT useless for their decipherment. In addition, the damages to the clay-tablets the cuneiform characters are written on are three dimensional, while CATT works with two dimensions. Attempts have been made to automatize the copying of cuneiform writing and inscriptions by P. Damerow/R. Englund/H. Nissen [Zur rechnergestützten Bearbeitung der archaischen Texte aus Mesopotamien (ca. 3200–3000 v.Chr.), MDOG 121, 1989, 139–151] and W. Hameter [Vorarbeiten für ein Unternehmen zur Herstellung druckfertiger Umzeichnungen von Inschriften mittels EDV, in: P. Ducrey et al. (edd.), Actes du Colloque „Epigraphie et Informatique", Lausanne 1989, 189–193].

2 At this point infrared photography, ultraviolet light and C_{14} dating may be mentioned as examples.

- The parchment and papyrus of manuscripts have been the „dinner" of worms, moths and mice, and many of the text gaps to be reconstructed today have been caused by such „dinners." Similar text gaps have also been caused by other physical damage: weather and human malice have broken inscriptions partly or worn parts of them away. In all these cases, today there are text gaps which must be reconstructed as far as possible.
- The ink of a manuscript has faded or crumbled away in the course of time. Sometimes even infrared photography can only detect very tiny shades which cannot be understood as the former characters. The parchment which was very precious in ancient times has sometimes been reused (palimpsest): the first text was scraped from the parchment, and/or it was simply written over. In both cases it is very difficult to read the palimpsest.
- The parchment of a manuscript has darkened in the course of centuries and milleniums or it has absorbed humidity and become rotten or mouldy, which not only caused text gaps but also darkened passages. In both cases the black or brown ink of a manuscript no longer contrasts the darkened parchment and the text is not readable.[3]
- A special problem of scrolls are the so-called mirrorwritings. If the ink of a scroll got wet, it sometimes pasted itself to the backside of the next winding of the scroll. The result is a mirrorwriting consisting of fragmentary characters and text gaps, since the wet ink usually only pasted itself in part to the backside of the next winding. Today both the home column[4] and the mirrorwriting can only be deciphered with great difficulty.

1.2 The Method of Reconstruction

The method described below is not meant to replace the normal procedure of decipherment, reconstruction, and transcription of damaged manuscripts and inscriptions, but only to supplement it: for instance, for the reconstruction of darkened texts, it is advisable to use an infrared photograph, even if the operations of CATT described below are implemented.

[3] This is due especially to the constant daylight to which the parchment of some manuscripts was exposed after their discovery: e. g. some manuscripts from cave four of Qumran are today totally black but were readable shortly after their discovery.

[4] The „home column" may be defined as the column from which a mirrorwriting has been separated.

The method of Computer Aided Text-Reconstruction and Transcription (CATT) uses image editing software in dealing with the several different types of damage done to manuscripts and inscriptions. Image editing programs try to transfer the photographic darkroom into the desktop computer. They are able to execute everything which is normally done in image editing by a photographic laboratory – from photo composition to the manipulation of exposure times. Normally image editing software is used for photo publication and as scanner support software and not for the reconstruction of damaged manuscripts, inscriptions, or even paintings. Therefore CATT may be described as a „misuse" of already available image editing programs. Two basic functions of these programs are used for this purpose:

- To separate any previously marked area of an image and insert it into any other image.
- To manipulate the gray-level or color of each point of an image.

1.2.1 The Operations of CATT

Before one is able to work on a damaged manuscript or inscription with a computer, the manuscript or inscription must be encoded, for which different procedures exist. A manuscript can be photographed by a digital camera, it can be filmed by a camcorder and then be digitalized by a videograbber-board, or it can be scanned. Of these methods, at the moment only scanning is workable: a camcorder cannot produce the image quality necessary for CATT and a digital camera capable of producing the requested quality is far too expensive.

A scanner looks and works like a photo-copying machine.[5] It encodes an image point by point (pixel). If a picture is scanned in a monochrome mode, a particular gray-level is assigned to every pixel.[6] The amount of gray-levels and the scanning resolution must be configured for each scanning. For CATT, 256 gray-levels and a resolution of at least 300 dpi (dots per inch) are the minimum.[7]

But not only the configuration of a scanner is of importance, the quality of the scanned image is also essential. Scanning should be

[5] Scanning will not be explained in this manual, because the user's guide of each of the programs explained below gives a detailed description of each scanning operation.

[6] Scanning in a color mode is not advisable, because colored images need an extreme amount of storage – in RAM as well as on the hard disk. A color photograph of 9 × 13 cm can require up to 20 MB.

[7] For the different types of scanners see Chapter 2.1: „Scanner."

done neither from the original manuscript or inscription, nor from printed plates: while it is self evident that inscriptions carved in heavy stones cannot be placed on a scanner, manuscripts should not be scanned with a normal flatbed scanner because its intensive light can do great damage to the parchment or papyrus of the manuscript. Printed plates on the other hand do not have enough gray-levels and have a resolution far too low for CATT's operations (at most 200 dpi). To obtain good results, it is necessary to work only with photographs taken directly from the text one wants to decipher. If colored photographs are available, they should be scanned in a monochrome mode, otherwise one must use monochrome photographs.[8]

Magnification

Normal magnification alone can often give the crucial hint for the decipherment of a manuscript or an inscription. Image editing programs can magnify any area of an image such as otherwise can only be done by a microscope. If magnified to a certain degree, the dots of an image are displayed as squares, which is often of help if characters are to be identified or compared.

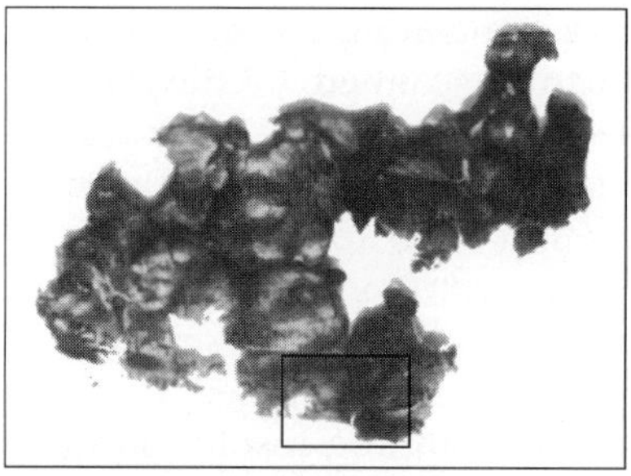

4Q180 fragment 3 (4Q Ages of Creation).

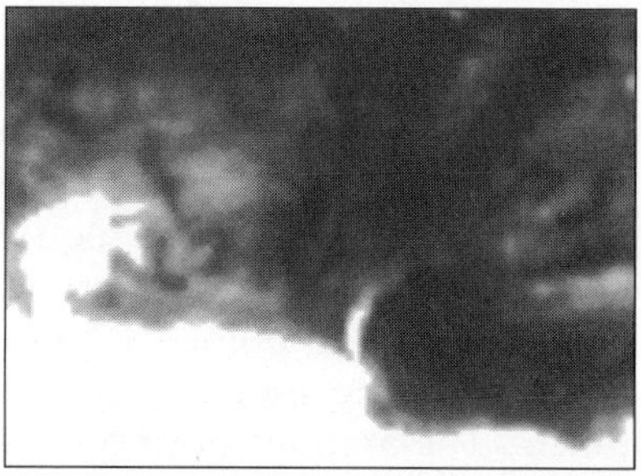

Detail of 4Q180, magnified.

PAM 41719: Courtesy of the IAA.

[8] Another form of scanning is Kodak's Photo-CD: the negative or slide is scanned by a developer and stored on the Photo-CD in a special file format. If negatives are available, it may be a good idea to use the Photo-CD, whose quality should be sufficient for CATT.

Darkened and Faded Texts

As mentioned above, tiny shades of former characters which cannot be recognized by the human eye, but can be detected by a computer, are sometimes preserved in darkened or faded passages of a manuscript. Image editing software is equipped with several functions for adjusting the gray-levels of pixels in an image. In this way, even tiny shades preserved in darkened or faded text passages can be processed to visibly contrasted characters. Most of these functions have been developed for the calibration of printed plates in image publication. In principle all the functions described below serve the purpose of enhancing and increasing the contrast of nearly contrastless text passages. There is no single function by which all darkened and faded texts can be reconstructed with good results: different kinds of faded or darkened texts require different methods of reconstruction.

Image Analysis by Histograms

For the editor of an antique manuscript, it is often very difficult to decide whether characters have been preserved in a darkened or faded part of a manuscript, or if nothing was ever written there at all. Analytical functions of image editing programs are of importance for this task: they can represent any part of an image as a so-called histogram.

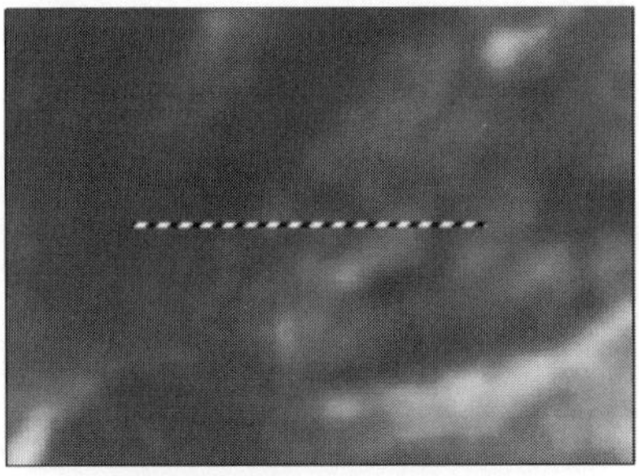

A line marked for image analysis.

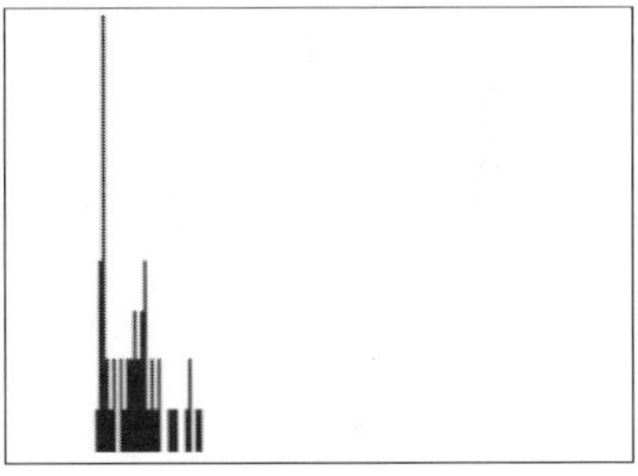

Histogram calculated along the marked line.

PAM 41719: Courtesy of the IAA.

A histogram is the graphic representation of the pixel distribution of an image in the form of a curve, ordered according to the respective gray-levels and amount of pixels. Its horizontal axis represents the gray-levels of an image in values ranging from 0 to 255 and the vertical axis shows the amount of pixels. Zero (0) stands for black, found on the left-hand side of the curve, and 255 is white, found on its right-hand side. If more than just a few gray-levels are detected in a histogram of a darkened or faded text, tiny shades of former characters have probably been preserved in the manuscript.

! Analysis of an image with the help of a histogram does require experience. It is advisable to first create histograms of faded or darkened parts of a text which are known to preserve characters. Afterwards these histograms can be compared with histograms taken from parts of a text which are not known to contain characters.

Negative

A first help in reconstructing darkened or faded parts of a text is to invert its image to a negative since contrast can sometimes be recognized by the human eye better in a negative than in a positive. To invert an image to a negative, an image editing program exchanges the values of the gray-scale levels with their numerative opposites.

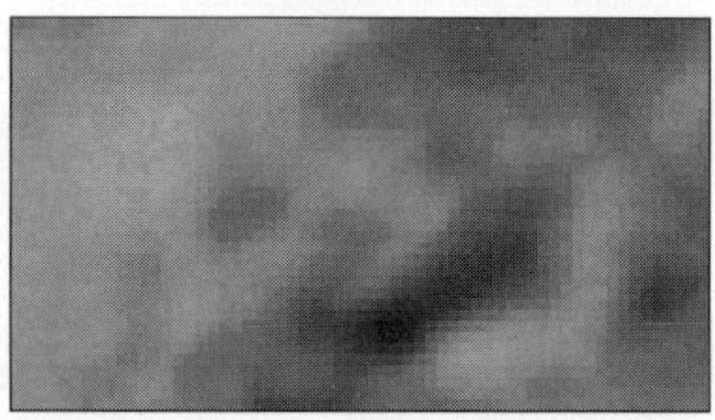

Detail of 4Q180 3 (left), inverted to a negative and enhanced in contrast (right).

PAM 41719: Courtesy of the IAA.

Regulation of Brightness and Contrast

Similar to the way in which contrast and brightness can be adjusted on the screen of a normal TV, image editing software is able to adjust the contrast and brightness of an image inside the computer – either

Detail of 4Q180 3 (left), enhanced in contrast and brightness (right).

PAM 41719: Courtesy of the IAA.

of selected sections or of the whole image. This function enables the study of a single photograph with different „exposure times," which is of great help in deciphering darkened passages of manuscripts.

Gamma Correction

As explained in the introduction to this section, the recognition of contrasts by the human eye differs from their representation in print or on the screen. To compensate for this difference, a further function has been developed, which can help in reconstructing darkened or faded text passages: the so-called gamma correction enables non-linear manipulation of the gray-levels or colors of the pixels in an image, i. e. not all pixels of a certain gray-level or color are assigned to a new value, only part of them. The result is a text whose readability is increased – especially in the darkened text passages.

Detail of 4Q180 3 (left), enhanced by gamma correction (right).

PAM 41719: Courtesy of the IAA.

Gray/Color Map

The gray/color-map-function enables the manipulation of individually selected gray-levels of an image. This is normally done using a curve whose horizontal axis represents the input gray-level (= the original one), while its vertical axis represents the output level (= the new one). In this way, all pixels of a certain gray-level can be assigned to a new gray-level value, e. g. all totally black pixels can be reassigned to white or 20 % gray etc.

Detail of 4Q180 3 (left), enhanced using the gray/color map (right).

PAM 41719: Courtesy of the IAA.

Equalization

Equalization works in a similar way. If the contrasts of an image or part of an image consist of only a few gray-levels, equalization can process the slightly lighter gray-levels along a previously created curve to be bright and the slightly darker ones to be dark, and the contrast is increased. The result is that tiny shades of former characters can be made readable again.

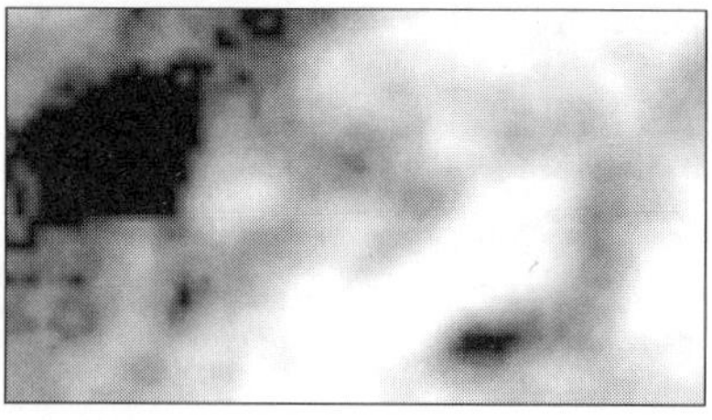

Detail of 4Q180 3 (left), enhanced using equalization (right).

PAM 41719: Courtesy of the IAA.

Comparison and Joining of Fragments

With different tools and procedures, text passages, fragments, and columns of a manuscript can be separated and stored individually. Afterwards these separated parts (hereafter called image excerpts or selected areas) can be inserted into any digitalized photo of a manuscript or inscription.

This function of image editing programs is extremely helpful if fragments of a manuscript or an inscription are to be compared or joined. In this context, H. Stegemann's method of reconstructing scrolls out of scattered fragments must be mentioned.[9] Often scrolls have crumbled into unconnected fragments. Many clusters have been found, e.g. in cave four of Qumran, consisting of fragments baked together. The fragments of these clumps were often pasted together when the former scroll was still intact, i.e. the windings of a scroll baked together and the scroll then disintegrated into clumps (hereafter these „portions of scrolls" are called layers). In the course of time, some of these layers disintegrated and their fragments were scattered, while other fragments have been separated in modern times with great patience by specialists since their discovery, without the sequence of the fragments having been recorded. Since the sequence of the windings of a scroll are preserved in the sequence of the pasted fragments of a layer, the location of unconnected fragments within a scroll can be deduced if they can be assigned to certain layers and if their location within these layers can also be found.

Border structures of fragments pasted together are relatively similar to each other. If fragments of similar or somewhat similar shape which have the same type of characters and parchment or papyrus can be identified, it is highly probable that they once formed a layer. Because alterations in the form of fragments in a layer abide by certain laws, one is able to locate the position of a fragment within the sequence of fragments in a layer with relative accuracy.

- In a first operation all fragments to be compared must be selected and stored separately in independent files. Afterwards the files will be compared in pairs by which one of the two files to be compared or joined must be inserted into the file of the second fragment.
- To enable the comparison of border structures, the inserted fragment must be displayed in a transparent mode. Similar to the ad-

[9] H. Stegemann, Methods for the Reconstruction of Scrolls from Scattered Fragments, in: L. H. Schiffman (ed.), Archaeology and History in the Dead Sea Scrolls, The New York University Conference in Memory of Yigael Yadin, Journal for the Study of the Pseudepigrapha, Supplement Series 8, Sheffield 1990, 189–220.

1QH 18

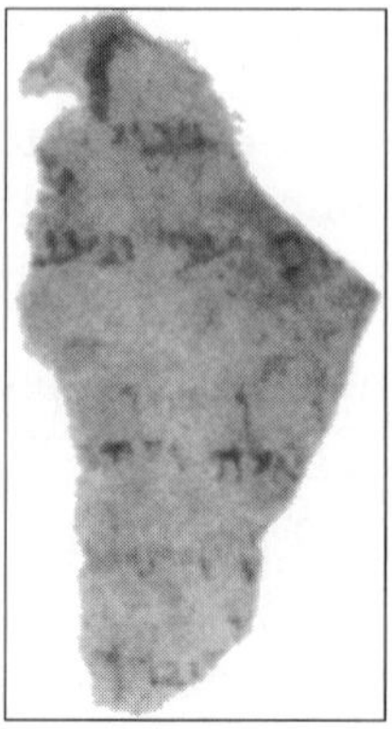

1QH 22

1QH 18 and 1QH 22 joined.

Courtesy of the Shrine of the Book.

justment of gray-levels with image editing software, all pixels of a certain range of gray-levels can be configured transparent, e. g. all light pixels of an image as a separate group. In this way the parchment of a manuscript can be defined transparent while its characters stay intransparent. In addition the inserted fragment will be surrounded by a blinking marque, if a special selection function, called the magic wand, has been used for the selection of the fragment.

In this way the border structures of fragments can be compared with great efficiency. Stegemann's method is of course not restricted only to the comparison of fragments, but it cannot be explained here in detail. It may be mentioned that the comparison of holes and text gaps caused by physical damage – also of importance for the reconstruction of broken scrolls – can be done similar to the comparison of fragments.

Mirrorwriting

The relocation of mirrorwritings to their respective home columns can be done in a similar way:

1. In a first operation the backside of the column or fragment on which the mirrorwriting is pasted must be selected and stored individually. Afterwards the mirrorwriting must be mirrored back, in order to bring the script into the line.

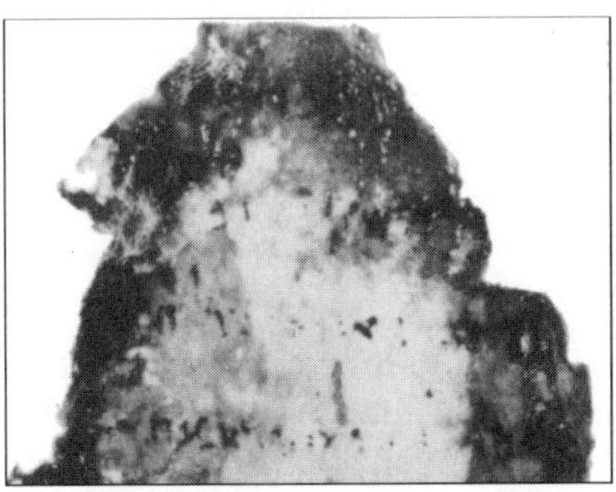

Detail of 11QTemp XXXVIII.

Detail of the corresponding mirrorwriting.

Courtesy of the Shrine of the Book.

2. In a second step the remirrored mirrorwriting is inserted into the file containing its home column. Again the transparency configuration of the insert function is of great help. By using it, all light pixels of an image – which represent the mirrorwriting's parchment – can be declared transparent, while its dark pixels – representing the mirrorwriting's characters – will stay intransparent.
3. Sometimes the exact relocation of a mirrorwriting is very difficult. In this case, the inserted mirrorwriting should be inverted to a negative – once again using the transparency configuration as described above. In this way the parchment of the mirrorwriting will remain intransparent while its characters and character fragments will be displayed transparent. The characters and character fragments of the mirrorwriting's home column can be inserted into the mirrorwriting like a stencil. After the relocation of the mirrorwriting and before it is fixated, its gray-scale should be re-inverted to a positive.

The mirrorwriting inverted to a negative and relocated to its home column.

The relocation finished.

Courtesy of the Shrine of the Book.

Character Fragments

At the edges of text gaps and fragments, often only small parts of former characters are preserved. The identification of these character fragments is usually very difficult. For this purpose, image editing software provides two different ways of creating letter-templates:

– A well preserved character is selected by drawing a rectangular marque around it. The contrast of the rectangular area selected is

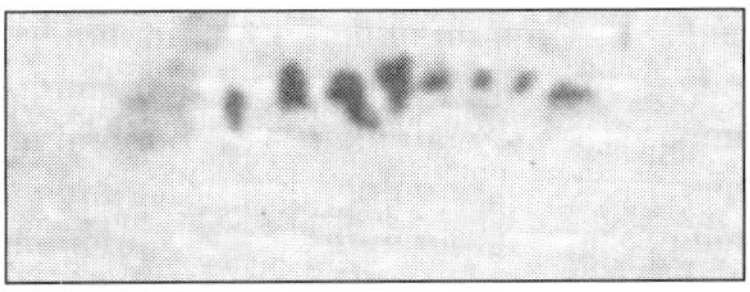

Character fragments in $1QSI_{25}$.

Letter-template generated from a character found in $1QSI_{25}$.

Character fragments in line 25 identified using the letter-template.

Courtesy of the Shrine of the Book.

then increased and its gray-scale inverted to a negative. The rectangular image excerpt is then stored in a new file, named, for instance, after the character stored in it. Before the letter-template can be inserted into the file containing the character fragments to be reconstructed, the transparency configuration of the insert function must be activated: all light pixels should be defined as transparent. The letter-template-file summoned by the insert command will now appear as a transparent white letter enclosed in a non-transparent dark environment. This letter-template can be moved to any location within the photo one is working on.

- Image editing software allows you to surround any well preserved character with a blinking marque by a tool called the „magic wand tool". This marque can be saved and inserted into the file containing the character fragment to be identified. Again the letter-template can be moved and placed within the photo one is working on as wanted.

Comparison of Characters

As noted above, it is often necessary to compare the characters of different manuscripts. Letter-templates can also be used for this pur-

Reconstruction of Text Gaps

One of the most difficult tasks in reconstructing damaged manuscripts and inscriptions is the reconstruction of text gaps. Normally a text gap, as well as the characters of a text, must be carefully measured. Afterwards the average size of the characters of a manuscript or inscription and the amount of characters which can be placed in the text gap must be calculated. Only then can a proposed reconstruction be verified or falsified, according to the sum of characters needed. Using image editing software, one is able to select and store single characters or whole words, which can afterwards be inserted into the text gap of interest. In this way text gaps can be reconstructed in the ductus of the scribe of an manuscript or the stone-cutter of an inscription.

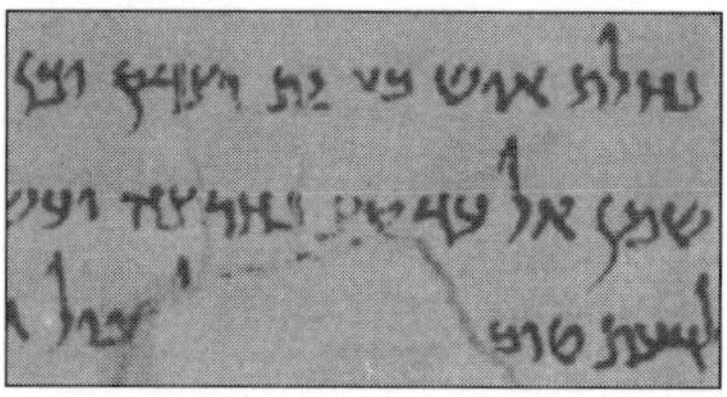

Text gap in $1QSIV_{26}$.

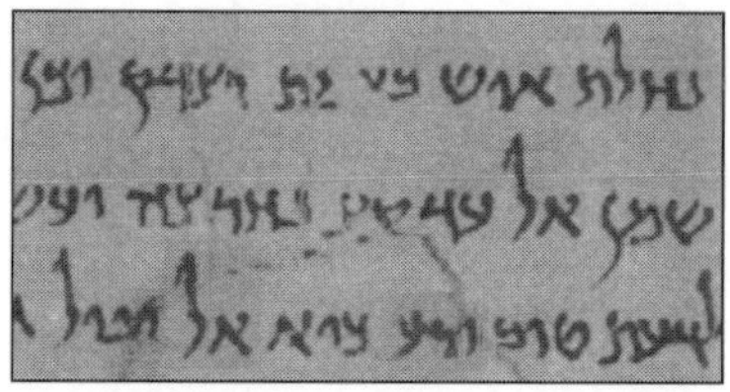

The text gap reconstructed*.

Words and characters extracted from 1QS.

* For the reconstruction see H. Stegemann: Zu Textbestand und Grundgedanken von 1QSIII, 13-IV, 26, RdQ 13, 1988, 95–131, 108.

Courtesy of the Shrine of the Book.

Chapter 2

Hard- and Software Requirements

The method of CATT has been developed on IBM compatible PC's running with MS-DOS, but comparable image editing software also exists for the MacIntosh. If damaged manuscripts or inscriptions are to be reconstructed with the aid of a computer not running with DOS, the operations described in chapters one and three can easily be transferred to imaged editing software running on another system: equalization or monitor gamma, for example, should also be available with image editing software running on these systems.

In this chapter, some basics of DOS and the graphic user interface (GUI) Windows 3.1 will be explained. It is however not my intention to give detailed instructions on how to use DOS or Windows. Both are released with excellent users guides and – in addition – a good number of manuals are available on both of them. For experienced users of Windows and DOS, it won't be neccessary to read this chapter. For these users, only the first section will be of interest, where the hardware requirements for CATT will be described. But for beginners on DOS and Windows, the two following sections will probably be of help.

2.1 Hardware

High quality image processing is one of the most demanding tasks for a desktop computer. Only a few years ago, most of the operations of CATT could have been performed only on a mainframe. Since the fastest desktop computers available at reasonable prices are the IBM compatible machines, the method of CATT has been developed for and is used on these computers. There is however – as mentioned above – no reason why CATT should not work on a MacIntosh or any other system if the appropriate software is available: just look for the necessary functions and tools in an image editing program and proceed as described in chapter one.

In the following tables, hardware configurations of a desktop computer for operating CATT are given; the first table describes a minimum configuration and the second a medium one:

Minimum Configuration

- Processor: 386-DX-40
- RAM: 8 MB
- Hard disk: 200 MB
- Graphic board: SVGA (resolution: 800×600, colors: 256, video RAM: 512 KB)[1]
- Screen: SVGA, non-interlaced (resolution: 800×600, colors: 256, size: 15″ diameter)
- Pointing device: any mouse or digitizer which works with the resolution of the screen and the graphic board.

Medium Configuration

- Processor: 486-DX-33
- RAM: 16 MB
- Hard disk: 500 MB
- Graphic board: SVGA truecolor graphic board (resolution: 1024×768, colors: 16 700 000, video RAM: 1 MB)[2]
- Screen: SVGA, non-interlaced (resolution: 1024×768, colors: 16 700 000, size: 15″ diameter)
- Pointing device: any mouse or digitizer which works with the resolution of the screen and the graphic board.

Printer

For any configuration a HP compatible laser printer with PostScript capabilities is advisable; but even then images cannot be printed with good quality; for this purpose a high resolution Linotype must be used.

Laptop

If the reconstruction of texts is to be done with the damaged manuscripts or inscriptions directly at hand, e.g. in a museum or

[1] The faster the graphic board, the better the results.
[2] The faster the graphic board, the better the results.

even – with some inscriptions – at the excavation site, a computer is usually not at hand. In this case, a laptop must be used, although normally laptop screens are not adequate for CATT's purposes: most laptops use a high quality passive black and white LCD display[3] which provides at most 64 gray-levels. Even with a colored passive LCD display, the representation of contrasts does not reach CATT's standard. Only an active LCD display which is able to work with 256 colors or more should be used – a technique which is also named TFT display.

Scanner

As described in the first chapter, scanners should be used to digitize images of damaged manuscripts. Different types of scanners are presently available, of which three are of interest for CATT:

1. The hand scanner is the least expensive type; it must be held in the hand and gets acceptable results in many cases. A hand scanner should only be purchased if very few columns or pages are to be read. If more text must be reconstructed, a hand scanner will be too complicated in use: scanning with hand scanners needs a good amount of time and great patience.
2. In this case, a flatbed scanner should be used. This scanner looks and works like a photo-copying machine and gets better results than the hand scanner.
3. The best quality can be reached when a negative or slide is scanned. Film-scanners must be used for this. But – as always – high end quality is available only for a high end prize: film-scanners normally cost about $15 000 or more.

In this context Kodak's Photo-CD must be mentioned, since for the Photo-CD, negatives or slides are scanned by the Kodak Company with a high quality film-scanner and stored on a computer readable CD.[4] The Kodak company advertised support of 4×5″ negatives for summer 1993. At the moment, only normal negatives or slides can be scanned. If you decide to use the Photo-CD, contact your local Kodak dealer to get detailed information.[5]

To produce the quality necessary for CATT, every scanner – whether it is a hand scanner or a flatbed scanner – must be able to

---

[3] A technique which is, for instance, also to be found with wrist watches.

[4] To use the Photo-CD, your computer must be equipped with a CD-ROM drive which supports the new CD-ROM-XA standard.

[5] PhotoTouch 2.01 do not support the Photo-CD.

scan with at least 300 dpi[6] and 256 gray-levels. A film-scanner must be able to scan with an even higher resolution.

! Often scanners are advertised which can supposedly scan with a resolution of 600 dpi or more. This resolution is often not the physical resolution of the scanner itself, but is reached by software manipulation (interpolation).

Magneto Optical Disk

As already mentioned, digitized images need a large amount of storage space: therefore even a computer equipped with a hard disk of 300 MB or more can run out of storage. For this problem, a new technique can be of help, the magneto optical disk: similar to a CD, data is stored with laser technology, but, unlike a CD, a magneto optical disk is rewritable.

! For scholars working on the Dead Sea Scrolls, it will be of interest to know that Dr. Timothy Lim of the Oxford St. Hugh's College is digitizing images of the photographic plates of the Dead Sea Scrolls for publication by Oxford University Press.

2.2 Software

In addition to an image editing program, the operating system MS-DOS (version 5.0 or above) and the graphical user interface Windows 3.1 are necessary for CATT.[7]

2.2.1 Operating System

After a computer running with DOS has been booted (initialized), the so-called prompt will be displayed on the screen: `C:\>`. All commands typed in the keyboard will be displayed next to this prompt, e. g. the graphical environment with which DOS is equipped is activated by the `dosshell` command.[8] Every command must be confirmed with the *Enter* key. Capitalization of commands will be ignored by DOS. If a running DOS command must be stopped, the keys *Ctrl* + *C* must

[6] 300 dpi (= dots per inch) means that the sides of a square inch consist of 300 dots each, and a full square inch contains 90 000 dots.

[7] Word processors will not be discussed here, because the edition of reconstructed manuscripts with word processors is not a part of CATT's operations.

[8] The Dosshell can be quit by pressing *Alt* + *F4*.

be pressed simultaneously. If the last command issued should be repeated, the *F3* key can be used to recall it to the screen.

The DOS prompt indicating that drive *D:* is valid.

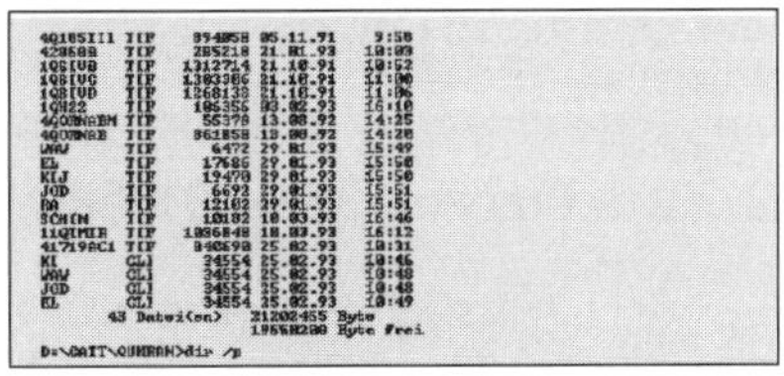

The `dir` command showing the content of a directory `qumran`.

File management is of importance for CATT, as well as for all other computer operations. Any data used by a computer is stored in a file, e. g. a scanned image or a text. A filename under DOS consists of two parts: The name of the file – at most eight characters – and, separated by a period, an extension of three characters which marks the type of the file (file format). The file `pstyler.exe` is, for example, the execute file (`.exe` = execute) of the image editing program PhotoStyler 1.1. File formats of importance for CATT are the executable formats `.com` and `.exe` and the graphic file formats `.bmp`, `.eps`, `.gif`, `.pcx`, and `.tif` (TIFF).[9]

Drives and Directories

Files are stored by the computer on different storage media, called drives: the hard disk and the floppy drives. Each drive is referred to by a character followed by a colon: normally the hard disk is addressed as `c:`[10] and the floppy drives are called `a:` and `b:`. On floppy disks, as well as on a hard disk, DOS creates directories in which files can be stored. Actually even a disk itself is referred to by DOS as a directory, the so-called root directory or root. A directory can be described as a kind of file folder, in which any number of files can be stored, as long as there is free storage on the disk. A disk may be described as a filing cabinet containing several file folders. In addition to files, directories can also be stored in directories, then called subdirectories. The directories of a disk are managed by the oper-

[9] `.eps` marks a PostScript image file.

[10] If a computer has more than one hard disk, additional hard disks are referred to as `d:`, `e:` etc.

ating system as a tree, which can be visualized with the `tree|more` command.[11]

To work under DOS with drives, directories, and files, the following commands are needed.[12]

2.2.2 Drives and Directories

`a:` To change the current drive, type the name of the drive to which you want to change at the DOS prompt, for example `a:`.

`md` To create a directory, use the commands `md` or `mkdir` (make directory). The name of the directory to be created must be given after this command and a space must be typed between the command and the name: e. g. `md␣qumran`.

`cd` To change the current directory, type `cd` or `chdir` (change directory), and the name of the directory. Command and name must be separated by a space. To change to the next higher directory use the `cd..` command. The current directory is displayed by DOS as a part of its prompt: `C:\WINDOWS>` indicates the Windows directory as being current.

A single backslash set after the `cd` command symbolizes the root: `cd␣\` will change to the root directory of the current drive. Because the `cd` command allows changes only from a main directory to a subdirectory and back, the backslash must always be set if you want to change directly from one main directory to another: The command `cd␣\qumran` given in the Windows directory will change to the Qumran directory.

The backslash is also to be set between a main directory and a subdirectory, here it marks a next directory: The

11 The command `tree` will display the directories of the current drive in the form of a tree, the option `|more` will separate this tree into portions only as large as the screen. If the switch `/f` is added in front of `|more`, the files stored in the directories will also be displayed.

12 MS-DOS (version 5.0 and above) provides users with help for its commands if the switch `/?` is set after the command of interest: the command `copy /?` will call helpful information about the copy command to the screen.

command cd␣\qumran\1qs given in the Windows directory will change from the Windows directory to the 1QS subdirectory of the Qumran directory.

rd — To delete a directory, the rd or rmdir command (remove directory) must be used. This command works only if given outside the directory to be deleted. The deletion of directories is allowed by DOS only if all files and subdirectories of a directory have previously been erased.

Files

Switches, Options, and Wildcards

Several options, switches,[13] and wildcards are of importance for DOS' file mangement. The most important are:

/s — A command provided with this switch will be executed not only for the current directory but for all directories.

/p — The results of a command configured with this switch will be displayed on the screen in pages, in order that results, which are larger than one screen in content, can be viewed.

/w — Normally DOS works with only one screen column. The /w switch will display the results of an executed command in up to five columns.

|more — The more option works similar to the /p switch, and should be used with the type[14] and the tree commands, for which /p does not work.

? * — Two different wildcards can be used with DOS: the question mark (?) represents one character, while the asterix (*) represents several characters.

Commands

copy — With this command files can be copied. Following the command, the file to be copied and its destination must be named. Drive and directory of the file to be copied are

[13] Each switch is written following a slash.

[14] The type command displays the contents of a file on the screen.

considered to be part of the file name. A space must be set between command, filename, and destination, respectively: The command `copy␣a:\1qsi.tif␣c:\qumran` will copy the file 1QSI of the TIFF file format from a floppy disk in drive `a:` to the Qumran directory of the hard disk `c:`.

If a different filename is indicated for the destination file, the file will be copied to a file of this new name: the command `copy␣a:\1qsi.tif␣c:\qumran\serekh.tif` will copy the file `1qsi` of the TIFF file format from a floppy disk in drive `a:` to a file `serekh` of the same file format in the Qumran directory on the hard disk `c:`. If this file does not exist, it will be created automatically.

By using wildcards, groups of files can be copied: the command `copy␣a:\*.tif␣c:\qumran` will copy all files of the TIFF file format from the floppy disk in drive `a:` to the Qumran directory of the hard disk `c:`.

`del` By using the `del` command, files can be deleted. Wildcards can also be used with this command. The syntax and the use of wildcards is the same as with the `copy` command.

! The command `del *.*` will erase all files in the current directory. Sometimes files are deleted by this command by accident. If this happens, do not perform any further disk operations (copying, saving etc.). Files are not deleted totally by DOS: only the first byte, which is the first character of the file name, is erased. But, DOS will write new data on the sector(s) of a disk previously occupied by a deleted file making file restoration impossible; therefore nothing should be stored after an accidental deletion of files. The DOS `undelete` function can restore the first character of the name of a deleted file. In this way a previously deleted file can sometimes be recovered with the DOS `undelete` command.[15]

`ren` By using the `ren` command, files can be renamed. The syntax of the command and its use of wildcards is

[15] The `undelete` command is well documented in the DOS manual, in addition users will be guided by DOS after the `undelete` command is given.

the same as with the `copy` command: the command `ren␣1qs.tif␣serekh.tif` will rename the file 1QS of the TIFF file format to a file named Serekh of the same file format.

`dir` The `dir` command (dir = directory) is used for different purposes:

- If the command is given without any additions, all files of the current directory will be listed on the screen.[16]
- If only a selection of files should be displayed, wildcards must be used as described for the `copy` command.
- If the `/s` switch is used in connection with the `dir` command all files of all subdirectories of the current directory will also be displayed.
- The `/o` switch is also of help for the `dir` command: it sorts the files of a directory. Several parameters exist for this switch:

  `/o:n` All files will be sorted alphabetically according to their file names.

  `/o:e` All files will be sorted alphabetically according to their extensions.

- The `dir` command can also be used to search for files: change to the root directory and type the `dir` command, the `/s` switch, and the name of the file you're looking for at the DOS prompt: the command `dir␣1qsi.tif␣/s` will search for the file 1QSI of the TIFF format in all directories of the current hard disk. If you don't want to change to the root directory, type `dir␣\1qsi.tif␣/s` for the same effect.
- Because the `dir` command also displays the amount of bytes used by a file (i. e. the file's size) and calculates the total amount of bytes used by all files listed, it can also be used to calculate the size of a directory or the amount of storage needed by a certain group of files. If the `/s` switch is set, the size of a directory including its subdirectories can also be calculated.

[16] If there are more files in a directory than can be displayed on the screen at one time, the switch `/p` allows you to view them in pages.

`backup` Because of the large size of the graphic files necessary for CATT, it is often impossible to store them on a single floppy disk. Normally floppy disks have at most 1.2 or 1.44 MB (= megabyte) of storage space while image files often have a size of 2 MB or more. The `backup` command can be used to copy these files in parts to several floppy disks: The command `backup␣c:\qumran\1qsi.tif␣a:` copies the file 1QSI of the TIFF file format to the floppy disk in drive `a:`. When all the storage capacity of this floppy disk is used up, you will be asked to put the next one in the drive.

`restore` When the file is to be copied back to a hard disk, it must be done with the `restore` command: the command `restore␣a: d:\qumran\1qsi.tif` will copy the file 1QSI of the TIFF file format to hard disk `d:`. You will be asked to insert the next floppy disk into drive `a:` when the first part of the file has been copied.

! When using the backup command, a file can only be restored to a directory with the name of the directory from which it has been copied: in the example above, the file 1QSI of the TIFF file format can be restored to any drive but only to a directory named `qumran`.

! The commands `backup` and `restore` are compatible in all DOS releases from MS-DOS 3.3 to MS-DOS 6.0.

2.2.3 Windows

The many different and sometimes confusing commands, switches, and parameters of DOS indicate that the operating system of a desktop computer is extremely powerful but also very complicated to use. Sometimes it reminds one more of a programming language than of a system that should enable and simplify the use of a computer and its data. For this reason, the so-called graphical environments or GUIs (Graphical User Interface) have been developed. They can be described as graphical translators between the computer system (starting with the operating system of the computer) and its user. All graphical environments have a common principal: they display the command structure of a program graphically, partly as symbols and partly as written commands. These symbols and commands are usually grouped, organized, and represented by other symbols and commands. Every symbol or command can be activated with the help of special input devices, mostly a „mouse." The mouse is a graphical input device. Normally it is as large as the palm of one's hand and is equipped with two or three buttons. A small ball is found on the bottom of the mouse. If the mouse is moved over a surface, e.g. a writing table, the ball is rolled. In this way, the computer is able to detect and store the movements. On the screen, the mouse is displayed as a small pointer or mark which moves analogous to the movements of the mouse. If the mouse-pointer is placed on a symbol or command and the left mouse-button is pressed (= to click), the function or application represented by the command or symbol will be called or executed.[17] In addition to this graphical method of using a GUI, the environment can also be run from the keyboard by using key combinations and typed in commands.

Because most image processing programs available for IBM compatible computers run under Windows 3.x, this graphical environment will be explained briefly below.[18]

Windows has four main purposes[19]:

- To simplify the use of the PC.
- To allow easy data exchange between different Windows programs (hereinafter Windows programs will be called „applications").
- To hold several applications in memory and run them at the same time (multi-tasking).
- To use – unlike DOS – the whole RAM of the PC.

As explained above, functions and applications of GUI's are represented graphically. In Windows, each function and application is displayed in and handled as a window, e.g PhotoStyler, seen on page 26. Any window can be reduced to a symbol or enlarged to full or partial screen size if the minimize and maximize buttons are used, both found in the upper right-hand corner of a window and equipped with an arrow, pointing upwards or downwards, respec-

17 Some commands need a confirmation in order to be executed; this confirmation can be given for instance by pressing the left mouse-button two times (= to doubleclick).

18 Naturally a detailed user guide for Windows can't be given here. Windows is released with an excellent manual and, in addition, books introducing and explaining Windows are available. For example: file management is very simple and efficient with Windows' file manager; nevertheless it will not be described here.

19 For an inexperienced Windows user it might be advisable to run Windows while reading this paragraph. To run Windows, type `win` at the DOS-prompt and press *Enter*.

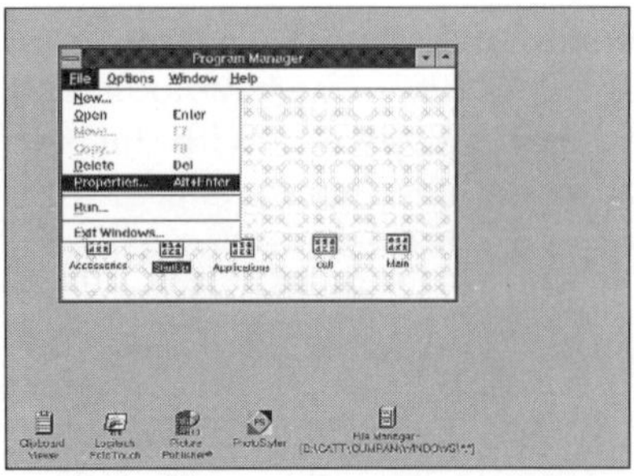

Windows „*Program Manager*“ with program groups.

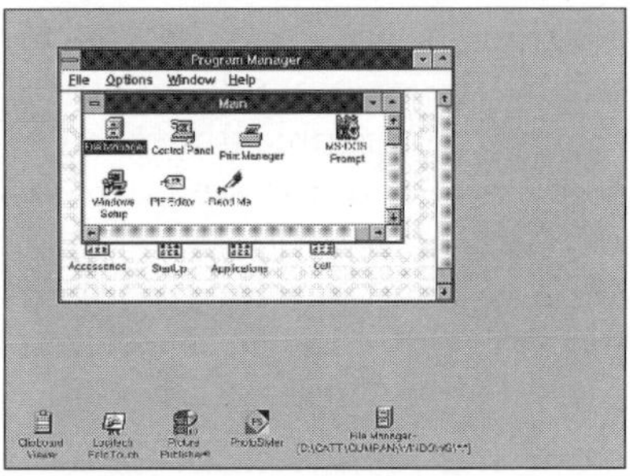

The „*Main*“ program group opened.

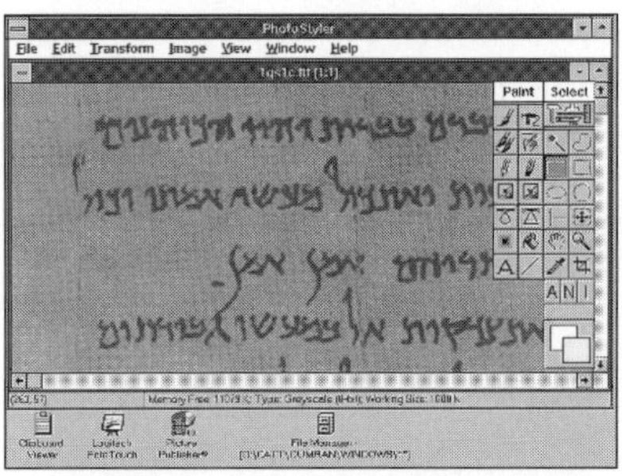

A Windows program, PhotoStyler, opened.

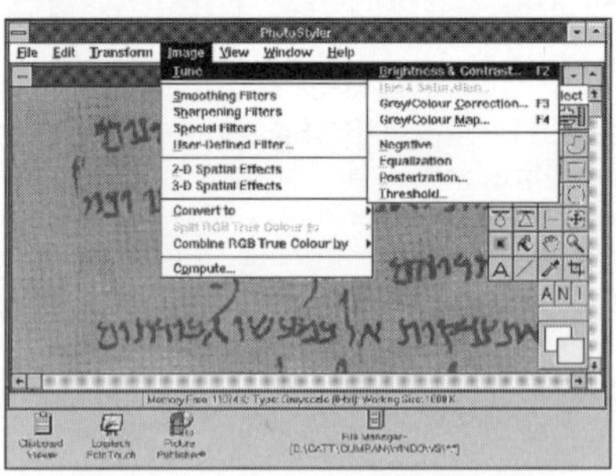

Menu with submenu of PhotoStyler.

tively. To close an application, doubleclick the square displayed in its upper left-hand corner.[20]

The basic window of Windows is its *„Program Manager."* If not configured otherwise, the *„Program Manager"* will always be opened when Windows is run. At the top of the program managers window, a small ribbon is displayed, in which several commands (*menus*) are seen (*„File," „Options," „Window," „Help"*). If one of these commands is clicked, additional commands will be displayed in a box which opens. Each menu (e.g. the *„File"* menu) represents a group of commands which correspond in function to the title of the menu. Sometimes such a menu consists partly or entirely of submenus: in the *„Image"* menu of PhotoStyler, several submenus are organized, among others the *„Tune"* submenu (see page 26). In this way the commands of Windows and its applications are organized and grouped in a logically structured hierarchy.

Several rectangular symbols are found in the *„Program Manager's"* main field. Each of these symbols represents a further window containing Windows applications (program groups). These will be „opened" when doubleclicked. Some of the applications which are organized in the program groups are part of the normal Windows release while others must be bought separately, e.g. image processing packages. Each application is represented again by a symbol (icon), whose shape corresponds to the function of the application, e.g. the file manager of Windows is symbolized by a filing cabinet. If one of these icons is clicked, the application symbolized will be executed.

In addition to menus, commands, program groups, and icons, Windows and its applications also provide graphically represented and executed functions. If the contents of a certain window are too large to be displayed all at once, Windows will equip this window with scroll bars. If the arrows at the end of such a bar are clicked, the contents of the window will be scrolled.[21] Alternatively the mouse-button can be placed on the square attached to a scroll bar: if the mouse is moved while the left mouse-button is held pressed, the content of the window will be scrolled in the direction the mouse moves. The function of every button used by Windows and its appli-

[20] To run two or more applications at the same time, their windows must both be opened, either reduced to a symbol or as a full size window. For multi-tasking with Windows see the Windows users guide.

[21] To scroll the window, place the mouse-pointer on one of the arrows and hold the left mouse-button pressed – the window will be scrolled as long as the mouse-button is pressed.

cations can be identified by words, characters or symbols displayed on them.

Most of the graphic and image processing applications of Windows are equipped with so-called toolboxes. A *tool* can be defined as a function of a program represented by an icon, e. g. a brush. This function will be activated if the icon is clicked. Several of these icons grouped together and displayed in a special area of the application's program window are called a toolbox (e. g. the toolbox of the graphical Windows application Paintbrush on page 29).

In addition, Windows and its applications use so-called dialogue boxes to set configurations and to communicate with their users – for instance, warnings are given in such dialogue boxes if data will be lost when the user exits a program without storing a file he or she has changed or created while working with the application. These dialogue boxes are again equipped with buttons, menus, and the like. For instance, PhotoStyler asks via a dialogue box if the changes done to the image file `1qsic.tif` found in the `\qumran` subdirectory of the `\catt` directory should be saved in this file before closing the program (page 29). If the „*Yes*" button is clicked, the changes will be saved; if the „*No*" button is clicked, they won't be saved. The „*Cancel*" button will abort the closing of the program and return to PhotoStyler.

Clipboard

The clipboard is a special application which will be explained here, because it is crucial for CATT. The clipboard is Window's intermediate, temporary storage area. Previously selected data can be copied to and called from the clipboard by every application.[22] The current data stored in the clipboard can be viewed using the clipboard viewer found in the „*Main*" program group.[23] To save data from the clipboard, click the „*Save As*" command of the clipboard viewer's „*File*" menu and the „*Save As*" dialogue box will be opened. Type a filename with the extension `.clp` in the „*Filename*" box,[24] and choose the directory the file shall be stored in by doubleclicking this directory on the tree displayed in the „*Directories*" box; then click the „*OK*" button.

[22] Clipboard usage with PhotoStyler, FotoTouch, and Picture Publisher is explained in the corresponding chapters on the programs in this book.

[23] To open the „*Clipboard Viewer*", doubleclick the „*Clipboard Viewer*" icon of the „*Main*" program group.

[24] All Windows clipboard files are marked by the extension `.clp`.

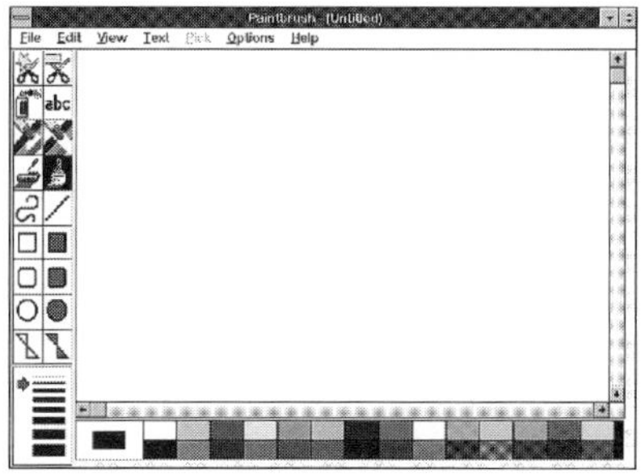

The toolbox of the Windows application Paintbrush.

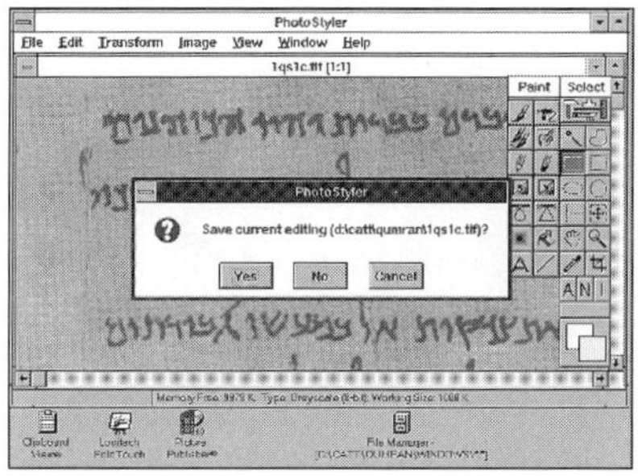

A dialogue box of Windows.

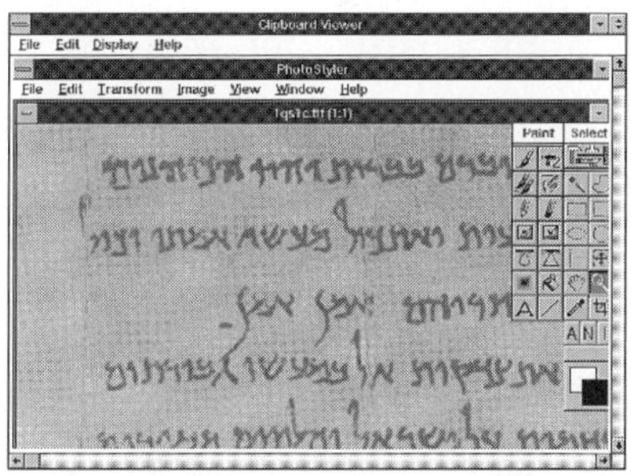

The Windows „*Clipboard Viewer*" displaying a screenshot of PhotoStyler.

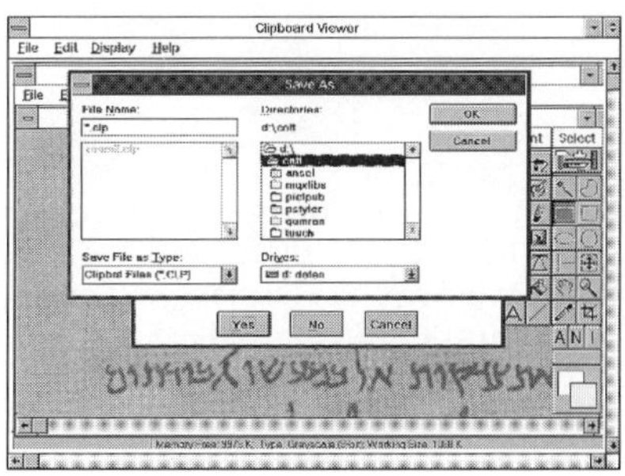

Saving the screenshot with the „*Clipboard Viewer*."

To call a previously stored file to the clipboard,[25] click the „*Open*" command of the „*File*" menu, and the „*Open*" dialogue box will be displayed. Open the directory in which the file to be loaded is stored by doubleclicking it on the tree displayed in the „*Directories*" box. A list of existing files with the extension `.clp` will be displayed in the second filename box. Doubleclick the file to be loaded or type its name in the first filename box and click the „*OK*" button (see page 29).[26]

When Windows is running, one is able to „take a photograph" of the screen by using the clipboard (screen shot). To take a screen shot of the whole screen, press the „*Print*" key. Afterwards open the „*Clipboard Viewer*" and save this copy of your screen as described above. Most of the plates in this book have been produced in this way.[27] To take a screenshot of the active window only, press the *Alt* and the *Print* key at the same time.[28]

Windows and High Resolution Graphic Boards

When operating CATT, it is important to know that Windows 3.1 normally runs the screen with a resolution of 640×480 points and only 16 colors, which is not nearly the quality needed for CATT (see page 16). Windows is released with only a few drivers for SVGA graphic boards, but additional drivers are available from Microsoft, and an SVGA driver for Windows 3.1 is usually released along with the SVGA graphic board. With the help of this driver, Windows should be configured to a resolution of about 800×600 points and at least 256 colors. How to set up the resolution and the number of colors is normally explained in the graphic board's manual as well as in the Windows user guide.

25 Only files with the extension `.clp` previously stored from the „*Clipboard Viewer*" can be loaded to the clipboard.

26 All Windows applications call and save files in this way, therefore it will not be explained again in detail.

27 To reach good quality in printing the screenshot, the Windows screen driver must be configured with a resolution of at least 800×600 points.

28 Attention, sometimes this window can be a dialogue box.

Chapter 3

CATT in Practice

The purpose of this chapter is to describe the commands which are necessary to execute the operations of CATT. This will be done for every program individually. Each program will be described in an introduction followed by an explanation of how to use the tools and commands common to all operations of CATT. Afterwards, detailed instructions will be given on how to execute the operations of CATT described in the first chapter of this book.

Before this can be done, the representation of images on the screen must be discussed: as already mentioned in the description of the operations of CATT, there is a significant difference between the recognition of contrast by the human eye and its representation on the screen of a computer: usually an image is perceived by the human eye as darker than its original. To bridge this difference, monitor gamma correction has been invented.[1] This is to be understood as constant calibration of every image displayed by a program on the screen. Since monitor gamma is only meant for the display on the screen, its corrections are not saved to an image file and are only part of the setup configuration of a program equipped with monitor gamma. Usually the default value of monitor gamma is 1.00, which means virtually no calibration at all. To display the contrast of an image such that it confers with the impression of the original, monitor gamma must be usually configured to a value of 1.48. Of all the programs discussed in the manual, monitor gamma is available with PhotoStyler 1.1, PhotoStyler 2.0, and Picture Publisher 3.1.

- To configure monitor gamma with PhotoStyler 1.1, the *„Preferences …"* command of the *„File"* menu must be clicked to call the *„Preferences Setup"* dialogue box. Click the *„Monitor Gamma …"* button of the dialogue box to open the *„Monitor Gamma"* dialogue

[1] For gamma correction see chapter 1, p. 7.

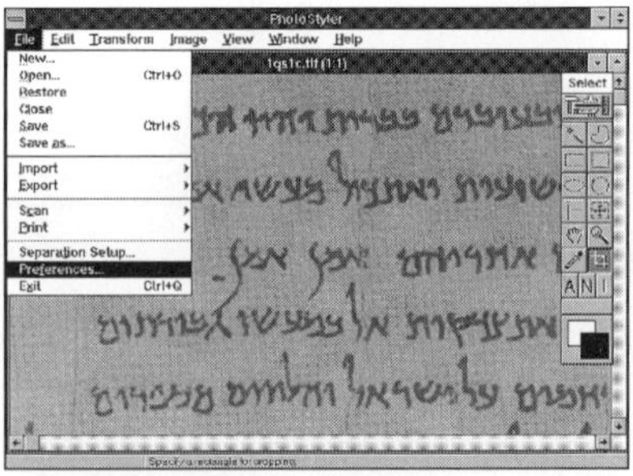

Calling the *„Preferences Setup"* dialogue box with PhotoStyler 1.1.

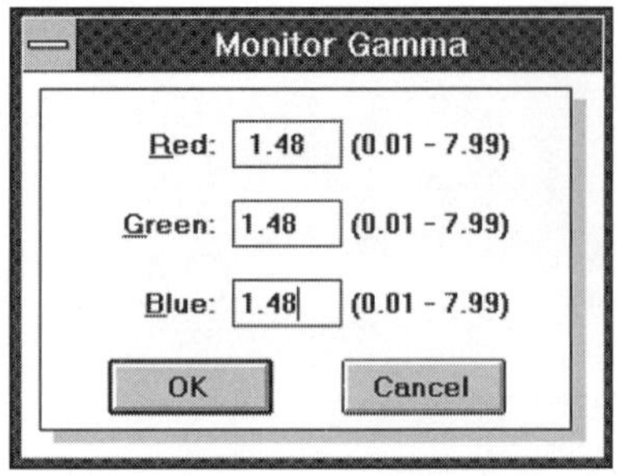

„Monitor Gamma" dialogue box of PhotoStyler 1.1.

box and then type the value 1.48 into each of the boxes entitled *„Red,"* *„Green,"* and *„Blue."* Afterwards click the *„OK"* buttons of both dialogue boxes or press *Enter* twice.

– With PhotoStyler 2.0, monitor gamma must be configured in the *„Monitor Profile"* dialogue box, which can be opened with the *„Monitor Profile ..."* command in the *„Color Management"* submenu of the *„File"* menu. Type the value 1.48 in the *„Target Gamma"* box of this dialogue box, and the representation of contrasts on the screen will be adjusted to the recognition of the human eye.

  Alternatively the slide bars named *„Red,"* *„Green,"* and *„Blue"* can be used. Red, green, and blue ribbons are found next to the slide bars, each one enclosing a brighter red, green, or blue ribbon: for each main color the brightness of the inner ribbon must be adjusted with the slide bars to match the brightness of the outer

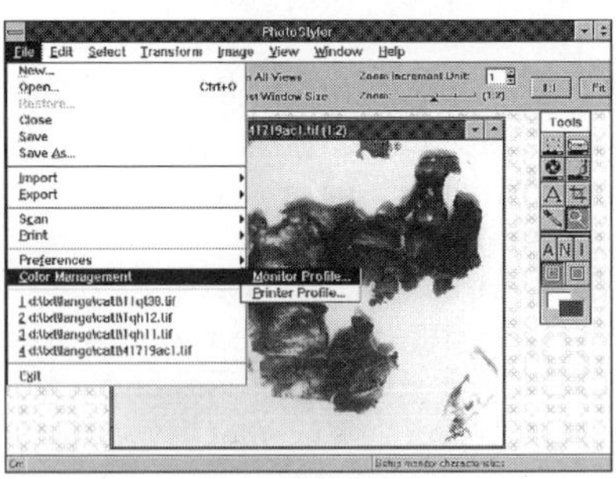

Calling the *„Monitor Profile"* dialogue box with PhotoStyler 2.0.

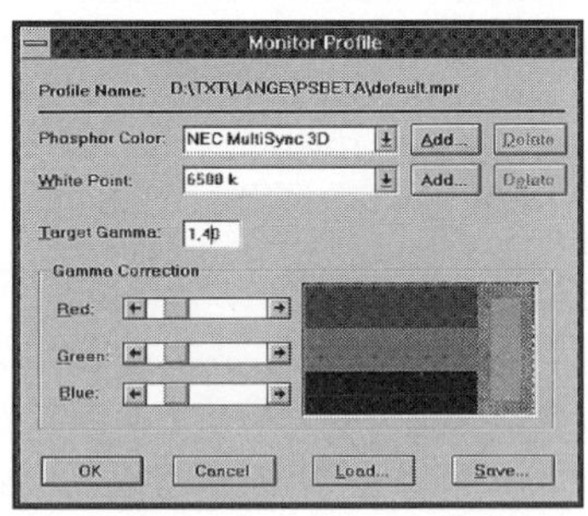

„Monitor Profile" dialogue box of PhotoStyler 2.0.

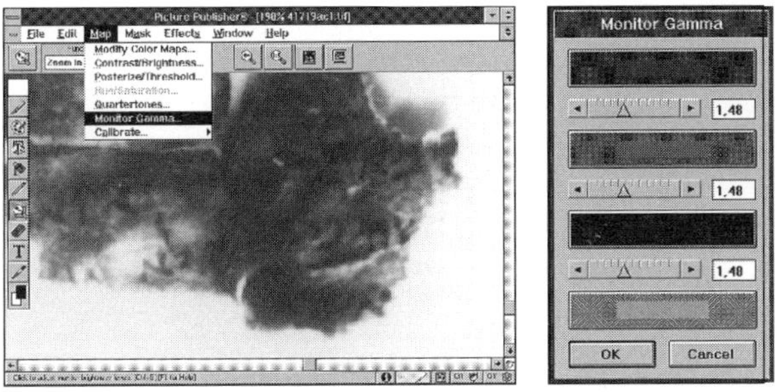

„Monitor Gamma" dialogue box of Picture Publisher and how it is called.

ribbon (place the mouse-pointer on the square-buttons of the slide bars, hold the left mouse-button pressed, and move the mouse).

– With Picture Publisher,[2] the *„Monitor Gamma"* dialogue box is called by the *„Monitor Gamma ..."* command of the *„Map"* menu. In this dialogue box, four colored ribbons are displayed (red, green, blue, and gray). Each ribbon contains another ribbon of the same color which is either displayed brighter or darker. A slide bar is found below each ribbon (except the gray one), which adjusts the brightness of the inner ribbon. For each color (except gray) the brightness of the inner ribbon must be adjusted to match the brightness of the outer ribbon, in order to reach the desired monitor gamma, or, for the same purpose type a value of 1.48 in each box found next to the slide bars.

! With Picture Publisher monitor gamma can only be configured when an image file is opened.

---

[2] For the monitor gamma correction of Picture Publisher see also 130 f.

3.1 FotoTouch 2.1

3.1.1 Introduction and Miscellaneous

In contrast to PhotoStyler and Picture Publisher, FotoTouch[3] is a low cost image processing package. It is sold along with Logitech's hand scanner Scanman 256 as scanner-support software. It does not support colors – only gray-levels. The program is described here because the Scanman 256 achieves reasonable results for CATT in scanning if only few images are to be reconstructed, and FotoTouch achieves comparable results in image processing.

Because FotoTouch is written as scanner-support software for a hand scanner, the program is able to join image excerpts or whole images onto the sides of the current image and not just insert them within its present borders – a capability which is not found with professional image processing packages. Nevertheless the program is not as well equipped with tools and functions as the professional packages. The program supports the file formats BMP, EPS, PCX, and TIFF[4] and the new „Twain" scanner standard.

Commands

Like other Windows programs, FotoTouch groups all necessary commands for file mangement in the *„File"* menu:

Open	To call a file, click the *„Open ..."* command of this menu or press *Ctrl + O*.
Close	To close a file and clear the screen, use the *„Close"* command or press *Ctrl + C*.
Save	To store an image, use the *„Save"* command. This function will also be executed if *Ctrl + S* is pressed.
Save As	The *„Save"* command will store all changes of the current image to its file once clicked. In this way the orig-

[3] The program is a renamed follow-up version of Ansel 1.0, reviewed in A. Lange, Computer Aided Text-Reconstruction and Transcription (CATT), Developed with the Dead Sea Scrolls, in: G. Brooke/F. Garçia Martinez, Congress Volume, International Meeting of the IOQS in Paris 1992 [title uncertain, Leiden 1993 in print].

[4] In addition to normal TIFF (named „TIFF uncomp." by Logitech) TIFF CCITT and a compressed TIFF are supported. Concerning the compressed TIFF, it should be mentioned that this format can't be read by all image processing programs.

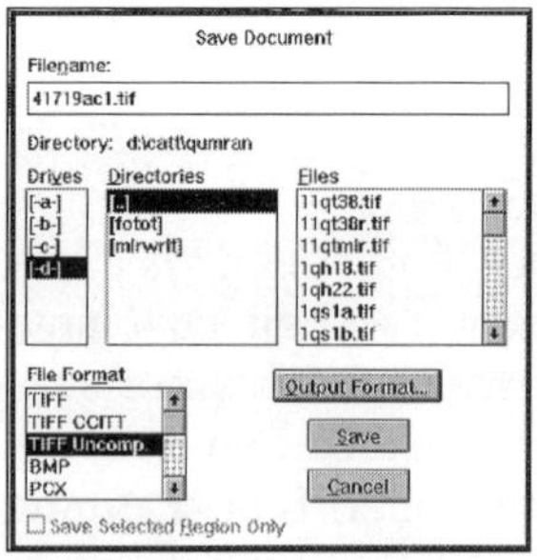

„Save Document" dialogue box of FotoTouch.

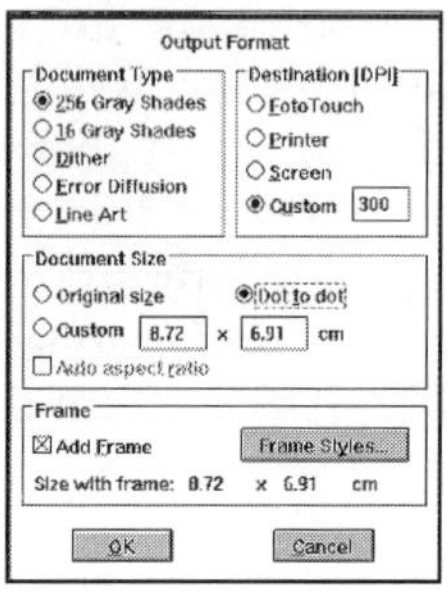

„Output Format" dialogue box of FotoTouch.

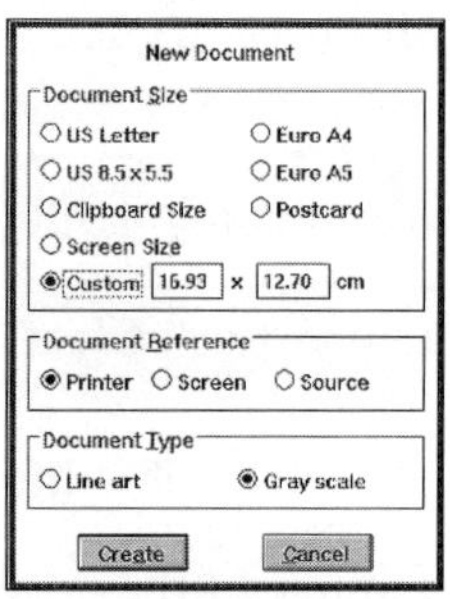

„New Document" dialogue box of FotoTouch.

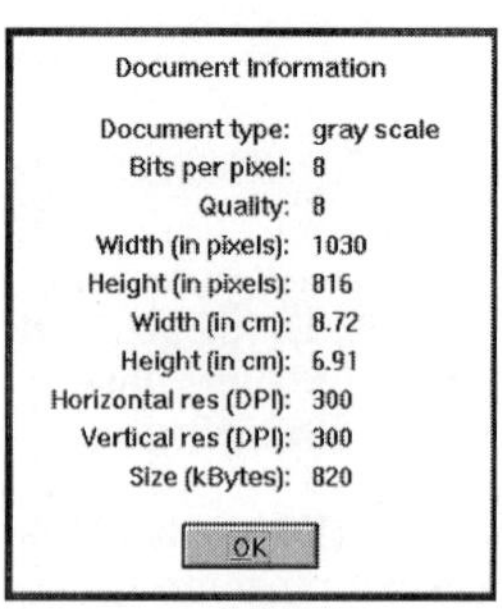

„Document-Information" dialogue box of FotoTouch.

inal image is lost. The „*Save As ...*" command enables one to store the selected image excerpts or the whole current image into a different file.[5]

! FotoTouch is able to store a previously selected area of an image to a new file, if the „*Save As ...*" command is used.

! Images or image excerpts can be configured in the „*Output Format*" dialogue box which can be called with the „*Output Format ...*" button of the „*Save Document*" dialogue box.

! If not otherwise specified in the „*Save Document*" dialogue box, FotoTouch will store a TIFF file in a compressed TIFF file format which cannot be processed by all image processing programs.

New

To create a new file, click the „*New ...*" command or press *Ctrl* + *N*. After the command has been clicked, the „*New Document*" dialogue box will be displayed. In this dialogue box, size, resolution, and gray-scale of the file to be created can be configured. To reach the 300 dpi required for CATT, use the „*Printer*" option if your printer is configured to such a resolution. Otherwise choose the „*Source*" option.[6] To reach the 256 gray-levels necessary for CATT, activate the „*Gray Scale*" option of the dialogue box.

! Configure the new file only as large as necessary. Graphic files with the resolution of 300 dpi and 256 gray-levels need an enourmous amount of space as well in RAM as on the hard disk. A graphic file with the measurements given in the picture on page 36 will need, even in FotoTouch's compressed TIFF, 2.929 MB.

Information

Information about the current image will be displayed if the „*Document-Info*" command of the „*View*" menu is clicked or *Ctrl* + *I* is pressed.

---

[5] After the command has been clicked, you will be guided by the „*Save Document*" dialogue box.

[6] In this case the Scanman must be configured to a resolution of 300 dpi or more.

Rulers

With the *„Show Ruler“* command of the *„View“* menu, ruler-lines can be put on the screen (alternatively press *F8*). The kind of measurements displayed with the ruler-lines can be configured in the *„Preferences“* dialogue box, which is called by the *„Preferences ...“* command of the *„File“* menu. The current measurement is displayed in the upper left corner of the program window, where the ruler-lines cross.

! The measurements displayed by the ruler-lines are not the measurements of the manuscript to be reconstructed, but of its scanned photograph, which is not usually scaled 1 : 1.

Exit

There are three ways to exit FotoTouch: a) click the *„Exit“* command of the *„File“* menu, b) doubleclick the square found in the upper left-hand corner of FotoTouch's program window, c) press *Alt + F4*.

Tools

For the selection of image excerpts, FotoTouch provides users with two different selection tools.

To select a rectangular area of the current image, click the *„Rectangular Selection“* tool and place the mouse-pointer next to the area to be selected. Hold the left mouse-button pressed and draw a rectangular marque around the area of interest.

The selection will be activated when the left mouse-button is released. To de-select a previously selected area, click one of the selection tools, place the mouse-pointer anywhere outside the selected area, and press the left mouse-button one time. To move a selected area, place the mouse-pointer anywhere inside the area, hold the left mouse-button pressed, and move the mouse.

To select an irregular formed area of the current image, click the *„Free Selection“* tool and draw a marque of any form around the area of interest by moving the mouse-pointer while the left mouse-button is pressed. Afterwards proceed as described above.

To scroll an image, click the *„Hand“* icon of the toolbox, place the mouse-pointer – now displayed in the shape of a hand – inside the current image, hold the left mouse-button pressed,

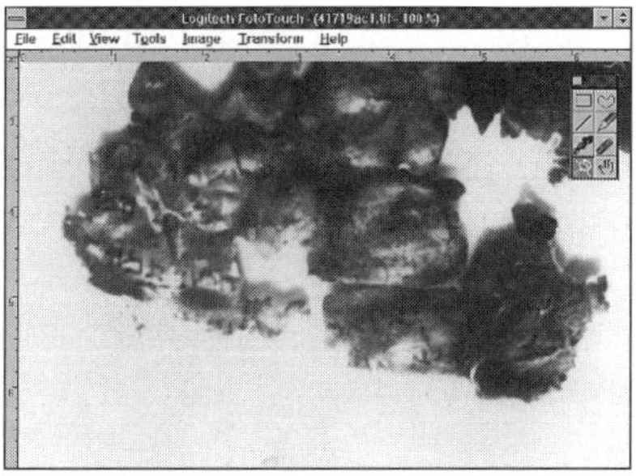

4Q180 3

Part of 4Q180 3 magnified

PAM 41719: Courtesy of the IAA

and move the mouse: the image will be scrolled according to the mouse movements.

3.1.2 Magnification

Once an image is called to FotoTouch's program window, magnification of images can be reached in three different ways:

- Click the *„Magnifying Glass"* icon of FotoTouch's toolbox. When returned to the current image, the mouse-pointer will be displayed in the shape of a magnifying glass. Place the mouse-pointer on the area to be magnified. Each time the left mouse-button is pressed, the image will be zoomed to double its previous size. Each time the right mouse-button is pressed it will be zoomed to half of its former size.
- The *„Zoom In"* and *„Zoom Out"* commands of the *„View"* menu enable one to zoom the current image in or out respectively. In this way magnification can be reached while working with another tool.
- Zoom operations can be executed with FotoTouch in the same way by using the + and – keys of the keyboard.

3.1.3 Darkened or Faded Texts

Negative

To invert the gray-scale of the current image to a negative, click the *„Negative"* command of the *„Image"* menu. A previously selected area of the current image can also be inverted to a negative if it is marked before the *„Negative"* command is executed.

! An altered image should be stored in a separate file leaving the original image intact.

Regulation of Brightness and Contrast

With FotoTouch contrast and brightness can be regulated in three different ways.

- For the regulation of contrast and brightness, FotoTouch provides users with a small toolbox which is shown or hidden once the *„Show Tone Controls"* command of the *„View"* menu is clicked or *F7* is pressed. Three sliders can be seen in this toolbox, each one equipped with an arrow. If the arrow of the left-hand slide bar is moved with the mouse-pointer, the brightness of the current image is increased or decreased. With the help of the central slide bar, the contrast of the current image can be regulated in the same way. If the arrow of the right-hand slide bar is moved with the mouse-pointer, the amount of highlights, shadows, and midtones of the current image will be adjusted – this function is named *„Tone"* by Logitech. Each slide bar can be reset to zero if its arrow is doubleclicked. To reach good results with darkened or faded texts, it is advisable to combine these three tools.
  If only a selected area of the current image should be enhanced in contrast and brightness, the previously described tools cannot be used: Click the *„Lighten"* or the *„Darken"* command of the *„Image"* menu to lighten or darken an image excerpt after it has been selected.[7]
- Brightness and contrast of the current image or of previously selected areas can also be manipulated if the *Alt* key and + or – are pressed simultaneously.

! If an image or a selected area of an image is lightened by the *„Lighten"* command or the keys *Alt* and +, its contrast will decrease. To compensate for this decreasement, execute the *„Sharpen"* command of the *„Image"* menu.

[7] The same results will be reached for the whole image if these commands are used and no image excerpt has been selected beforehand.

Fragment of 4Q185
PAM 43514: Courtesy of the IAA

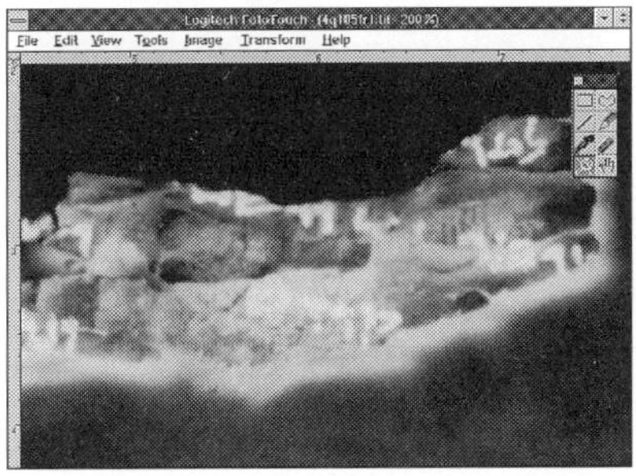

The same fragment inverted in gray scale to a negative.

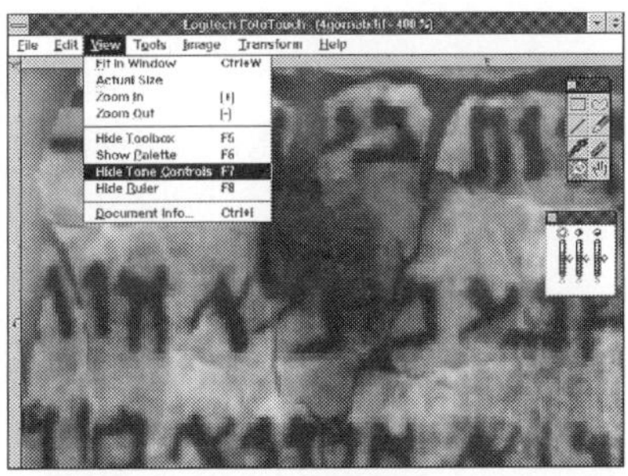

Part of 4QOrNab
PAM 42265: Courtesy of the IAA

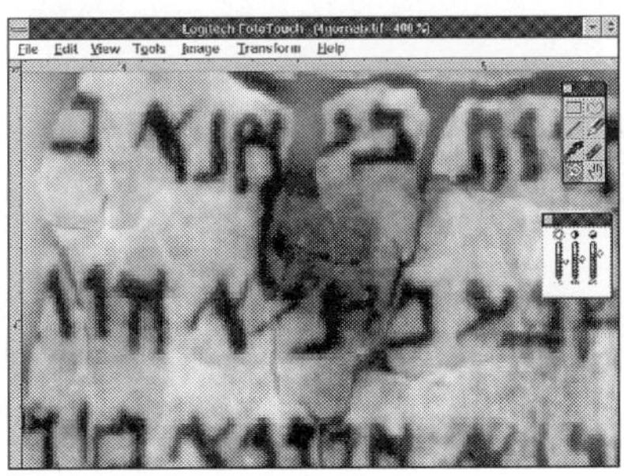

The same part of 4QOrNab enhanced in contrast and brightness.

! An altered image should be stored in a separate file leaving the original image intact.

Equalization

FotoTouch provides users with an excellent predefined equalization function. Configurable equalization is not available with FotoTouch but will seldom be needed, because its predefined equalization usually fits CATT's purposes.

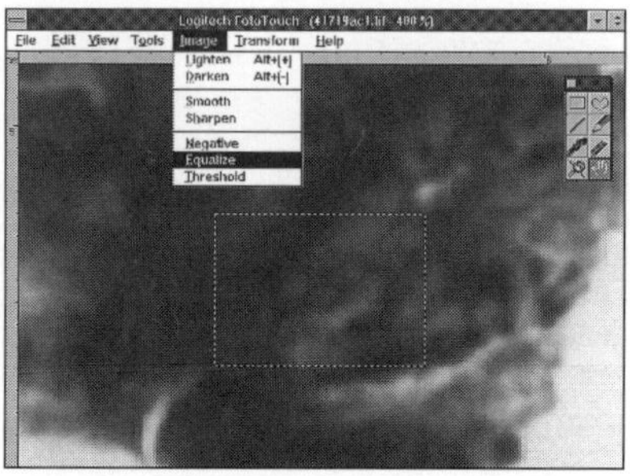

Part of 4Q180 3

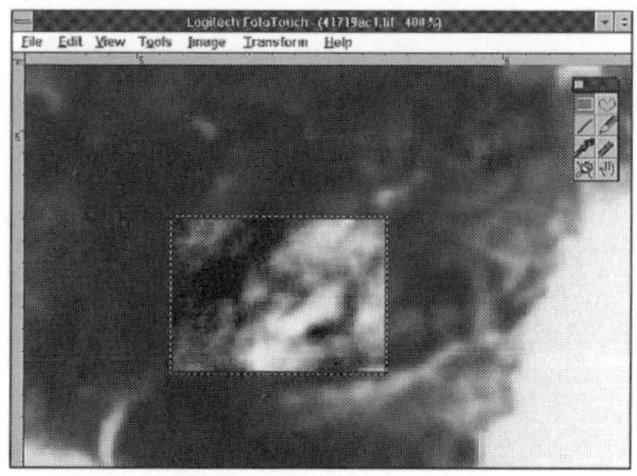

The same part of 4Q180 3 enhanced with equalization (כללה).

PAM 41719: Courtesy of the IAA

To use equalization, select the darkened or faded area of the current image with the help of the *„Free Selection"* tool, then click the *„Equalize"* command of the *„Image"* menu.

! An altered image should be stored in a separate file leaving the original image intact.

! If large faded or darkened parts of a manuscript are to be reconstructed, it is advisable to mark small parts of these darkened or faded areas and work on them individually to reach good results.

3.1.4 Comparison and Joining of Fragments

1. To join or compare fragments, the fragments of interest must be selected out of their image files. To do this, call the files containing the fragments and use the *„Rectangular Selection"* tool to draw a marque around the fragment to be selected. The selected fragment

should then be saved with the help of the *„Save As . . . "* command of the *„File"* menu.

2. Afterwards call the file containing the fragment with which the fragment just saved is to be compared or joined. To enable comparison and joining of fragments with FotoTouch, the transparency of the programs paste function must be configured, which can only be done if an image has been loaded beforehand. For this use the *„Paste Setup . . . "* command of the *„Edit"* menu to call the *„Paste Setup"* dialogue box, and choose the option *„Transparent."*

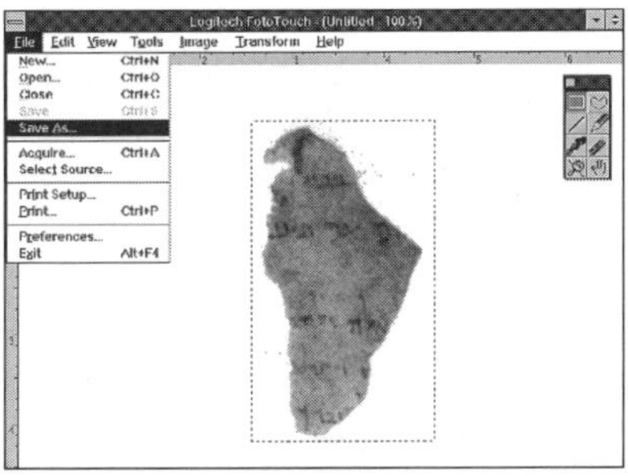

1QH 22 selected
Courtesy of the Shrine of the Book

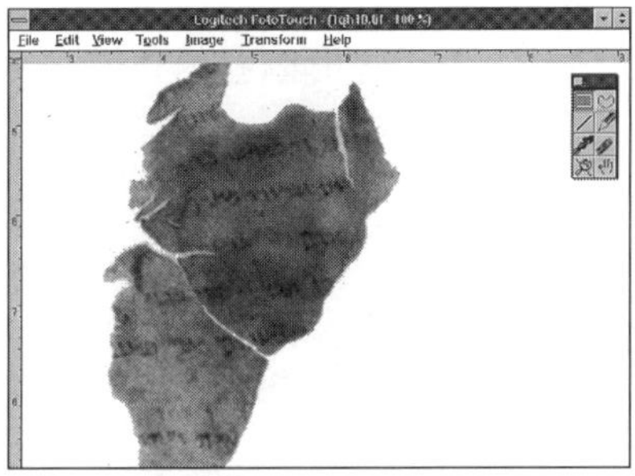

1QH 22 joined with 1QH 18
Courtesy of the Shrine of the Book

3. To insert a previously selected and saved fragment, click the *„Stitch From . . . "* command of the *„Edit"* menu (afterwards you will be guided by dialogue boxes). The inserted fragment will be displayed on the screen surrounded by a blinking rectangular marque. To move it, place the mouse-pointer inside the inserted fragment, hold the left mouse-button pressed, and move the mouse. To rotate or resize the inserted fragment, use the *„Deskew"* or the *„Scale"* command of the *„Transform"* menu.[8]
4. To compare the border structures of both fragments, place the inserted fragment on the fragment with which it is to be compared. To join them, place the inserted fragment next to the fragment with which it is to be joined, and click the current image anywhere outside the inserted fragment to fixate it.

As long as FotoTouch's transparency option is activated, only the inserted fragment will be visible, while the white background of the inserted fragment will not hide any part of the current image. Even the parchment of the inserted fragment will be displayed half-transparent, which is of great help if the location of the lines of the

[8] For a detailed explanation of how to use these commands see below (49).

fragments is to be compared. The *„Stitch From ...“* command will automatically enlarge the current image if the fragment to be inserted is too large and does not fit.

! The exact location and scale of the selected fragments should be noted.

3.1.5 Mirrorwriting

1. In a first operation the mirrorwriting to be relocated must be selected like any other fragment, as described above (see page 42). After being selected, the mirrorwriting must be mirrored back: for this use the *„Flip Horizontal“* command of the *„Transform“* menu. The remirrored mirrorwriting should be stored in a separate file with the *„Save As ...“* command of the *„File“* menu.
2. After the file containing the column from which the mirrorwriting has been separated is called, click the *„Stitch From ...“* command of the *„Edit“* menu to insert[9] the mirrorwriting into this file. To relocate the mirrorwriting, place it above its home column and fixate it as described above for the comparison and joining of fragments.

! Somtimes it is of great help to invert the inserted mirrorwriting to a negative. In this way the characters of the mirrorwriting will be displayed transparent while their surrounding parchment will be displayed black and intransparent. By this means, you are able to see the character fragments of the mirrorwritings home column through the transparent characters of the mirrorwriting.

! Because both – the parchment of the mirrorwriting as well as the parchment of its home column – are sometimes crumbled, it is advisable to relocate only small portions of a mirrorwriting in one operation and not the whole mirrorwriting.

3.1.6 Character Fragments

1. To identify character fragments, lettertemplates must be created. For this an intact character must be selected with the help of the *„Rectangular Selection“* tool. After having selected a character, use

[9] Ensure yourself that the *„Transparency“* option of FotoTouch's insert function is activated as described in the previous paragraph.

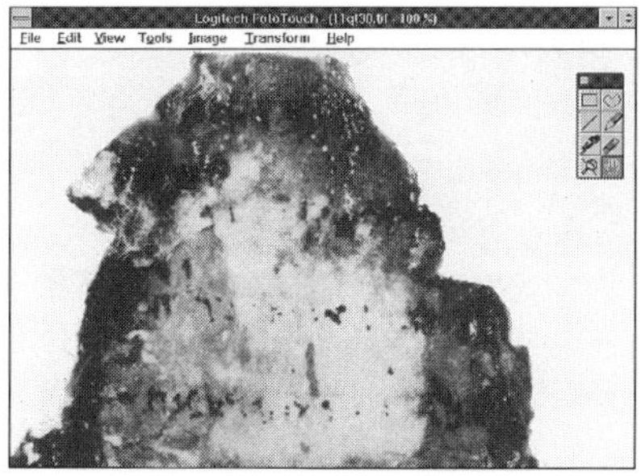

11QTemp XXXVIII

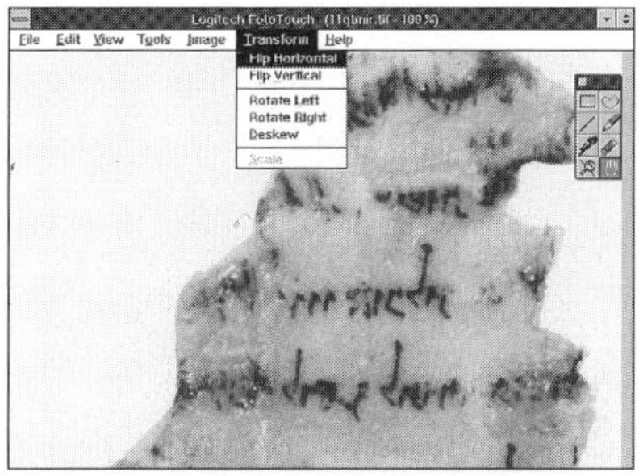

Remirroring the mirrorwriting of 11QTemp XXXVIII.

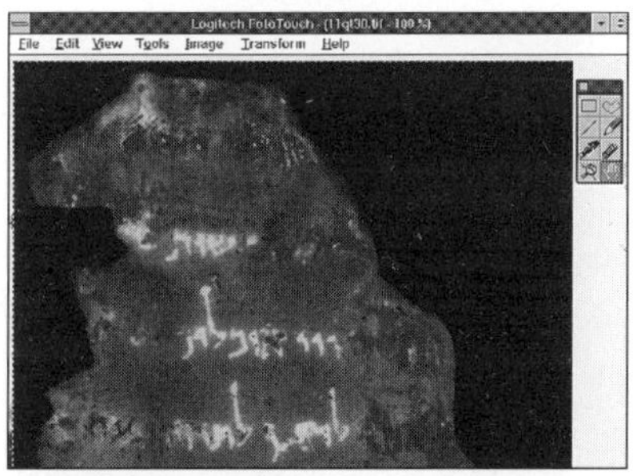

The pasted mirrorwriting inverted to a negative.

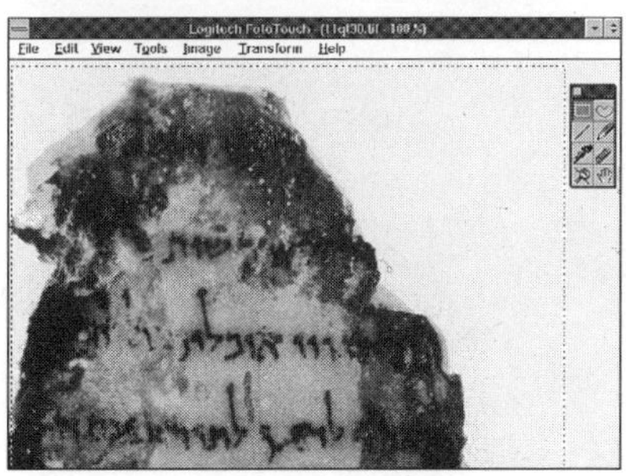

The mirrorwriting relocated.

11QTemp XXXVIII and mirrorwriting: Courtesy of the Shrine of the Book

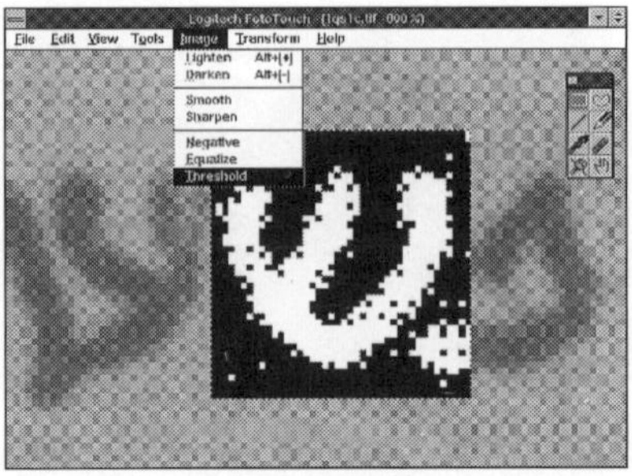

A character selected out of 1QS I_{23} and inverted to a negative.

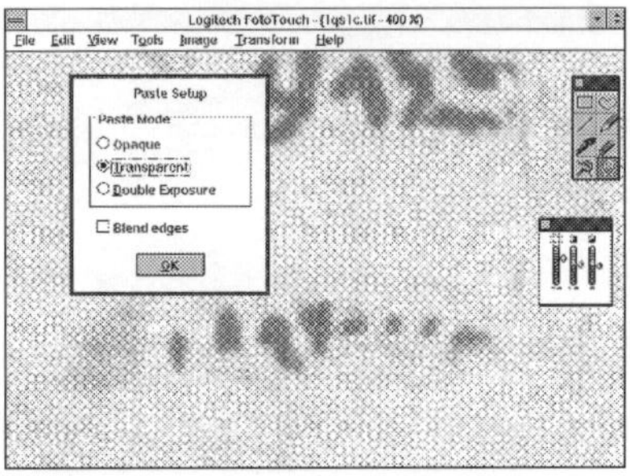

The *„Paste"* function of FotoTouch must be configured transparent.

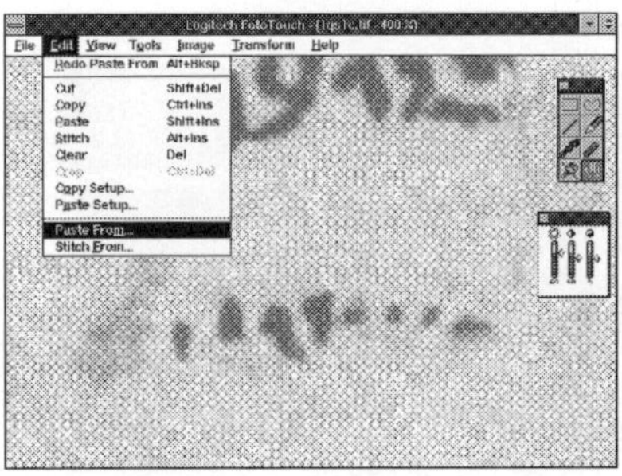

The lettertemplate pasted next to the character fragments to be identified.

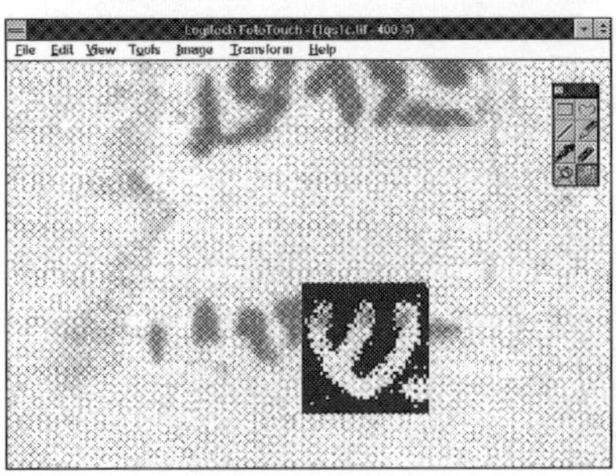

The character fragments identified as the Hebrew letter שׁ.

1QS I: Courtesy of the Shrine of the Book

the *„Negative“* command of the *„Image“* menu to invert the selected character to a negative and then enhance the contrast of the selected character with the help of the *„Threshold“* command of the *„Image“* menu. Thereafter the manipulated character should be stored to a separate file (use the *„Save As ...“* command of the *„File“* menu).

2. For using lettertemplates, it is essential to configure the paste function of FotoTouch to transparent before a lettertemplate is inserted: click the *„Paste Setup ...“* command of the *„Edit“* menu to call the *„Paste Setup“* dialogue box.
3. Insert a lettertemplate with the help of the *„Paste From ...“* command of the *„Edit“* menu into the file containing the character fragments to be identified (you will be guided by dialogue boxes): the lettertemplate will be displayed on the screen with its white pixels transparent, i. e. the characters, and its black pixels intransparent, i. e. the black background. To identify a character fragment, place the lettertemplate on top of it.[10]

! The exact location of the characters from which the lettertemplates have been derived should be noted.

! If the contrast of the lettertemplate cannot be enhanced by the *„Threshold“* command, use the *„Equalize“* command of the *„Image“* menu for the same purpose.

3.1.7 The Comparison of Characters

For the comparison of characters, e. g. necessary for paleographic purposes, proceed as described for the identification of character fragments.

3.1.8 The Reconstruction of Text Gaps

1. In a first operation all words and characters, which shall probably be inserted into the text gap to be reconstructed, must be selected and stored individually. To select them, use the *„Rectangular Se-*

---

[10] Place the mouse-pointer on the lettertemplate, hold the left mouse-button pressed and move the mouse. To fixate the lettertemplate, click anywhere on the current image outside the template. To delete the template, click the *„Cut“* command of the *„Edit“* menu or press *Shift + Del.*

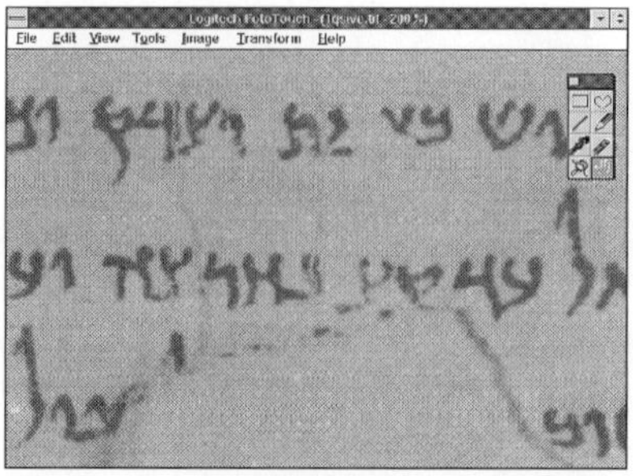

Text gap in 1QS IV_{26}

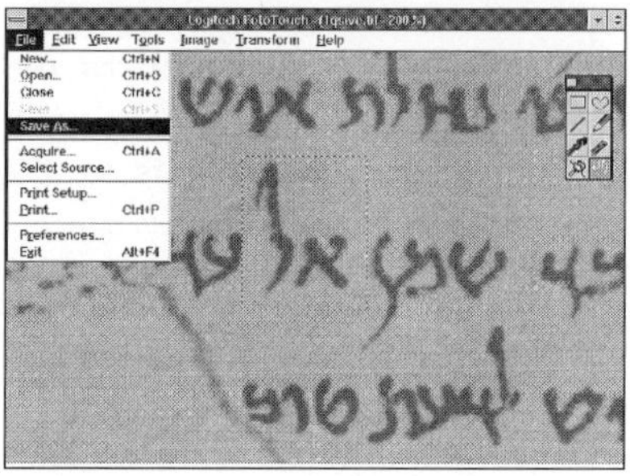

The word אל isolated in line 1QS IV_{26} and saved to a separate file.

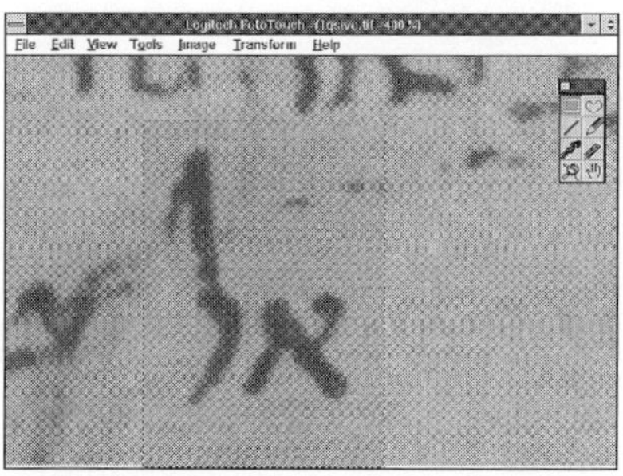

The word אל inserted into the text gap.

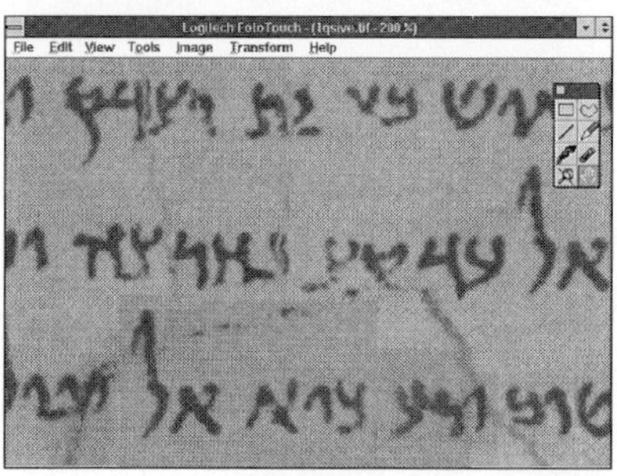

H. Stegemann's reconstruction of 1QS IV_{26} verified. (H. Stegemann, Zu Textbestand und Grundgedanken von 1QS III, 13-IV, 26, RdQ 13, 1988, 95–132, 107 f.)

Courtesy of the Shrine of the Book

lection" tool; to store them, activate the *„Save As ... "* command of the *„File"* menu.[11]

2. Call the *„Paste Setup"* dialogue box with the help of the *„Paste Setup ... "* command of the *„Edit"* menu to configure the insert function of FotoTouch to transparent.
3. In a next operation insert the words and/or characters just saved by the *„Paste From ... "* command of the *„Edit"* menu (you will be guided by dialogue boxes). Because the insert function of FotoTouch is configured to transparent, only the characters of the inserted image excerpts can be seen, while the surrounding parchment is displayed transparent. Place the inserted word or character at its location in the text gap and fixate it by clicking the surrounding current image.

! Note the location from where the inserted characters and/or words have been derived.

Scaling and Rotation of Images and Image Excerpts

To resize and/or rotate images or image excerpts, two commands of the *„Transform"* menu are to be used:

- Click the *„Scale"* command to resize an image. A rectangular marque equipped with four handles will be displayed around the image or image excerpt to be resized. Place the mouse-pointer on one of these handles, hold the left mouse-button pressed, and move the mouse. In a small dialogue box, the current width and height of the image or image excerpt being resized will be displayed, as well as the percentage of shrinking or extending.

! If an image excerpt of different scale must be adjusted to the scale of the current image, it is of great help to place e. g. a character of the image excerpt to be resized above a matching one of the current image and to resize the inserted image, until both characters are equal in size.

- To rotate an image or an image excerpt, click the *„Deskew"* command of the *„Transform"* menu. Afterwards the mouse-pointer will

[11] Make sure that the resolution of the new image file matches the resolution of the image-files from which the excerpts have been selected. To configure this resolution, click the *„Output Format ... "* button of the *„Save Document"* dialogue box.

be displayed in the shape of a double arrow. Place the mouse-pointer next to the surrounding marque of the image or image excerpt to be rotated, and draw a line parallel to the inclined fragment or image excerpt (hold the left mouse-button pressed and move the mouse). FotoTouch will calculate and correct the inclination automatically.

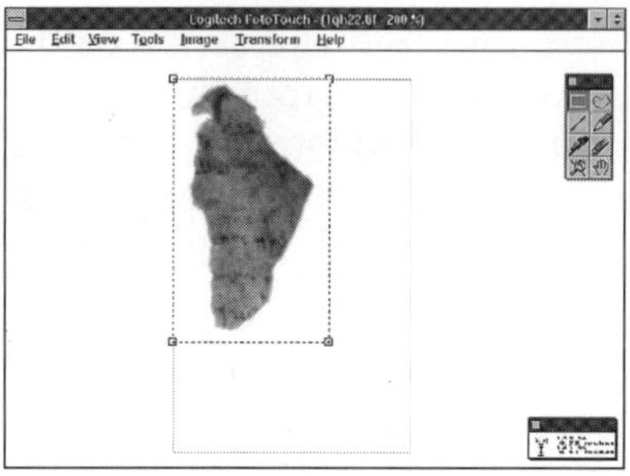

1QH 22 scaled.
Courtesy of the Shrine of the Book

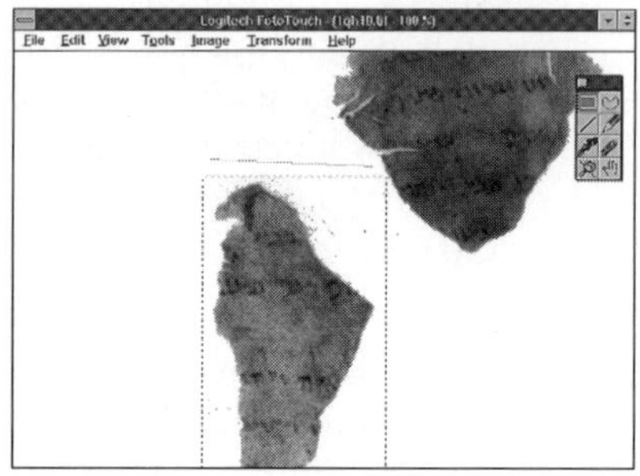

1QH 22 rotated
Courtesy of the Shrine of the Book

! FotoTouch does not rotate the rectangular marque surrounding the image or image excerpt, but only the area included in the marque. If the degree of rotation is too large, a part of an inserted fragment can be cut away.

3.2 PhotoStyler 1.1

3.2.1 Introduction and Miscellaneous

PhotoStyler has been developed by Ulead as a clone of the classical Macintosh image processing program, Adobe's Photoshop. Since Aldus bought Ulead, the program is Aldus' prime image processing package. Like all the programs described here, PhotoStylers runs under Windows 3.x. Nowadays the program has become the classical Windows image processing package. It provides a large amount of useful tools and functions for CATT. PhotoStyler supports the file formats BMP, EPS, GIF, PCX, TGA, and TIFF. TIFF-files can also be stored in the Macintosh TIFF-format.

The tools of PhotoStyler are organized in two separate toolboxes on the right-hand side of the program window. In the *„Paint"* toolbox, all painting tools are presented, e. g. a brush, a rubber, and a letter-icon, which activates the writing capacities of PhotoStyler when doubleclicked. In the *„Select"* toolbox tools are organized which help in selecting, moving, magnifying, and analysing images.

In a gray ribbon at the bottom of the program window, the so-called *„Status Bar,"* information and immediate context sensitive help are displayed.

Commands

Open — To call a file with PhotoStyler, click the *„Open ..."* command in the *„File"* menu or press *Crtl + O*, then you will be guided.

Close — To close a file, doubleclick the square at the upper left-hand corner of the file-window or click the *„Close"* command in the *„File"* menu.

New — To create a new file, click the *„New ..."* command in the *„File"* menu. A dialogue box entitled *„Create New Image"* will appear. Here the file to be created must be configured. As *„Data Type"* choose *„Greyscale(8-bit/pixel)."* The resolution of the file should be at least 300 dpi (see the plate on p. 52).

! Even if height and width of your new file are given in cm, configure the resolution of your new file in pixel/inch. The international standard measurement for the resolution of graphic files is dpi (= dots per inch).

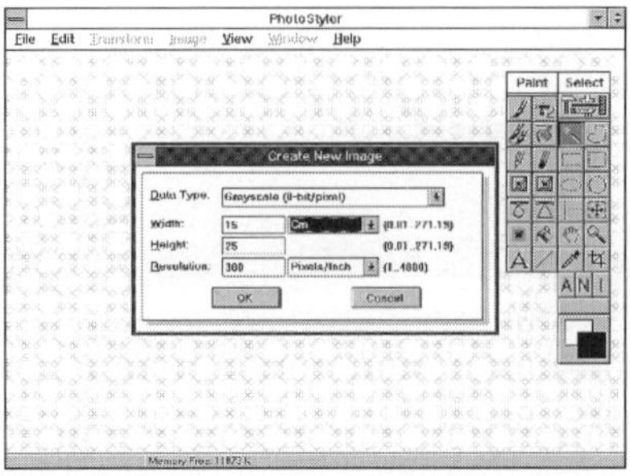

PhotoStyler's *„Create New Image“* dialogue box.

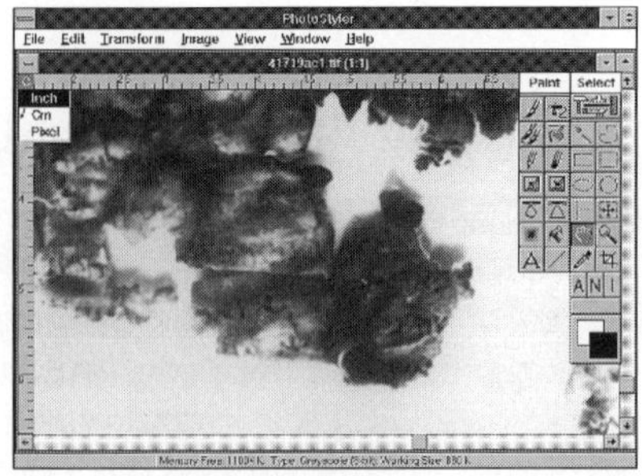

Part of PAM 41719 (4Q180 3) with ruler lines. Courtesy of the IAA

! Configure the new file only as large as necessary. Graphic files with a resolution of 300 dpi need an enormous amount of space in RAM and on the hard disk. A graphic file with the configuration as shown above (left) will need 5.109 MB of memory.

Save To save a file, click the *„Save“* command in the *„File“* menu or press *Ctrl + S*. If a new file is to be stored, the *„Save Image File“* dialogue box will be displayed. In this box, name, directory, and format of the file are to be given. Afterwards click the *„Save“* button.[12]

! If the results of your work on a text are stored with the *„Save“* command, the original image of the manuscript will be lost. Any manipulated image should be stored in a separate file using the *„Save As ...“* command.

Undo To undo or redo edits, click the first command of the *„Edit“* menu, named *„Undo“* or *„Redo“* respectively or press *Alt + Bksp*.

Rulers Ruler-lines can be shown or hidden. If the *„Rulers“* command in the *„View“* menu is clicked or *Ctrl + R* are pressed, horizontal or vertical ruler-lines will appear. The kind of measurement displayed (inch, cm, pixel) can be configured by clicking the button found where the rulers cross labeled *„I,“ „C,“* or *„P“* respectively as shown above (right).

[12] PhotoStyler is able to convert a DOS TIFF-file to the Macintosh TIFF. This application is very useful, if the results of your work will be published with an Apple system. For the conversion itself, see the PhotoStyler user manual, p. 71.

! The measurements displayed by the ruler-lines are not the measurements of the manuscript itself but of the scanned photo, which often differ significantly in size. To get the correct measurements of the manuscript, look for the ruler of the manuscript's photo and calculate the scale of the photo.

Tile — In PhotoStyler, every file is displayed in a separate window. If it is necessary to work with two or more files at the same time, open all files as described, and click the „*Tile*" command in the „*Window*" menu or press *Shift* + *F4*.

! Working with several graphic files at the same time requires a large amount of RAM. Hold only the files opened which are really needed.

Information — To get information about the current image, click the „*Information ...*" command of the „*View*" menu.

Exit — To quit PhotoStyler, click the „*Exit*" command of the „*File*" menu, doubleclick the square found at the upper left-hand corner of the program window, or press *Alt* + *F4*.

Tools

With the „*Magic Wand*" tool you are able to define any pixels of an image which are next to each other and have – in a certain range – the same gray-level as a selected area. To define this range, doubleclick the „*Magic Wand*" icon. A dialogue box will appear where the span of the range can be config-

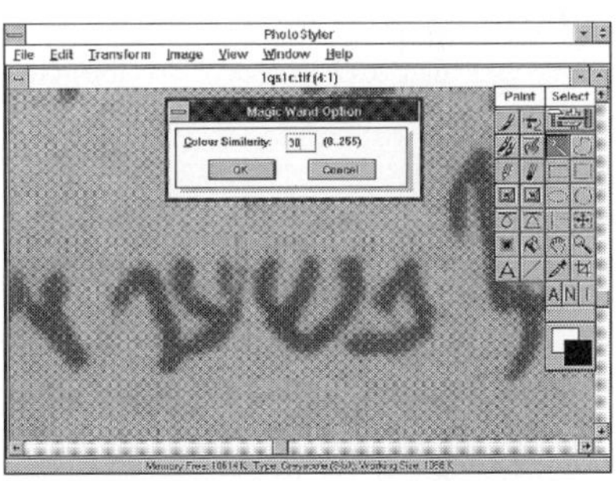

The wand range can be configured in the „*Magic Wand Option*" dialogue box.

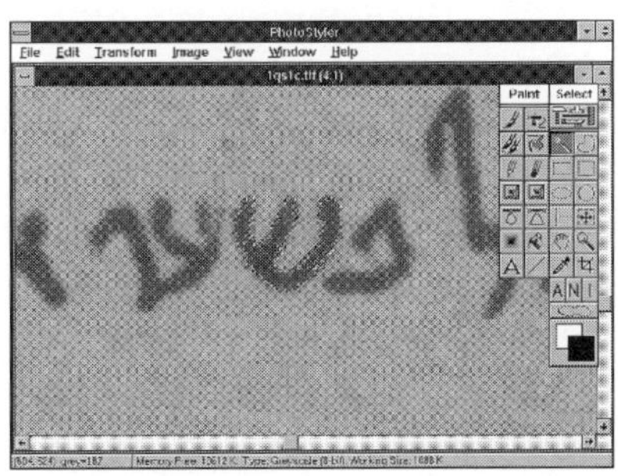

A black area selected with the „*Magic Wand*" tool.

ured. To analyze the range of gray levels of the area to be selected, move the mouse-pointer to the area to be selected. The gray level of the pixel the mouse-pointer is pointing at will be displayed on the left side of the status bar at the bottom PhotoStyler's program window. If, for instance, gray levels between 130 and 151 are found, the wand range should be set to 21. After the wand range is configured, click the area of interest and it will be masked with a blinking marque.

If you want to select an area of an image manually, click the „*Free Selection*" tool and move the mouse-pointer to the part of the image to be selected. Hold the left mouse-button pressed and move the mouse-pointer around the area to be selected, then press the left mouse-button two times – again the selected area will be masked by a blicking marque.

To select an area in the form of a rectangle, click the „*Rectangle Selection*" tool of the „*Select*" toolbox and proceed as described above.

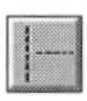

To define a line as a selected area, click the „*Line Selection*" tool and proceed as described above.

To scroll an image, click the „*Hand*" icon of the „*Select*" toolbox. When the mouse-pointer is moved back to the image, it will appear in the shape of a hand. Hold the left mouse-button pressed while moving the mouse and the image will follow the mouse movements. It is also possible to move the current image by using the horizontal and vertical scroll-bars of its window.

A special feature of PhotoStyler are its „*Selection*" buttons. With the „*A*" button *a*ll of the current image can be selected. With the „*N*" button any selected area can be deselected. With the „*I*" button any previously selected area can be *i*nverted – an application which is, for instance, very helpful for isolating fragments.

The „*Selection Status Indicator*" indicates the kind of selection.

For the „*Text*" tool see the user guide of PhotoStyler.

Clipboards

With PhotoStyler users are able to choose whether to work with the Windows clipboard or a clipboard designed especially for PhotoStyler, the so-called *„Private Clipboard."* While the Windows clipboard enables you to exchange data between all Windows programs, it is not especially designed for image processing and therefore some of CATT's operations can't be done using it. On the other hand the private clipboard of PhotoStyler is not able to exchange data with other Windows programs.[13]

- To call the clipboard from inside PhotoStyler, click the *„Clipboard …"* command in the *„Edit"* menu. In the *„Clipboard"* dialogue box, click the *„Load"* button to load and the *„Save"* button to store clipboard data to and from the hard disk respectively. Afterwards you will be guided by dialogue boxes.
- To change the clipboard, use the circles of the *„Clipboard"* dialogue box entitled *„Windows"* and *„Private."*

3.2.2 Magnification

To zoom any part of an image with PhotoStyler, click the *„Magnifying Glass"* icon of the *„Select"* toolbox. When placed on the area to be magnified, the mouse-pointer will change to the shape of a

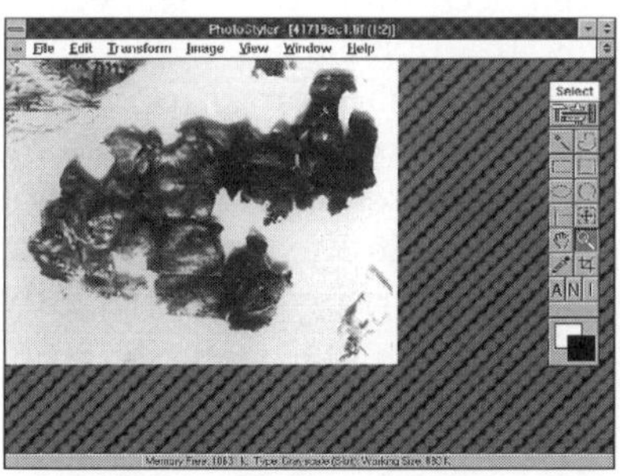

4Q180 3

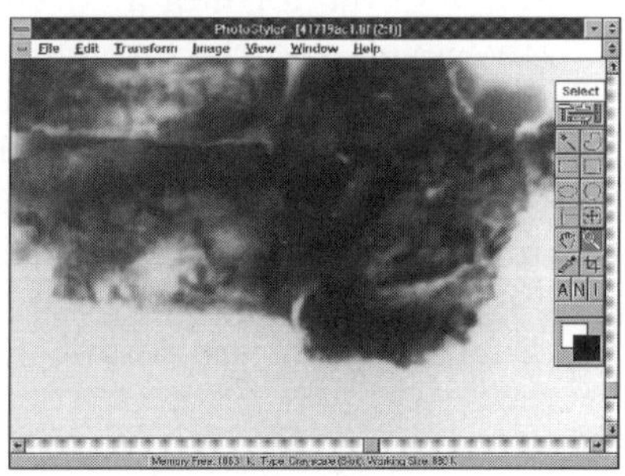

Part of 4Q180 3 magnified.

PAM 41719: Courtesy of the IAA

[13] We have had good experiences using the private clipboard for the program's internal data-exchange, for instance for inserting selected characters and/or fragments into an image, and the Windows clipboard at the same time to produce hardcopies of the screen. The plates of this manual have been produced in this way.

magnifying glass. Every time the left mouse-button is pressed, the image will be magnified (2:1, 3:1, 4:1 etc.). To reduce the current image to a scale of 1:1, press the right mouse-button.

If an image should be reduced, click the „*Zoom Out*" command in the „*View*" menu, choose one of the scales displayed in the submenu, and the image will be zoomed out to this scale.

3.2.3 Darkened or Faded Texts

Image Analysis by Histograms

Before reconstructing darkened or faded passages of a text, it is sometimes necessary to detect whether there have been any characters preserved or not. Histograms can be used for this purpose:

- To create a histogram, the area to be analyzed must be selected as explained above. Afterwards press *F3* to process a histogram and to open the „*Grey/Colour Correction*" dialogue box. A histogram is seen in this dialogue box. To magnify the histogram, click the toolbox icon of the dialogue box and a pull down menu will be opened. Click the „*Enlarge Histogram*" command of this menu to magnify the histogram and the „*Reduce Histogram*" command to reduce it.
- In dealing with histograms it is important to remember that a histogram is a graphic representation of the pixel distribution of an image in the form of a curve, ordered according to the respective gray-levels and the amount of pixels. If all pixels are of the same or nearly the same gray-level (the gray-levels from 0 to 255 are represented by the horizontal axis, their amount is represented by the vertical axis), there are no characters preserved. This does not imply that there were never any characters in the analyzed area, but that they have not been preserved. If some pixels of a slightly different value are found, this may indicate that characters are preserved here.

! PhotoStyler provides users with a „*Line Selection*" tool (see above); some of our most informative histograms have been produced by processing lines.

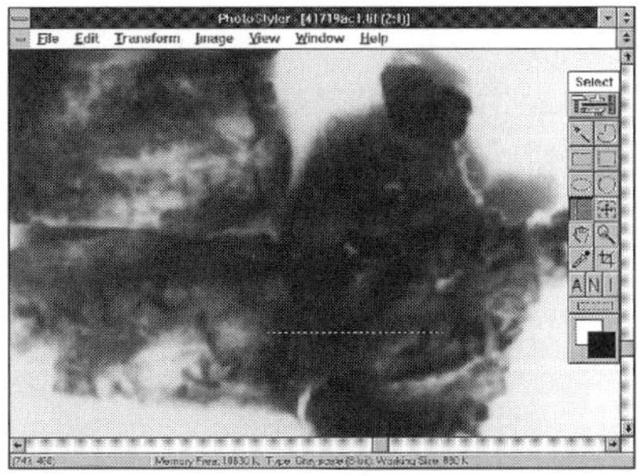

Line selected out of the magnified area.

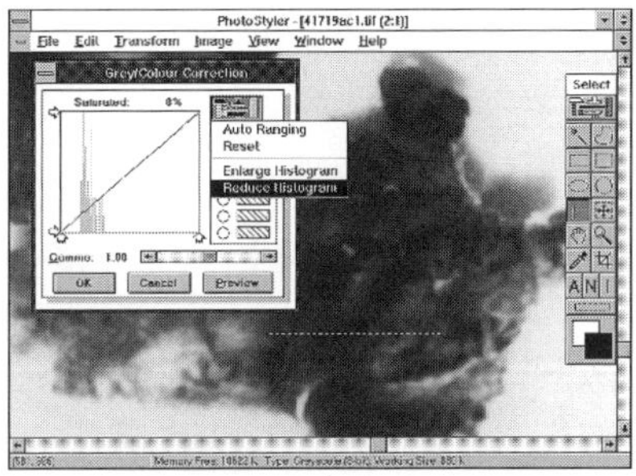

Histogram calculated along the line.

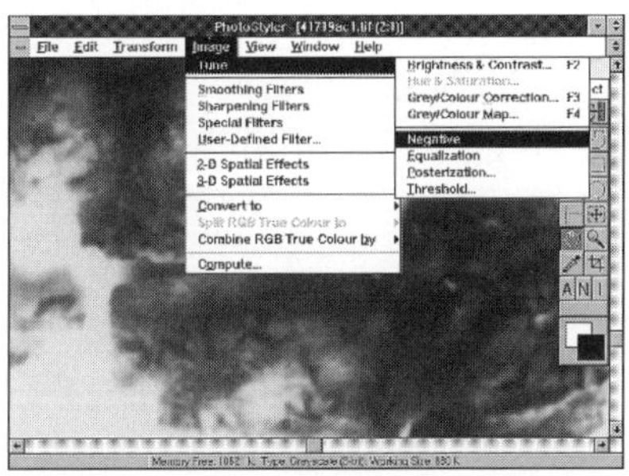

„Negative" command of the *„Tune"* submenu.

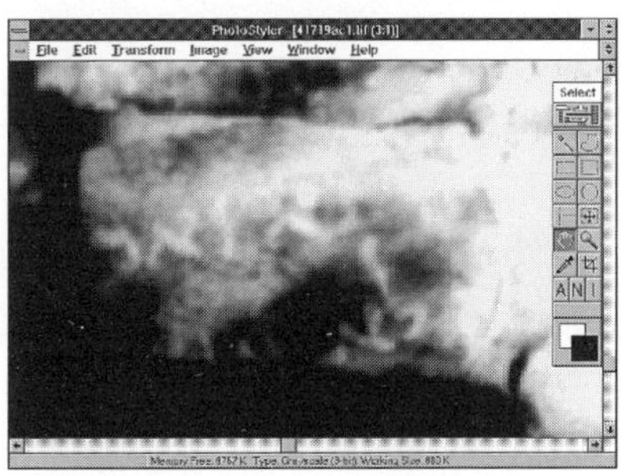

Negative made using the *„Negative"* command

PAM 41719: Courtesy of the IAA

Negative

To create a negative with PhotoStyler, click the „*Negative*" command of the „*Tune*" submenu of the „*Image*" menu. The gray-scale of the current image will be inverted to a negative. Press *Alt + Backspace* to undo the inversion and press it a second time to redo it.

Previously selected areas can of course also be inverted to a negative. For this purpose, select the area of interest as described above and click the „*Negative*" command.

! An altered image should be stored in a separate file leaving the original image intact.

Regulation of Brightness and Contrast

- To regulate brightness and contrast of an image, click the „*Brightness & Contrast*" command of the „*Tune*" submenu of the „*Image*" menu, or press *F2*. A dialogue box with two scroll bars will be displayed on the screen. Place the mouse-pointer on the buttons of the scroll bars, hold the left mouse-button pressed and move the mouse. Brightness and contrast will be regulated in accordance to the movements of the buttons, respectively.
- Click the „*Preview*" button if the results of the regulation are not displayed simultaneously. To reset the preview, click the „*Reset*" button, and to fixate the regulation, click the „*OK*" button.
- If brightness and contrast are to be regulated in a separated area only, select the area as described above before calling the „*Brightness & Contrast*" dialogue box.

! An altered image should be stored in a separate file leaving the original image intact.

Gamma Correction

- If the image of a manuscript is to be enhanced with the help of gamma correction, click the „*Grey/Colour Correction*" command of the „*Tune*" submenu of the „*Image*" menu or press *F3*. Move the button of the „*Gamma*" scroll bar in the dialogue box, and the image will be altered accordingly (place the mouse-pointer on the scroll bar button, hold the left mouse-button pressed, and move the mouse).

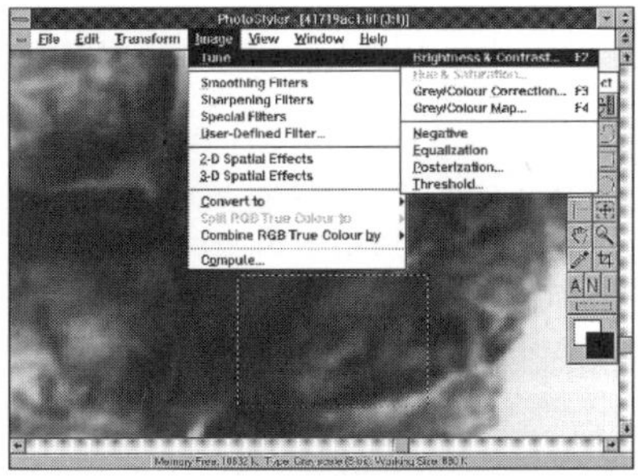

„*Brightness & Contrast*“ command of the „*Tune*“ submenu.

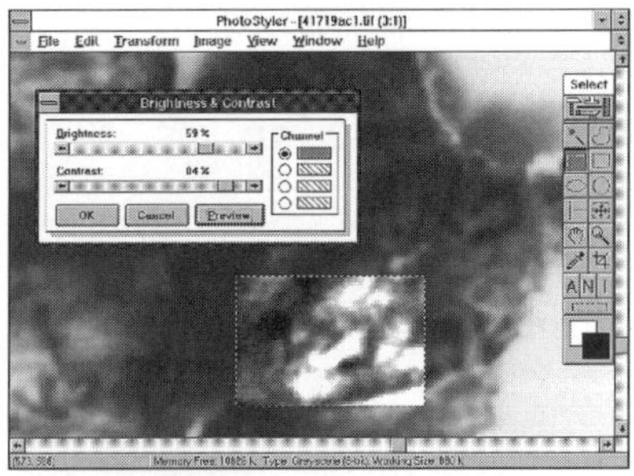

Selected area regulated in brightness and contrast (כללה).

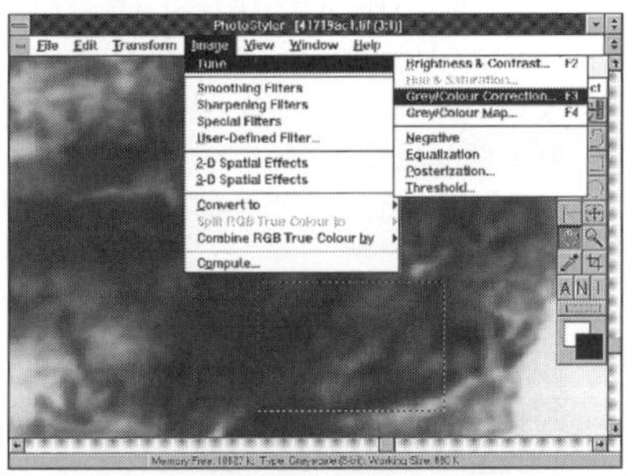

„*Grey/Color Correction* ... “ command of the „*Tune*“ submenu.

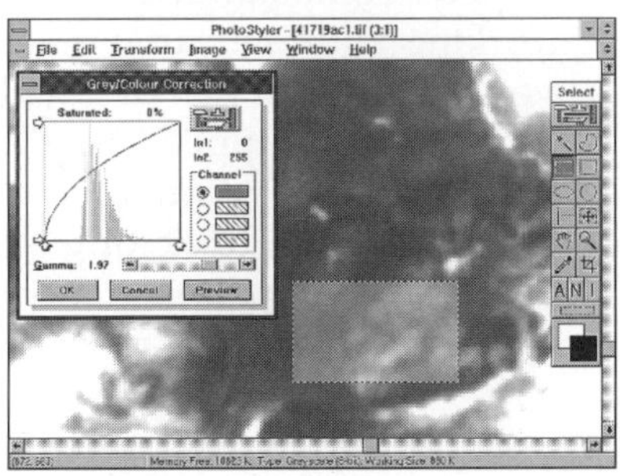

Selected area manipulated with gamma correction (כללה).

PAM 41719: Courtesy of the IAA

- Values above 1.00 lighten the image while values below 1.00 darken it. Click the „*Preview*“ button to preview alterations which are not displayed on the screen simultaneous to the scrolling of the scroll bar (to reset the preview, click the „*Reset*“ button) and the „*OK*“ button to fixate the enhancement.
- To enhance only a selected area of the fragment or manuscript, mark it before calling the gamma correction.

! An altered image should be stored in a separate file leaving the original image intact.

Gray/Color Map

- It is often of great help to assign a new gray-level to all pixels of an appointed gray-level by using the „*Grey/Colour Map*“ of PhotoStyler. It is called with the „*Grey/Colour Map*“ command of the „*Tune*“ submenu of the „*Image*“ menu or by pressing *F4*. The then displayed „*Grey/Colour Map*“ dialogue box provides users with a map, which „displays the value of the darkest pixels on the left and the brightest on the right. The mapping curve that runs across the map shows the actual brightness values of the pixels at each point across the map. The horizontal axis of the „*Grey/Colour Map*“ graphs the original gray- or color-values (input), where zero is black and 255 is white. The vertical axis graphs the new values (output).“ [14]
- Move the mouse-pointer to the curve, hold the left mouse-button pressed, and alter the curve as wanted, to reassign gray levels.
- The „*Toolbox*“ button of the „*Grey/Colour Map*“ dialogue box offers some additional helpful applications. The „*Piecewise*“ command displays some handles on the gray/color map curve, which make working with the curve much easier, but does not achieve results as good as when working without the handles. Helpful predefined curves can be applied by the commands „*Gamma,*“ „*Logarithm,*“ and „*Equalize.*“ [15] With the help of the „*Reset*“ command, the image can be restored to its original state. Use the „*Save*“ command to save a current mapping curve, and the „*Load*“ command to reload it.

---

[14] Aldus PhotoStyler User Manual, Version 1.1, p. 257.

[15] The gamma and the equalize curves are also available without the „*Grey/Colour Map.*“ See paragraphs „Gamma Correction“ and „Equalization.“

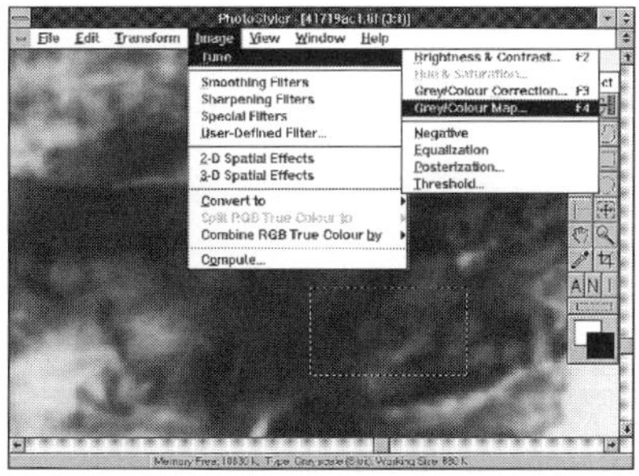

The *„Grey/Colour Map"* command of the *„Tune"* submenu.

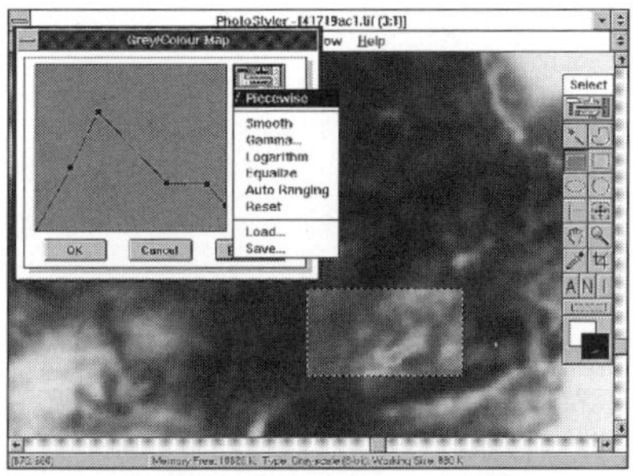

Selected area manipulated by the curve seen in the *„Grey/Colour Map"* dialogue box (כללה).

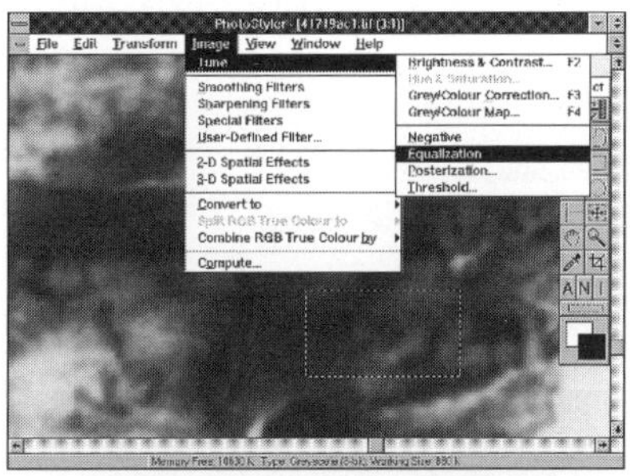

The *„Equalization"* command of the *„Tune"* submenu.

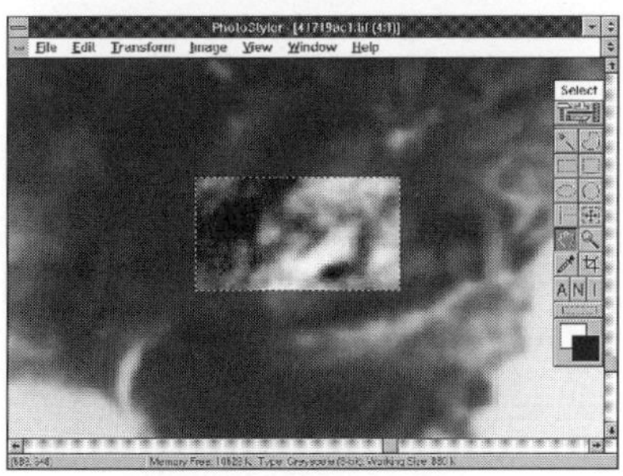

Selected area enhanced with the *„Equalization"* command (כללה).

PAM 41719: Courtesy of the IAA

- To manipulate only a selected area of the current image, mark it as explained above before calling the *„Grey/Colour Map."*

! An altered image should be stored in a separate file leaving the original image intact.

Equalization

1. PhotoStyler provides users with an excellent predefined equalization. Mark the area of the manuscript image to be reconstructed and call the *„Equalization"* command of the *„Tune"* submenu of the *„Image"* menu.

2. If a good reconstruction can't be reached by predefined equalization, call the *„Grey/Colour Correction"* dialogue box by clicking the corresponding command of the *„Tune"* submenu of the *„Image"* menu or press *F3*. A histogram of the image selection will be processed and displayed.[16] Moving the small arrows on the lower horizontal axis with the mouse will regulate the input range of the original digital image and the contrast will be increased. Moving the small arrows on the left vertical axis will regulate the output

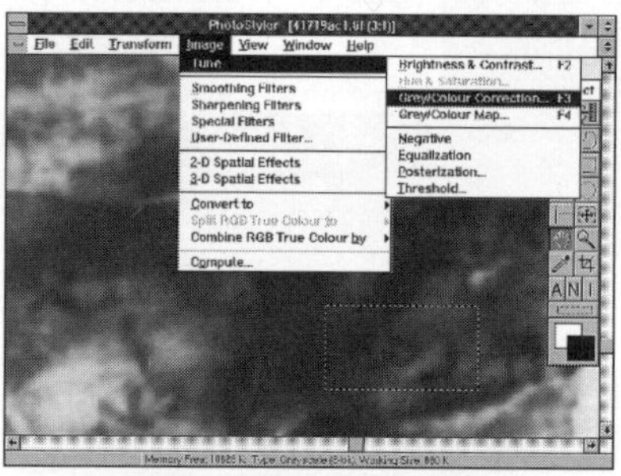

The *„Grey/Colour Map"* command of the *„Tune"* submenu.

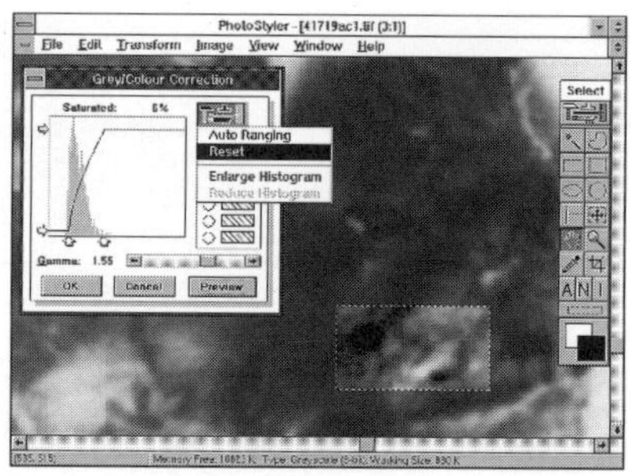

Selected area manipulated by the curve seen in the *„Gray/Colour Map"* dialogue box (כללה).

PAM 41719: Courtesy of the IAA

---

[16] The histogram can be enlarged and reduced with the corresponding commands which will be displayed if you click the *„Toolbox"* icon.

range of the enhanced image and the contrast will be decreased. The „*Reset*" command, displayed after the „*Toolbox*" icon is clicked, will restore the manipulated image to its original state.

! Both functions should only be used on selected areas of an image. Using equalization for a whole image won't help you in reconstructing your text because a fragment or a manuscript usually isn't darkened or faded to the same degree.

! Especially if large faded or darkened parts of a manuscript are to be reconstructed, it is advisable to mark small parts of the darkened or faded parts and work on them individually, to reach good results.

! Using the „*Grey/Colour Correction*" instead of the „*Equalization*" command enables users to combine equalization and gamma correction.

! An altered image should be stored in a separate file leaving the original image intact.

3.2.4 Comparison and Joining of Fragments

1. To compare two fragments, in a first operation one of the fragments should be selected from the original scanned photo and stored in a separate file. The „*Magic Wand*" tool should be used for this purpose:

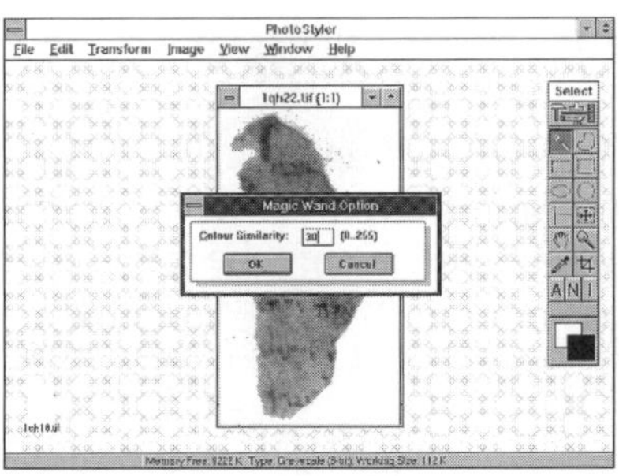

The wand range can be configured in the „*Magic Wand Option*" dialogue box.

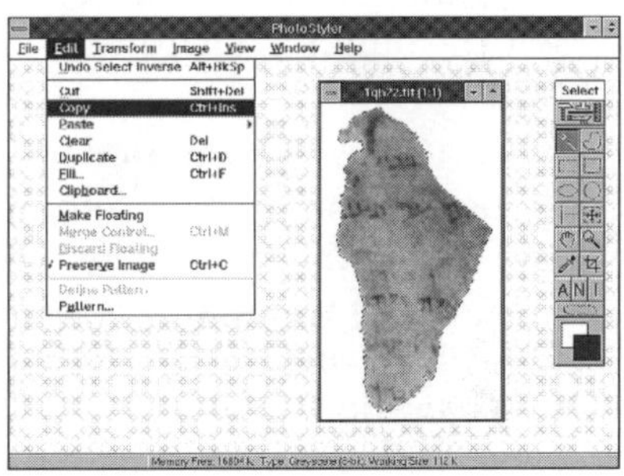

Fragment selected with the „*Magic Wand*" tool.

1QH 22: Courtesy of the Shrine of the Book

- To configure the wand range, doubleclick the *„Magic Wand"* icon of the *„Select"* toolbox. In the now opening dialogue box, the color similarity should be configured to 30. If this configuration does not work, the gray-level-range of the area surrounding the fragment of interest should be analyzed with the mouse-pointer (see above), and the color similarity of the magic wand range should be set according to the range detected.
- Move the mouse-pointer to the area surrounding the fragment of interest and press the left mouse-button. The white environment surrounding the fragment will be defined as a selected area (for the *„Magic Wand"* tool see the introduction to PhotoStyler). To invert the orientation of the selected area from the white environment to the enclosed fragment, click the *„I"* button of the *„Select"* toolbox. Then copy the now selected fragment with the help of the *„Cut"* or *„Copy"* command of the *„Edit"* menu to PhotoStyler's private clipboard (see the introduction to PhotoStyler) or press *Shift* + *Del* or *Ctrl* + *Ins* respectively.

2. In a second operation the file containing the fragment to be compared must be called, and the selected fragment must be inserted from the private clipboard of Photostyler into this file by using the *„As Selection"* option of the *„Paste"* command found in the *„Edit"* menu or pressing *Shift* + *Ins*.

3. In a third operation the transparency of the insert function must be configured:[17] press *Ctrl* + *M* to call PhotoStyler's merge control. To see only the border structure of the inserted fragment, configure the *„Floating Opacity"* box of the *„Merge Control"* dialogue box to the value 1. The border of the inserted fragment will be marked with a blinking marque while the rest of the fragment will be transparent.

   Place the mouse-pointer on the inserted fragment, hold the left mouse-button pressed, and move the mouse: the inserted fragment will follow the movements the mouse. To change the transparency level of the inserted fragment, again call the *„Merge Control"* dialogue box (press *Ctrl* + *M*) and choose the *„If Darker"* or *„ Always"* configuration.

4. Sometimes it is necessary to compare the direction and position of the lines of both fragments with each other. For this purpose con-

[17] The insert function of PhotoStyler can be configured in the *„Merge Control"* dialogue box.

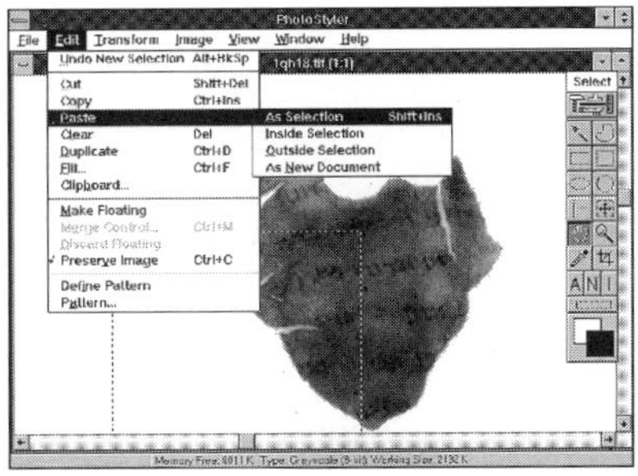

Pasting the selected fragment into another file.

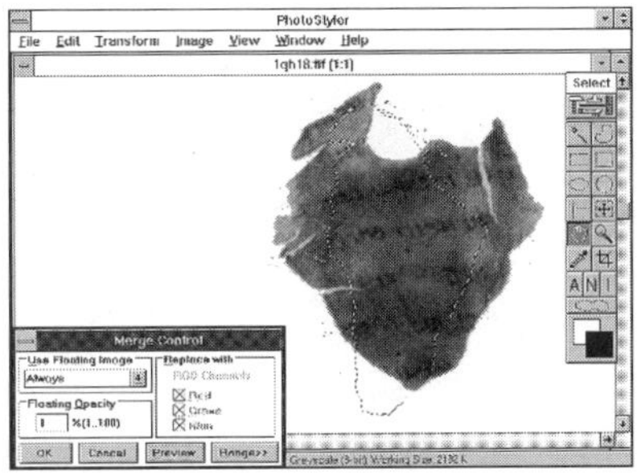

The pasted fragment is configured transparent.

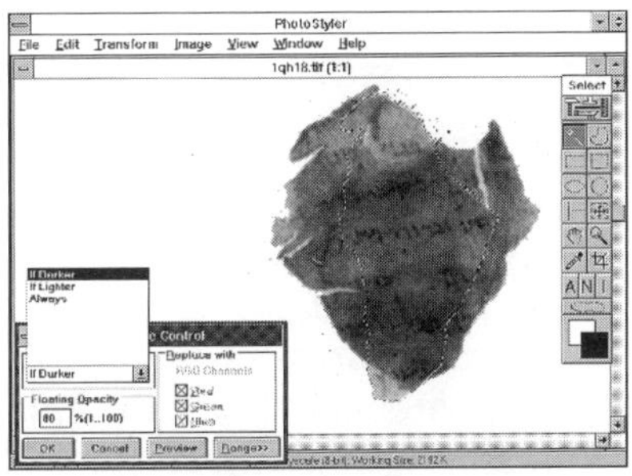

The pasted fragment is configured only partly transparent.

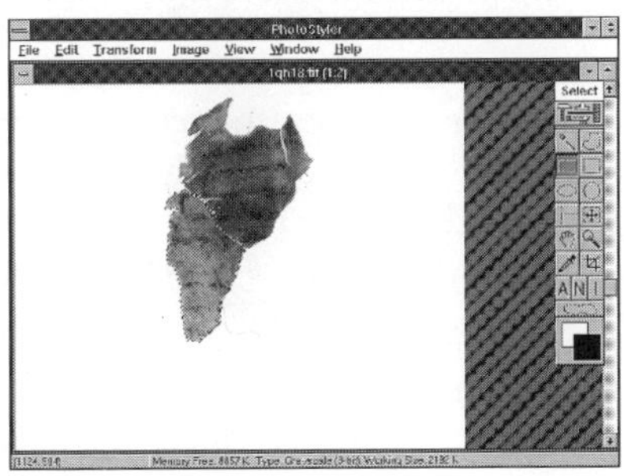

Joined fragments.

1QH 18; 22: Courtesy of the Shrine of the Book

figure the merge control with the „*If Darker*" option and try several values for the „*Floating Opacity*" – use the „*Preview*" button of the „*Merge Control*" dialogue box to preview the tested configurations. You will get a transparent inserted fragment of which only its dark passages – e. g. its characters – are not transparent.

5. To join the fragments side by side, select them in any way which seems appropriate, copy them to PhotoStyler's private clipboard and then insert them into the file of the fragment to be compared using the „*As Selection*" option of the „*Paste*" command found in the „*Edit*" menu or pressing *Shift* + *Ins*. Once inserted and moved to the right place, the „*N*" button of the „*Select*" toolbox should be clicked to unselect and fixate the inserted fragment.

! Sometimes the image into which the selected fragment should be inserted does not provide enough room. In this case, create a new file and insert all the fragments to be joined or compared into this file. Be sure to keep in mind that graphic files need an enormous amount of the computer's memory. One may easily run out of RAM, even if the PC equipped with 8 MB or more of RAM.

3.2.5 Mirrorwriting

1. To relocate a mirrorwriting, it must be selected in a first operation out of the original scanned photo and stored as a separate file. For this purpose, use the „*Magic Wand*" tool as described above (see 3.2.4 Comparison and Joining of Fragments on p. 63). The selected mirrorwriting should be copied to PhotoStyler's private clipboard with the „*Cut*" or the „*Copy*" command of the „*Edit*" menu [18] (alternatively press *Shift* + *Del* or *Ctrl* + *Ins*), and saved from this clipboard as a CLI file.

2. In a second operation the file containing the mirrorwriting's home column – i. e. the column from which it has been separated – must be called to the screen, and the mirrorwriting must be inserted from PhotoStyler's private clipboard into this image. For this, click the „*Paste*" command in the „*Edit*" menu and choose the „*As Selection*" option or press alternatively *Shift* + *Ins*.

   If the mirrorwriting is no longer stored in Photostyler's private clipboard, call it back to the clipboard. For this, click the „*Load ...*"

[18] The Windows clipboard isn't suitable for the relocation of mirrorwritings. If it is used for this purpose, the selected area is always stored in the form of a rectangle.

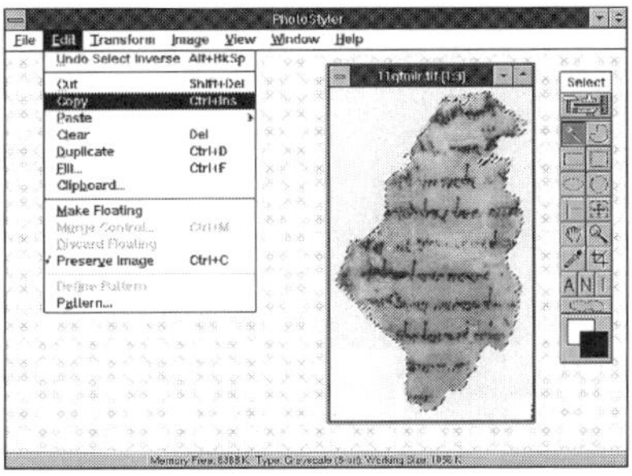

Selected mirrorwriting of 11QTemp XXXVIII copied to the clipboard.

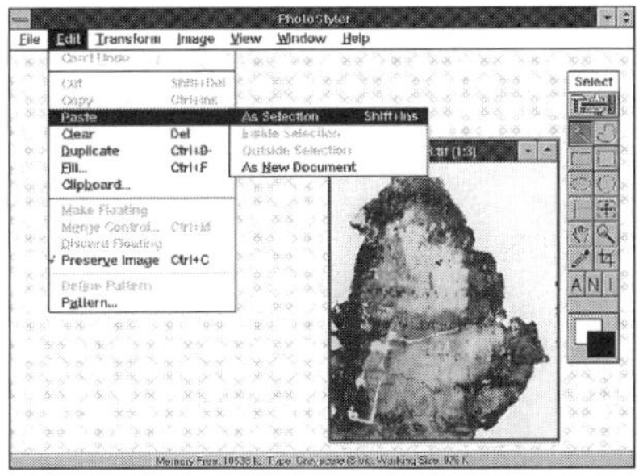

Pasting the mirrorwriting into the file of its home column.

11QTemp XXXVIII and mirrorwriting: Courtesy of the Shrine of the Book

button in PhotoStyler's „*Clipboard*" dialogue box – afterwards you will be guided (the „*Clipboard*" dialogue box is called with the „*Clipboard ...*" command in the „*Edit*" menu).

3. After this the mirrorwriting, which of course preserves the characters in the wrong order, must be „mirrored back": for this, click the „*Flip Horizontal*" command of the „*Transform*" menu.[19]

4. In a fourth operation the transparency of the insert function must be configured:[20] press *Ctrl + M* to call the „*Merge Control*" dialogue box. For the relocation of mirrorwritings, our experience has shown that it is best to choose the option „*If Darker*" in the „*Use Floating Image*" pulldown menu. Afterwards try several values for the „*Floating Opacity*" to reach the best transparency. Click the „*Preview*" button to preview and the „*OK*" button to fixate the configuration. In this way dark areas of the inserted mirrorwriting will be configured non-transparent (i. e. the characters) while its bright areas will become transparent (i. e. the parchment).

5. In a fifth operation the relocation itself can be done. To move the mirrorwriting on the screen, place the mouse-pointer on the mirrorwriting, hold the left mouse-button pressed, and move the mouse. The mirrorwriting will follow the mouse movements. To fixate the mirrorwriting after successful relocation, click the „*N*" button of the „*Select*" toolbox.

[19] For the scaling of the fragment, which will be necessary if the photo of the mirrorwriting and the photo of the column or fragment from which it has been separated are of different scales, see the last paragraph of this section.

[20] The insert function of PhotoStyler can be configured in the „*Merge Control*" dialogue box.

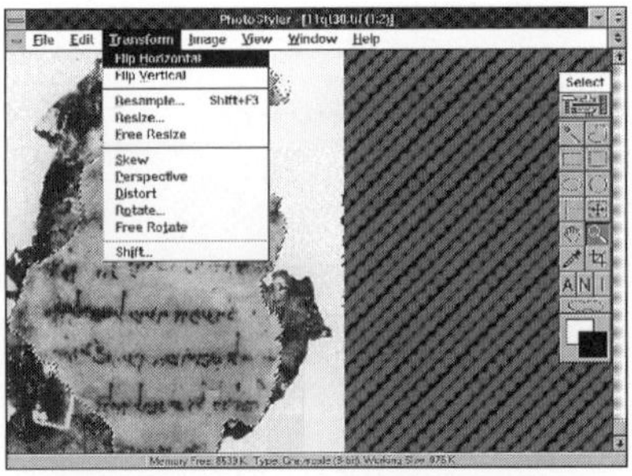

Remirroring the mirrorwriting.

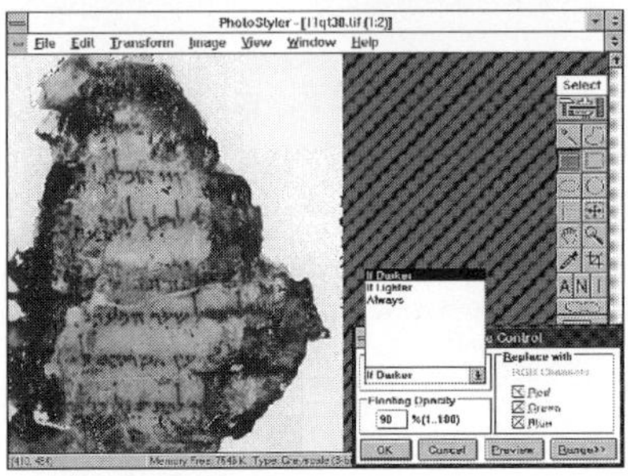

The pasted mirrorwriting is configured transparent.

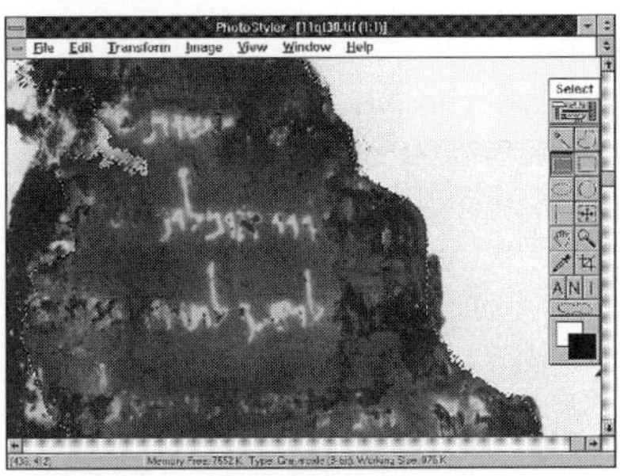

The pasted mirrorwriting inverted to a negative.

The mirrorwriting relocated.

11QTemp XXXVIII and mirrorwriting: Courtesy of the Shrine of the Book

! If you try to relocate a large mirrorwriting in a single operation, you will probably run short of RAM. In this case it is advisable to select several small parts out of the mirrorwriting and relocate them individually. For this, use the *„rectangle selection tool"* of the *„Select"* toolbox.

This is also advisable, because both, the parchment of the mirrorwriting as well as the parchment of its home column, are sometimes crumbled.

! Sometimes it is helpful to invert the inserted mirrorwriting to a negative. In this way the characters of the mirrorwriting will be displayed transparent while their surrounding parchment will be displayed black and non-transparent (the inserted mirrorwriting has to have been configured previously to transparent). In this way it is possible to see the character fragments of the mirrorwriting's home column through the transparent characters of the mirrorwriting.

3.2.6 Character Fragments

With PhotoStyler there are two different methods of creating and using lettertemplates, depending on the configuration of the merge control and the selection tool used to select characters from which lettertemplates can be derived:

1. Magnify a well preserved character and select it with the help of the *„Magic Wand"* tool (for the *„Magic Wand"* tool see above). As wand range (color similarity) several values should be tested. After being marked, copy the character by using the *„Copy"* command of the *„Edit"* menu to PhotoStyler's private clipboard[21] (alternatively press *Ctrl* + *Ins*).

   Afterwards go to the character fragments to be identified, insert the well preserved character with the *„Paste"* command of the *„Edit"* menu and choose the *„As Selection"* option of the *„Paste"* (alternatively press *Shift* + *Ins*).[22]

   Now press *Ctrl* + *M* to call the *„Merge Control"* dialogue box. In this dialogue box, the *„Use Floating Image"* pull down menu is to

[21] For PhotoStyler's private clipboard see above. The Windows clipboard cannot be used for this operation.

[22] PhotoStyler will insert the well preserved letter out of the clipboard to any marked area of an image or, if there is no selected area, the character in the clipboard will be inserted at the upper left corner of the current image.

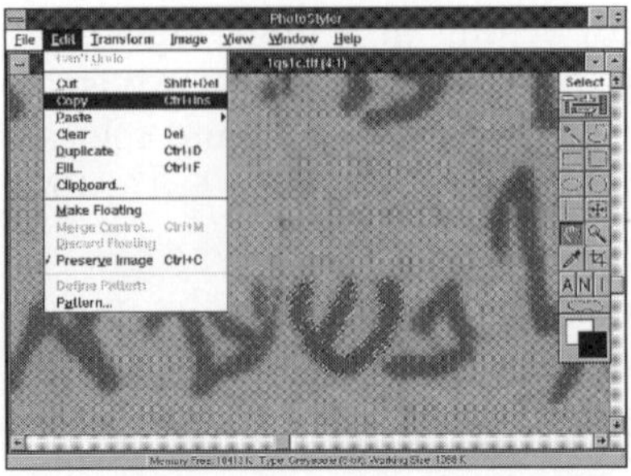

Character selected with the *„Magic Wand"* tool and copied to the clipboard.

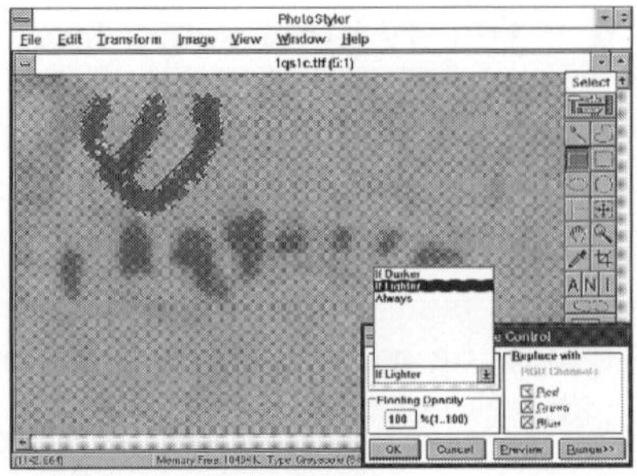

Selected character pasted next to the character fragments to be identified.

1QS $I_{23.25}$: Courtesy of the Shrine of the Book

be configured with the *„If Lighter"* option. Then click the *„Preview"* button to preview the transparency reached or the *„OK"* button to activate it. If it is not suffiencient, try another *„Floating Opacity"* value. In this way a transparent character can be created whose edges are marked by a black and white marque.

This lettertemplate can be moved around on the screen as wanted: place the mouse-pointer on the lettertemplate, hold the left mouse-button pressed, and move the mouse.

2. Use the *„Rectangle Selection"* tool to select a well preserved character in a rectangle and copy it – as described above – to the clipboard.[23]

   Then insert the character with the *„Paste"* command of the *„Edit"* menu to the character fragments to be identified. Invert the inserted character with the *„Negative"* command to a negative and enhance its contrast with the *„Equalization"* command (both commands are found in the *„Tune"* submenu of the *„Image"* menu).

   After this, call the *„Merge Control"* dialogue box by pressing *Ctrl + M* and configure the *„Use Floating Image"* pull down menu with the *„If Darker"* option. The result is a transparent character surrounded by an non-transparent dark environment. This lettertemplate can be moved and fixated as usual.

[23] For this operation either the Windows clipboard or PhotoStyler's private clipboard can be used.

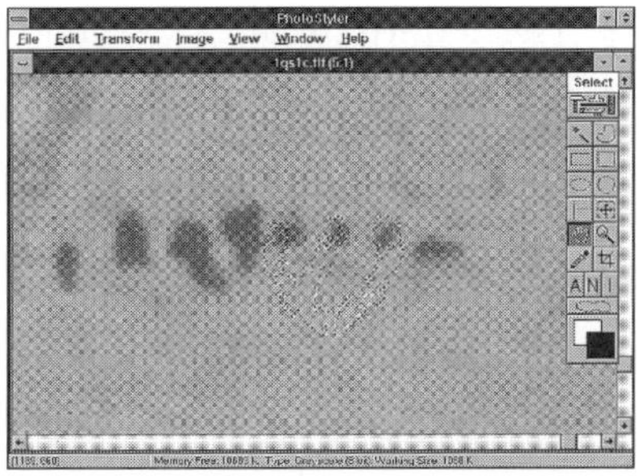

Character fragments identified with transparent lettertemplates.

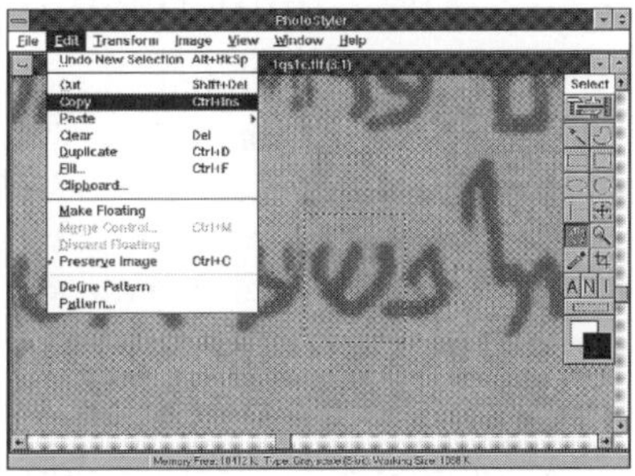

Character selected and copied to the clipboard.

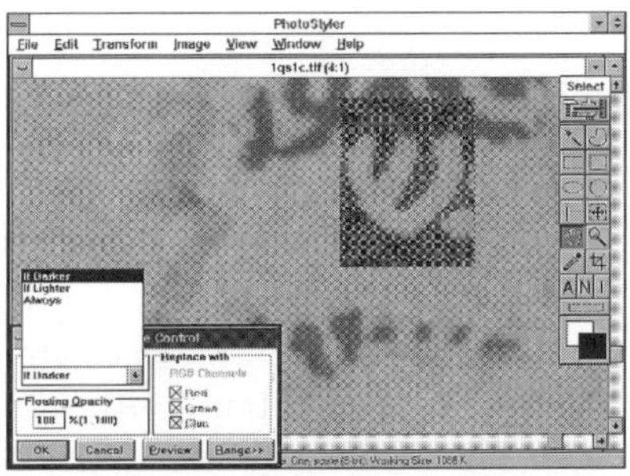

Character inverted to a negative, pasted next to character fragments, and configured transparent.

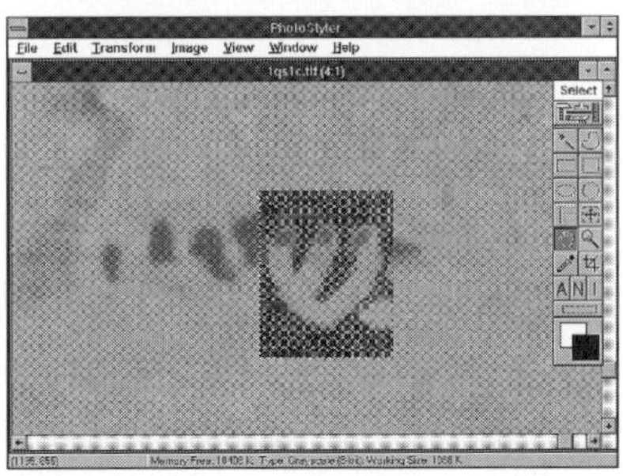

The character fragments identified as the Hebrew letter ש.

1QS $I_{23.25}$: Courtesy of the Shrine of the Book

! The lettertemplates can be stored after being copied to the clipboard; in this case, the inversion to a negative and equalization should be done *before* copying a well preserved character to the clipboard.

! It is recommended to note the exact location from where the lettertemplates have been derived, and, if possible, the scale of the image.

3.2.7 The Comparison of Characters

If characters of different manuscripts are to be compared (paleography), you can proceed in a similar way, as described in 3.2.6. There is only one difference: instead of one text (= image file), two or more must be held opened.[24] Now mark the character of interest, load it into PhotoStyler's private clipboard, and insert it into the image containing the character to be compared.

! It is recommended to note the exact location from where the lettertemplates have been derived, and, if possible, the scale of the image.

3.2.8 Reconstruction of Text Gaps

In a similar way text gaps[25] can be reconstructed with the ductus of the scribe of a certain scroll.

1. Select the words or characters probably to be inserted into a text gap, and copy them with the „*Copy*" command of the „*Edit*" menu to PhotoStyler's private clipboard, or use the keys *Ctrl* + *Ins*. Then save the selected characters to file by using the „*Save* ..." button of the previously called „*PhotoStyler Image Clipboard*" dialogue box (for this click the „*Clipboard* ..." command of the „*Edit*" menu).

2. Mark the part of the text gap where the selected word or character shall be placed with the „*Rectangular Selection*" tool, and call the stored word or character to PhotoStyler's private clipboard using the „*Load* ..." button of the „*PhotoStyler Image Clipboard*" dialogue

[24] For this call the files successively and click the „*Tile*" command in the „*Windows*" menu (or press *Shift* + *F4*) to arrange the files next to each other on the screen.

[25] Text gaps caused by physical damage are often named *lacunae* in the literature on the Dead Sea Scrolls.

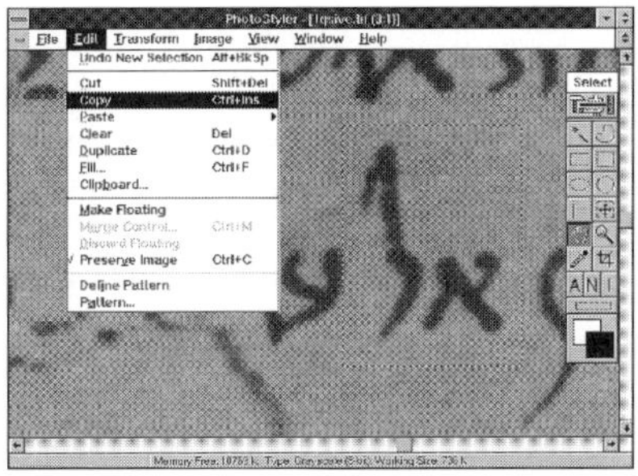

Selected word (אל) copied to the clipboard.

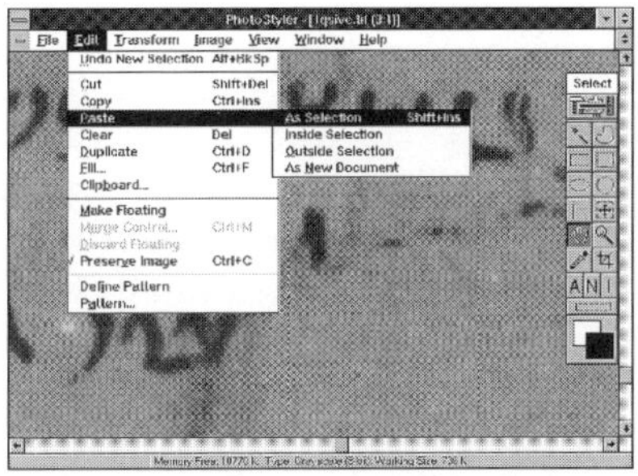

Pasting the selected word to the text gap.

The selected word placed in the text gap.

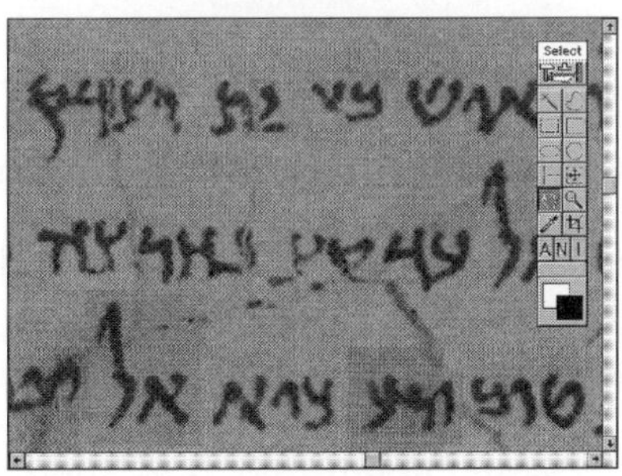

H. Stegemann's reconstruction of 1QS IV_{26} verified. (H. Stegemann, Zu Textbestand und Grundgedanken von 1QS III, 13-IV, 26, RdQ 13, 1988, 95–132, 107 f.)

1QS $I_{25.26}$: Courtesy of the Shrine of the Book

box. Then insert the character into the selected area by clicking the „*As Selection*" option of the „*Paste*" submenu of the Edit menu (alternatively press *Shift* + *Ins*).

3. If there are character fragments at the edges of the text gap to be reconstructed, try to use lettertemplates as described above.

! It is recommended to note the exact location from where the words and/or characters used for the reconstruction have been derived.

Scaling and Rotation

For all the operations described in points 3–7, it's sometimes necessary to work with images scanned from photos of different scale and inclination. To deal with these problems, PhotoStyler 1.1 provides users with several different functions for the resizement and rotation of images, all found in the „*Transform*" menu.

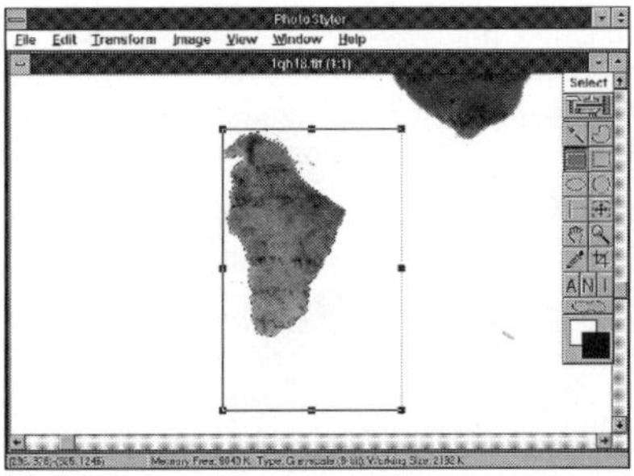

Scaling a fragment with the „*Free Resize*" command.

1QH 22: Courtesy of the Shrine of the Book

– The „*Free Resize*" command[26] is helpful in scaling inserted selected areas. After a fragment or character has been inserted into an image of a different scale, click the „*Free Resize*" command and the inserted area will be surrounded by a rectangle equipped with handles.
  If the handles located on the horizontal or vertical lines are pulled with the mouse, the inserted area will be enlarged either horizontally or vertically. The handles located on the corners of the rectangle will enlarge the inserted area in both directions at the same time if pulled by the mouse.

[26] For the commands „*Resample* ..." and „*Resize* ..." see PhotoStyler's user guide.

Before resizing, place an object – e.g. a character of the inserted area – above a matching one in the image into which the object is to be inserted. If the merge control has been configured to transparent, the size of both characters can be equaled by using the „*Free Resize*" command.

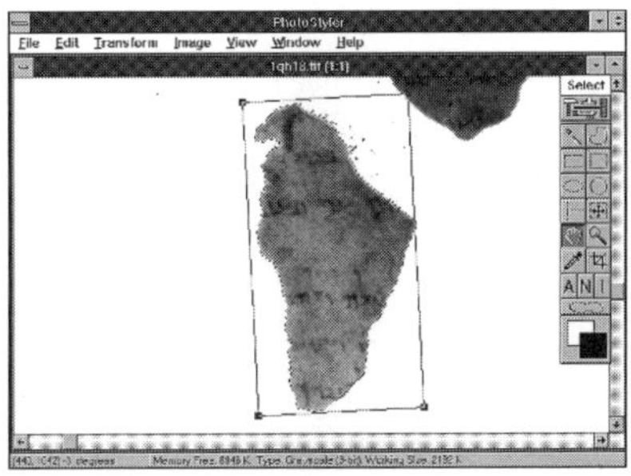

Rotating a fragment with the „*Free Rotate*" command.

1QH 22: Courtesy of the Shrine of the Book

– Often inserted fragments, mirrorwritings, and characters have an inclination which does not fit to join, relocate, or compare them. To rotate these inserted areas, click the „*Free Rotate*" command of the „*Transform*" menu before fixating the inserted image excerpt. The marque of the inserted excerpt will be equipped with four handles. Place the mouse-pointer on one of these handles, hold the left mouse-button pressed, and move the mouse – the inserted image excerpt will be rotated according to the mouse movements.[27]

[27] Alternatively use the „*Rotate*" command of the same menu to change the inclination of an inserted image excerpt. For this see the introduction to PhotoStyler's commands.

3.3 PhotoStyler 2.0

3.3.1 Introduction and Miscellaneous

Since the release of version 1.1, Aldus has equipped PhotoStyler with many additional commands and tools, organized in several menus, submenus, toolboxes, and tool classes.[28] To make access to and use of these commands and tools easier, PhotoStyler 2.0 is designed as a highly customizable program, by providing users with a „*Quick Command Palette*“ and a „*Custom Tool Group*.“ The program supports the file formats BMP, DCS, EPS, GIF, JPEG, MAC, PCD (PhotoCD), PCT (PICT), PCX, RLE, SCT, TGA (Targa), and TIFF. TIFF-files can also be stored in the Macintosh TIFF-format. The new „*Twain*“ scanner Standard is also supported.

Commands

Open — To call a file with PhotoStyler, click the „*Open ...*“ command in the „*File*“ menu or press *Crtl + O*, then you will be guided by the „*Open Image File*“ dialogue box. If you want to have a short look at a „thumbnail“ of the file before opening it, use the „*Preview*“ button in this dialogue box.

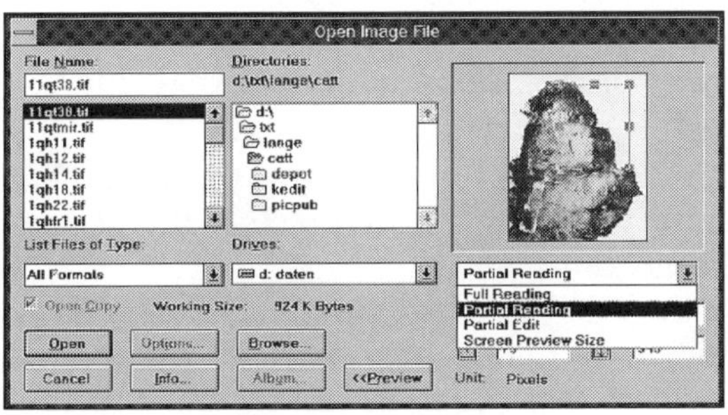

PhotoStyler's „*Open Image File*“ dialogue box. The rectangle marks the area to be loaded.

! The last five files opened are listed by PhotoStyler 2.0 at the bottom of the „*File*“ menu. Click one of these files, and it will be recalled to the screen.

[28] This documentation of PhotoStyler 2.0 has been made on a very early but stable beta-version, which has been kindly given to me from Aldus Germany. For that reason, you may find some things slightly different than the final version. But following this description, you should be able to reconstruct damaged texts with PhotoStyler 2.0. If the program differs from this description, please read its manual.

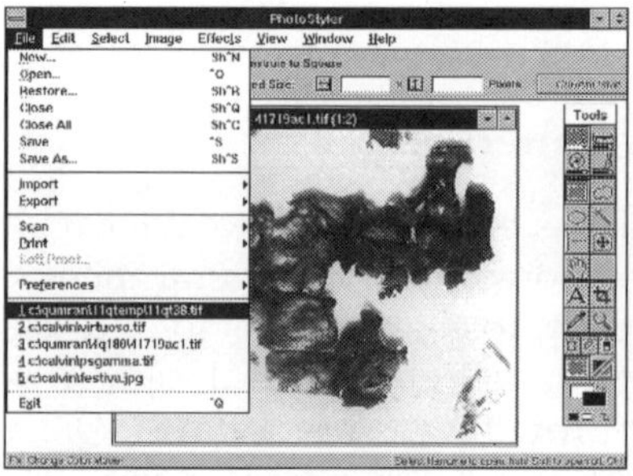

The file `11qt38.tif` marked for recalling.

! PhotoStyler displays every file in a separate window. If it is necessary to work with two or more files at the same time, open all files as described and click the „*Tile*“ command in the „*Window*“ menu or press *Shift* + *F4*.

! Working with several graphic files at the same time requires a large amount of RAM. Hold only the files opened which are really needed.

! It is often necessary to store a manipulated image in a separate file in order that the original image is not destroyed: PhotoStyler 2.0 will produce a new copy of each file when calling it to the screen if the „*Open Copy*“ option of the „*Open Image File*“ dialogue box is activated.

Close — To close a file, doubleclick the square at the upper left-hand corner of the file-window or click the „*Close*“ command in the „*File*“ menu.

New — To create a new file, click the „*New ...*“ command in the „*File*“ menu. A dialog box entitled „*Create New Image*“ will appear. The file to be created must be configured here. As „*Data Type*“ choose „*Grayscale (8-bit).*“ The resolution of the file should be at least 300 dpi (see the plate on the following page).

! Even if the height and width of your new file are given in cm, configure the resolution in pixel/inch. The international standard measurement for the resolution of computer graphic files is dpi (dots per inch).

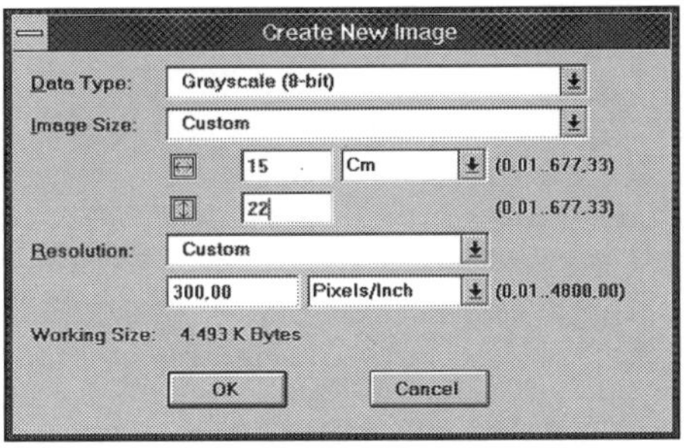

PhotoStyler's „*Create New Image*" dialogue box.

! Configure the new file only as large as necessary. Graphic files with a resolution of 300 dpi need an enormous amount of space in RAM and on the hard disk. A graphic file with the configuration as shown above will need about 5 MB of memory.

Save To save a file, click the „*Save*" command in the „*File*" menu or press *Ctrl + S*. If a new file is being stored, the „*Save Image File*" dialogue box will be displayed. In this box, name, directory, and format of the file are to be given. Afterwards click the „*Save*" button.[29]

! If the results of your work are stored with the „*Save*" command, the original image of the manuscript will be lost. Any manipulated image should be stored in a separate file using the „*Save As ...*" command, if the „*Open Copy*" option was not used when the file was loaded.

Restore To restore an image or a selected part of an image damaged by edits, use the „*Restore ...*" command of the „*File*" menu, afterwards you will be guided by a dialogue box.

Undo To undo or redo edits, click the first command of the „*Edit*" menu or press *Alt + Bksp* or *Ctrl + Z*.

Rulers Ruler-lines on the edge of the screen can be shown or hidden, if the „*Rulers*" command in the „*View*" menu is clicked or *Ctrl + R* are pressed. Horizontal or vertical ruler-lines will appear. The kind of measurement (inch, cm, pica, pixel, point) displayed can be config-

[29] PhotoStyler is able to convert a DOS TIFF-file to the Macintosh TIFF-format. This application is very useful if the results of your work will be published with an Apple system. For the conversion itself see the user manual of PhotoStyler.

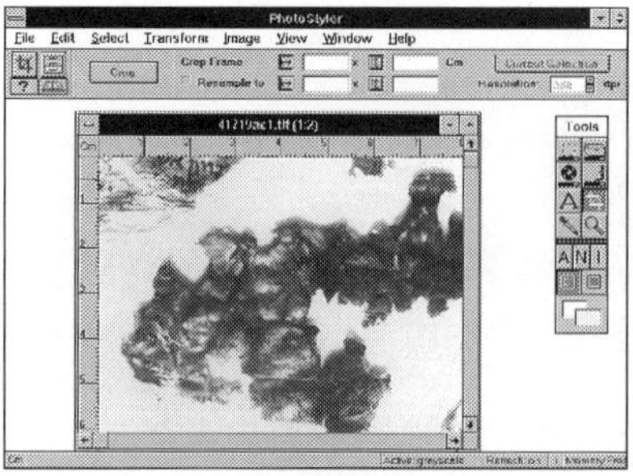

4Q180 3 with ruler-lines.
PAM 41719: Courtesy of the IAA

ured by clicking the button found on the left-hand side of the status line labeled *„In,“ „Cm,“ „Pc,“ „Px,“* or *„Pt“* respectively. The position of the mouse-pointer is indicated by a small line in the horizontal and the vertical ruler-line.

! The measurements displayed by the ruler-lines are not the measurements of the manuscript itself but of the scanned photo, which often differ significantly in size. To get the correct measurements of the manuscript, look for the ruler of the photo of the manuscript and calculate the scale of the photo.

Information — To get information about the current image, click the *„Image Information …“* command of the *„View“* menu, use the *„i“* button of the status line (i. e. the gray ribbon at the bottom of the program window), or press *F12*.

Exit — To quit PhotoStyler, click the *„Exit“* command of the *„File“* menu, doubleclick the square found at the upper left-hand corner of the program window, or press *Alt* + *F4* or *Ctrl* + *Q*.

Quick Command Palette

With PhotoStyler 2.0, commands often used can be organized in the *„Quick Command Palette,“* which may be described as a toolbox for commands. This is especially helpful if these commands are found in submenus.

- To open the *„Quick Command Palette,“* click the corresponding command in the *„Show/Hide“* submenu of the *„View“* menu or press *F11*.

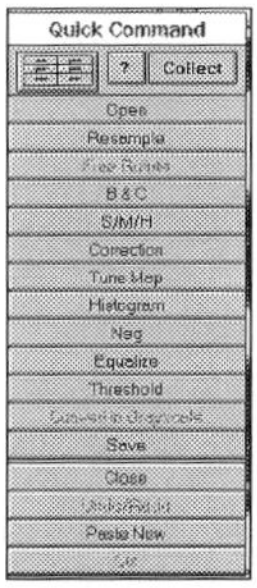

PhotoStyler's „*Quick Command Palette*" equipped with several commands.

- To modify the „*Quick Command Palette,*" click the „*Filing Cabinet*" icon found at its top: a pulldown menu is opened. To add additional commands to the palette, click the „*Modify* ..." command, then you will be guided by dialogue boxes. The new configuration of the „*Quick Command Palette*" can afterwards be saved and loaded with the „*Load* ..." and „*Save* ..." commands of the same pulldown menu.[30]

Tools, Tool Groups, Tool Ribbon, Status Bar

Instead of using two separate toolboxes, most of PhotoStyler's tools are grouped and hidden behind three icons, representing the different tools offered: a rectangle (selection tools), a wheel (special image editing tools), and a brush (painting tools). The tools grouped in this way are called „tool groups." If one of these icons is clicked, for instance the rectangle, the tool class represented will be displayed in a second toolbox, below the first one.

Custom Group

To combine different tools, a customized tool class can be defined.

To do this, call the „*Define Custom Tools*" dialogue box by doubleclicking the upper right-hand icon of the toolbox, equipped with a symbol representing the program's toolbox, or by using the „*Define Custom Tools* ..." command of the „*Preferences*" submenu of the „*File*" menu. A configured tool class can be saved and reloaded with the „*Save* ..." and „*Load* ..." buttons of this dialogue box.

[30] For more detailed information, see PhotoStyler's user guide.

To activate the custom tool group configured in this way, click the *„Custom Group"* icon in the toolbox.

Tool Ribbon

In addition, each tool can be configured in a gray ribbon, the so-called *„Tool Ribbon,"* found below PhotoStyler's menus. Four buttons are always found at the left-hand side of the *„Tool Ribbon"*:

By using the button equipped with the symbol of the currently activated tool, the current configuration of this tool can be saved: the next time this tool is activated, the saved configuration will again become valid.

Context sensitive help is available with the *„?"* button.

If the *„Filing Cabinet"* button is clicked, the *„Show/Hide"* sub-menu of the *„View"* menu will be opened. With the commands of this menu, the toolboxes, the status line, the *„Quick Command Palette,"* etc. can be shown or hidden.

With this button, a small image data base, named *„Album"* by Aldus, can be called.[31]

All other buttons, slides, pull down menus, and boxes are different for each tool and will therefore be explained along with the respective tools.

Status Bar

The *„Status Bar"* is a gray ribbon found at the bottom of the program window. Context sensitive first help and information is displayed on it: e. g. the gray-level of the pixel the mouse-pointer is pointing at.

The sort of measurement PhotoStyler's information is given in can be configured with the button found on the left-hand side of the *„Status Line"* – the current kind of measurement is displayed on it in abbreviations.[32] Click the button, to open a pull down menu, and choose the desired measurement.

[31] See section 3.4, p. 117.

[32] *„Px"* = pixel, *„In"* = inch, *„Cm"* = centimeter, *„Pc"* = pica, *„Pt"* = point.

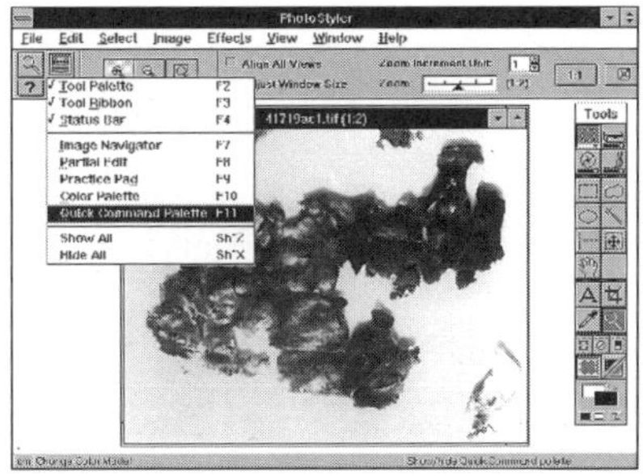

PhotoStyler's „*View*" menu called with the „*Filing Cabinet*" button of the „*Tool Ribbon*."

Detail of 4Q180 3
PAM 41719: Courtesy of the IAA.

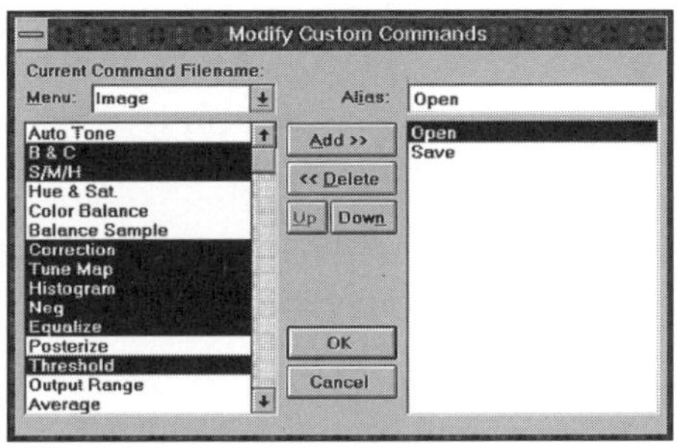

PhotoStyler's „*Modify Custom Commands*" dialogue box. The commands to be added to the „*Quick Command Palette*" are marked.

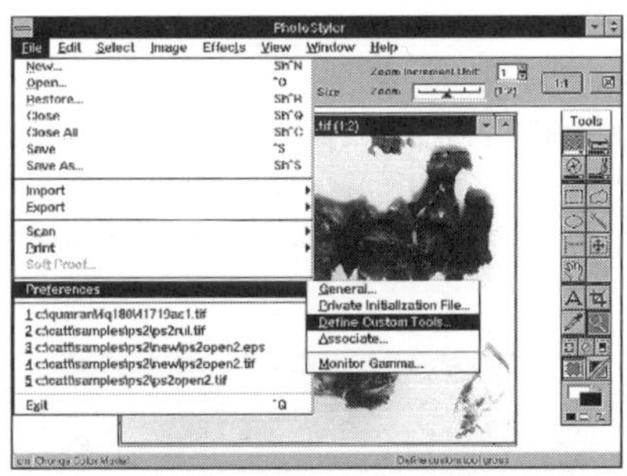

The „*Define Custom Tools*" dialogue box can be called with the „*Define Custom Tools ...*" command.

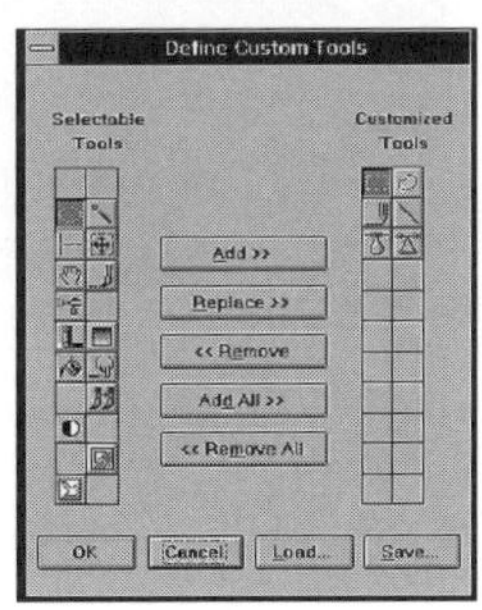

PhotoStyler's „*Define Custom Tools*" dialogue box. The tool to be added to the „*Custom Group*" is marked.

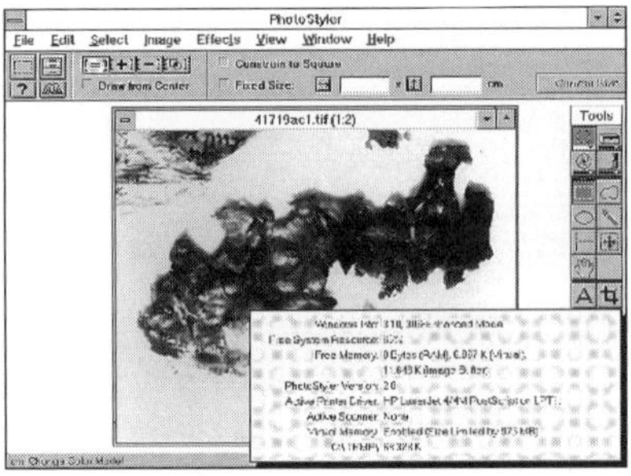

System Information.

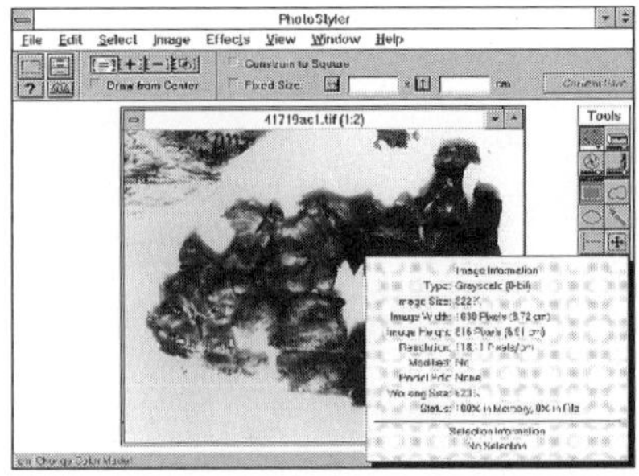

Information on the current image.

PAM 41719: Courtesy of the IAA

If the „*i*" button is clicked, information on the current image and a previously selected area is displayed.

If the „*Free*" button is clicked, system information will be displayed.

Tools

To select an area of the current image in the form of a rectangle, click the „*Rectangle Selection*" tool found in the „*Selection*" tool group, and move the mouse-pointer to the area to be selected. Hold the left mouse-button pressed and move the mouse – the area of interest will be surrounded by a blinking rectangular marque when the mouse-button is released.

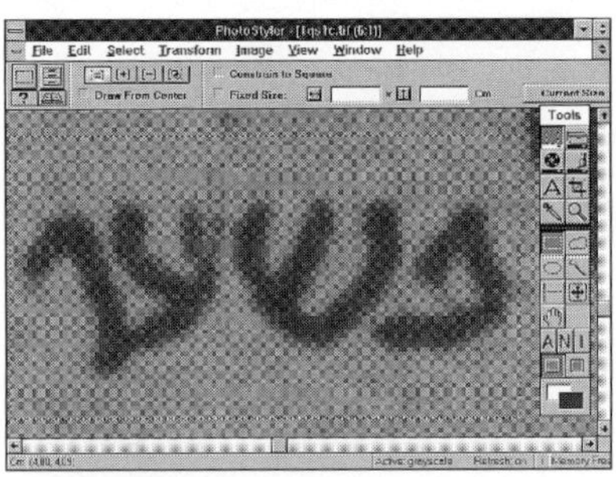

Letter selected with the „*Rectangle Selection*" tool.

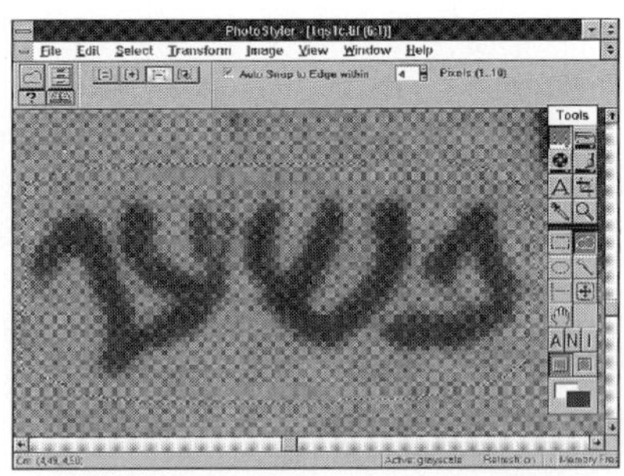

Letter selected with the „*Free Selection*" tool.

1QS I_{23}: Courtesy of the Shrine of the Book

To select an area of the current image manually, click the *„Free Selection“* tool found in the *„Selection“* tool group, and move the mouse-pointer to the area of interest. Hold the left mouse-button pressed and move the mouse around the area to be selected – the selected area will be surrounded by a blinking marque when the mouse-button is released.

To define a line as a selected area, click the *„Line Selection“* tool, found in the *„Selection“* tool group, and proceed as described above.

With the *„Magic Wand“* tool found in the *„Selection“* tool group, users are able to define any pixels of an image which are next to each other and have – in a certain range – the same gray-level, (for instance a character) as a selected area. To define the range of gray-level similarity, use the *„Similarity“* slide or the *„Similarity“* box of the *„Tool Ribbon.“* Then place the mouse-pointer on the area to be selected and press the left mouse-button.

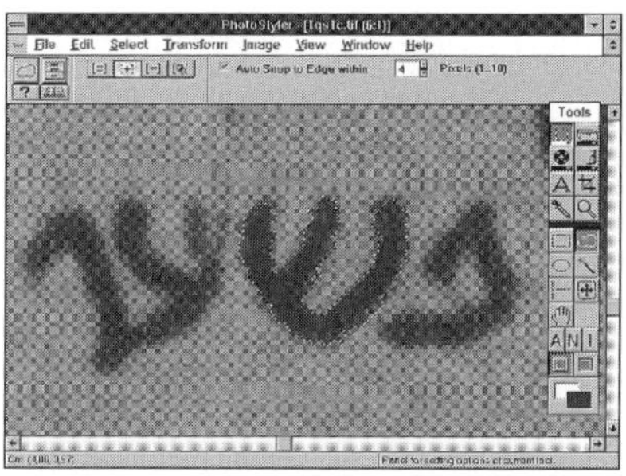

Letter selected with the *„Magic Wand“* tool. 1QS I_{23}: Courtesy of the Shrine of the Book

To analyze the range of gray-levels of the area to be selected, place the mouse-pointer on several different pixels of this area – the gray-level of the pixel the mouse-pointer is pointing at will be displayed in the long rectangle of the *„Status Bar.“* If for instance gray-levels between 130 and 151 are found, the wand range should be set to 21.

PhotoStyler's *„Select“* toolbox is one of its special features: with the first button, all of the current image can be selected. With the second button, any selected area can be de-selected. With the third button, any previously selected area can be inverted – an application which is, for instance, very helpful for isolating fragments (pp. 103–105). These funtions can also be executed by using the corresponding commands of the *„Select"* menu or pressing *Ctrl + A*, *Ctrl + N*, and *Ctrl + I* respectively.

With PhotoStyler 2.0, images can be scrolled in different ways:

- Click the *„Hand"* icon found in the *„Selection"* tool class, place the mouse-pointer – now displayed as a hand – on the current image, hold the left mouse-button pressed, and move the mouse. The image will be scrolled according to the mouse movements.
- Use the scroll bars, attached at the bottom and at the right-hand side of the image.

Click the button found at the lower right-hand corner of the current image, to call the *„Image Navigator"* dialogue box. In this dialogue box, the displayed area of the current image is marked by a rectangle. Place the mouse-pointer inside the rectangle, hold the left mouse-button pressed, and move the mouse: the current image will be scrolled to the new location of the rectangle.

For the *„Text"* tool, see PhotoStyler's user manual.

Partial Edit and Image Navigator

With PhotoStyler 2.0, users are provided with two additional functions to simplify working with large image files:

Partial Edit

„Partial Edit" enables users to edit selected portions of the current image if this image needs too much space in RAM to be edited as a whole. *„Partial Edit"* can be shown or hidden by clicking the *„Partial Edit"* command in the *„Show/Hide"* submenu of the *„View"* menu[33] or by pressing *F8*: a small bar equipped with several buttons is displayed when the *„Partial Edit"* is activated. Click the *„Partial ..."* button to call the *„Partial Edit"* dialogue box. The current image will be displayed in the dialogue box in a „thumbnail" view. Move the

33 The *„Show/Hide"* submenu can also be called by clicking the *„Filing Cabinet"* button of the *„Tool Ribbon"*.

rectangle found in this „thumbnail" view to select the image selection to be edited and use the handles found at the corners of the rectangle to enlarge or reduce the area of selection. To activate the selection, click the *„OK"* button of the *„Partial Edit"* dialogue box.

To recall the whole image, click the *„Fall"* button of the *„Partial Edit"* bar.

Image Navigator

Scrolling the current image is much easier using the *„Image Navigator"* of PhotoStyler 2.0. In addition, zoom operations can be executed with the *„Image Navigator"* using tools other than the magnifying glass. The *„Image Navigator"* is displayed in the form of a small dialogue box, which can be called by clicking the *„Image Navigator"* command in the *„Show/Hide"* submenu of the *„View"* menu[34] or by clicking the button found at the lower right-hand corner of the image window, where the scroll bars cross.

In the *„Image Navigator"* dialogue box, the current image is again displayed in the form of a „thumbnail" view. If the rectangle found in this „thumbnail" view is moved by the mouse, the current image will be scrolled according to the mouse movements.

For zoom operations, the *„Magnifying Glass"* buttons, the *„1 : 1"*-button, and the slide can be used.[35]

Clipboards

With PhotoStyler, users are able to choose whether to work with the Windows clipboard or a clipboard designed especially for PhotoStyler, the so-called *„Private Clipboard."* While the Windows clipboard enables you to exchange data between all Windows programs, it is not especially designed for image processing and some of CATT's operations can therefore not be done using it. On the other hand, PhotoStyler's private clipboard is not able to exchange data with other Windows programs.[36]

---

34 The *„Show/Hide"* submenu can also be called by clicking the *„Filing Cabinet"* button of the *„Tool Ribbon."*

35 For more detailed information PhotoStyler's user manual.

36 We have had good results using the private clipboard for the program's internal data-exchange, for instance for inserting selected characters and/or fragments into an image, and using the Windows clipboard at the same time to produce hardcopies of the screen (screen shots).

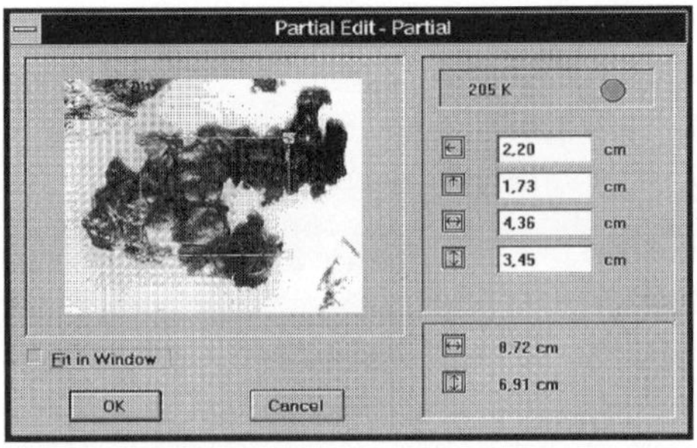

PhotoStyler's *„Partial Edit"* dialogue box.

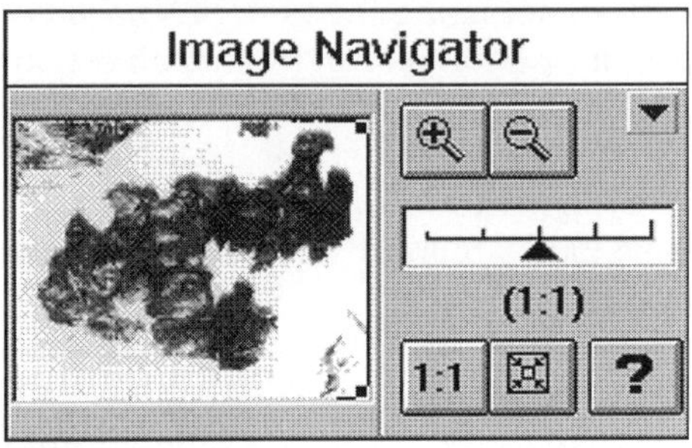

PhotoStyler's *„Image Navigator"*.

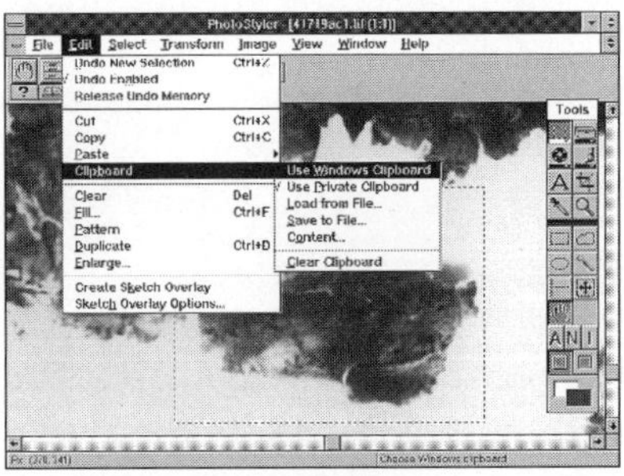

Both the Windows and Photo-Styler's private clipboard can be operated with the commmands in the *„Clipboard"* submenu.

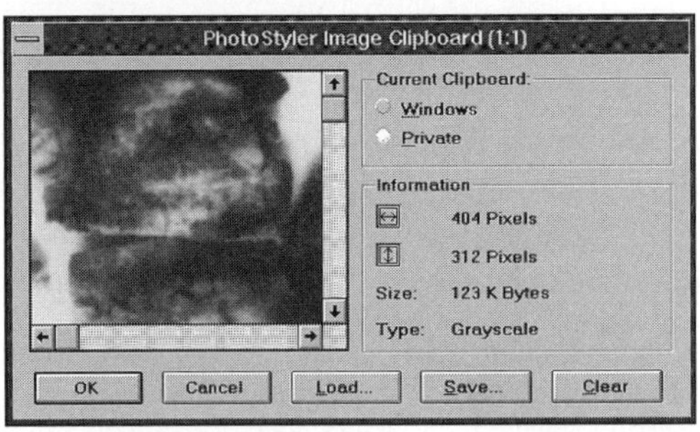

The *„PhotoStyler Image Clipboard"* dialogue box.

4Q180 3. PAM 41719: Courtesy of the IAA.

- To choose between both clipboards, click the „*Use Windows'*" or the „*Use PhotoStyler's*" command in the „*Clipboard*" submenu of the „*Edit*" menu. To save data from the clipboard to a file, use the „*Save* ..." command of the same submenu. To load a previously stored clipboard file into the clipboard, use the „*Load* ..." command.[37]
- To view the data stored in the clipboard, click the „*Content* ..." command in the „*Clipboard*" submenu of the „*Edit*" menu. With the buttons and options found in the now displayed „*Clipboard Content (1 : 1)*" dialogue box, the operations described in the previous paragraph can also be executed.

3.3.2 Magnification

Once an image is called to PhotoStyler's program window, magnification of images can be done in different ways.

Since the release of PhotoStyler 1.1, the capacities of the „*Magnifying Glass*" tool have been enhanced enormously. In this section, only the basic functions of the „*Magnifying Glass*" tool will be explained. When activated, several configurations and options for the „*Magnifying Glass*" tool are found in the „*Tool Ribbon.*"

If this button found at the left-hand side of the ribbon area is clicked, the configuration of the „*Magnifying Glass*" tool can be saved and will remain valid when the „*Magnifying Glass*" tool is activated at a later time.

To magnify the current image, click this button, place the mouse-pointer on the area of the current image to be magnified, and press the left mouse-button several times, until a satisfactory magnification is reached.

To reduce the current image, click this button and proceed as described above for magnification of the current image.

If this button is clicked, a rectangle will be displayed on the screen: the part of the image on which the rectangle is placed will be magnified. In effect this tool

37 With these commands the data stored in the clipboard can be saved as and loaded from nearly all known graphic file formats.

looks and functions like a real rectangular magnifying glass. To move it on the screen, place the mouse-pointer inside the rectangle, hold the left mouse-button pressed, and move the mouse.

This tool can also be used if the current image has already been magnified or reduced with another function.

The increment unit of zoom operations done with the *„Magnifying Glass“* tool can be configured by writing the value of increment in the *„Zoom Increment Unit“* box found on the right-hand side of the *„Tool Ribbon.“*

The current image can also be zoomed using the *„Zoom“* slide rule of the *„Tool Ribbon“*: place the mouse-pointer on the arrow of the slide rule, hold the left mouse-button pressed, and move the mouse. With the *„Zoom“* slide rule an image can be magnified or reduced without changing the configuration of the *„Magnifying Glass“* tool.

The current image can be reset to a scale of 1 : 1 by clicking the *„1 : 1“* button found on the right-hand side of the *„Tool Ribbon“* or by pressing the right mouse-button.

In addition, any area of the current image can be marked with a rectangle when the *„Magnifying Glass“* tool is activated: move the mouse-pointer – displayed in the shape of a magnifying glass – to the area of interest, hold the left mouse-button pressed, and move the mouse. When the left mouse-button is released, the marked area will be magnified.

View Menu

If the current image must be zoomed while you are working with other tools, the commands of the *„View“* menu can be used.

Zoom in — The *„Zoom In“* command is equipped with a submenu providing different scales of magnification. Open this submenu and click the scale of the magnification wished.

Zoom out — For the *„Zoom Out“* command, proceed as with the *„Zoom In“* command.

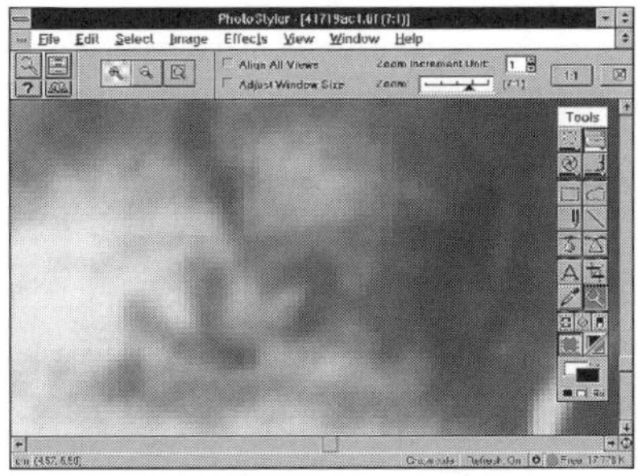

Detail of 4Q180 3 magnified.

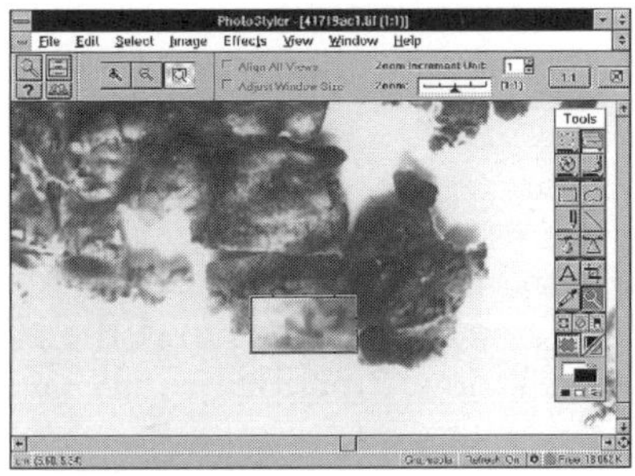

Detail of 4Q180 3 magnified.

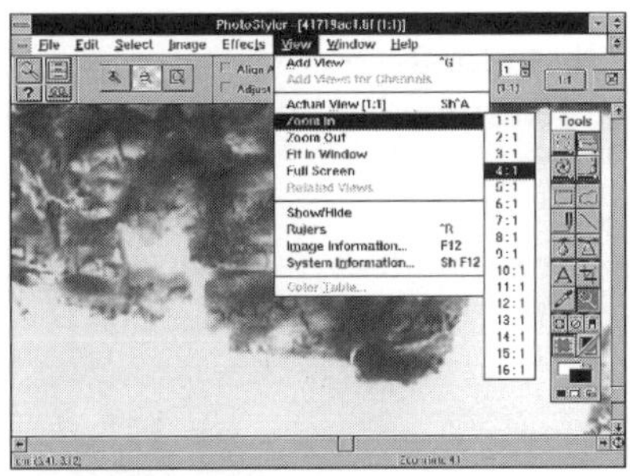

The *„Zoom In“* submenu of the *„View“* menu.

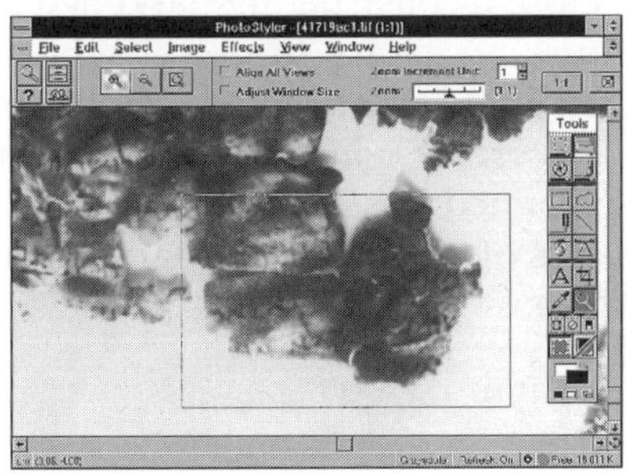

Detail of 4Q180 3 selected for magnification.

PAM 41719: Courtesy of the IAA

4Q180 3 zoomed out.
PAM 41719: Courtesy of the IAA.

Actual View With the *„Actual View (1 : 1)“* command, the current image can be zoomed to a scale of 1 : 1.

Zoom

Zoom operations can also be executed while working with other tools by using the buttons and the slide of the *„Image Navigator“* (for the global view function see above p. 87).

3.3.3 Darkened or Faded Texts

All dialogue boxes of the applications for gray-level manipulation are equipped with two test windows. By using these test windows, the results of an adjustment can easily be previewed in selectable parts of the current image. The buttons of these test windows are self-explanatory, and a detailed description must therefore not be given.

Image Analysis by Histograms

Before reconstructing darkened or faded passages of a text, it is sometimes necessary to detect whether or not any characters have been preserved. Histograms can be used for this purpose.

To create a histogram, the area to be analyzed must be selected as explained for the selection tools (see above p. 84–86). There are two ways of creating a histogram with PhotoStyler 2.0 after this has been done.

- Click the *„Histogram ...“* command in the *„Tune“* submenu of the *„Image“* menu to open the *„Histogram“* dialogue box, and a histogram of the current image selection will be calculated and displayed in the dialogue box after the *„Selection“* option has been clicked. Two buttons equipped with magnifying glasses are found there. They can be used to enlarge or reduce the displayed size of the histogram.

- Click the *„Tonal Correction …"* command in the *„Tune"* submenu of the *„Image"* menu to open the *„Tonal Correction"* dialogue box, and a histogram of the current image will be calculated and displayed in the dialogue box. To enlarge or reduce the histogram, use the two buttons of the dialogue box equipped with magnifying glasses.
- In dealing with histograms, it is important to remember that a histogram is a graphic representation of the pixel distribution of an image in the form of a curve, ordered according to the respective gray-levels and the amount of pixels (the gray-levels from 0 to 255 are represented by the horizontal axis, their amount is represented by the vertical axis). If all pixels are of the same or nearly the same gray-level, no characters have been preserved. This does not imply that there were never any characters in the analyzed area, only that they have not been preserved. If some pixels of a slightly different value are found, this may indicate that characters are preserved here.

! PhotoStyler provides users with a *„Line Selection"* tool (see p. 85) – some of our most informative histograms have been produced by processing lines drawn with this tool.

Negative

To create a negative with PhotoStyler, click the *„Negative"* command of the *„Tune"* submenu of the *„Image"* menu or press *Ctrl + 9*. The current image will be inverted to a negative. Press *Alt + Backspace* or *Ctrl + Z* to undo the inversion and press them again to redo it.

Previously selected areas can of course also be inverted to a negative. For this purpose, select the area of interest as described above and click the *„Negative"* command.

! An altered image should be stored in a separate file leaving the original image intact.

Regulation of Brightness and Contrast

- To regulate the brightness and contrast of an image, click the *„Brightness & Contrast …"* command of the *„Tune"* submenu of

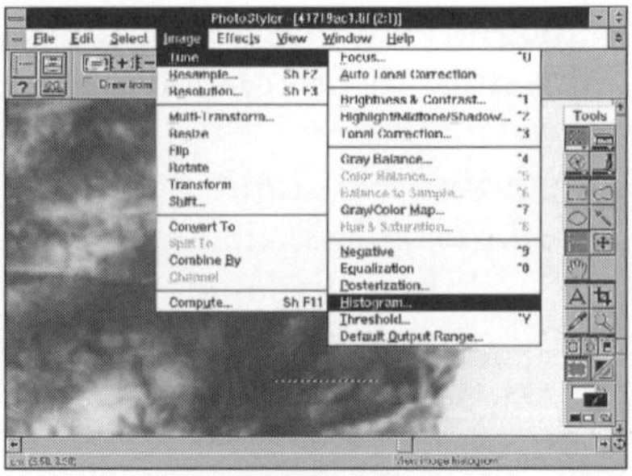

The *„Histogram"* command of the *„Tune"* submenu.

Detail of 4Q180 3. PAM 41719: Courtesy of the IAA.

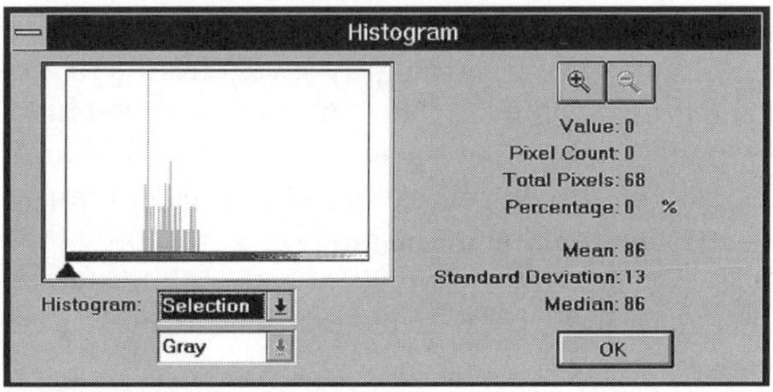

PhotoStyler's *„Histogram"* dialogue box with histogram.

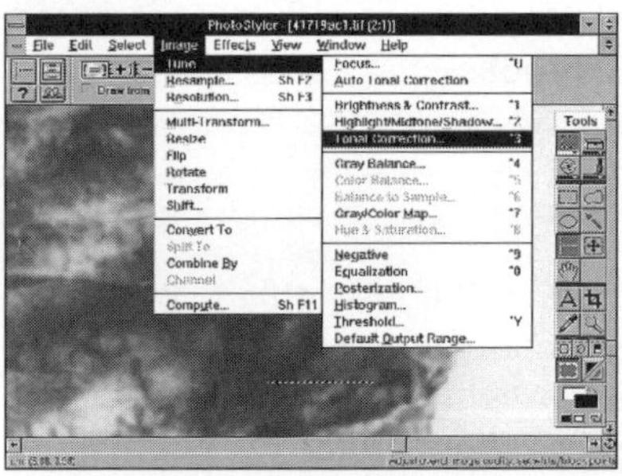

The *„Tonal Correction ..."* command of the *„Tune"* submenu.

Detail of 4Q180 3. PAM 41719: Courtesy of the IAA.

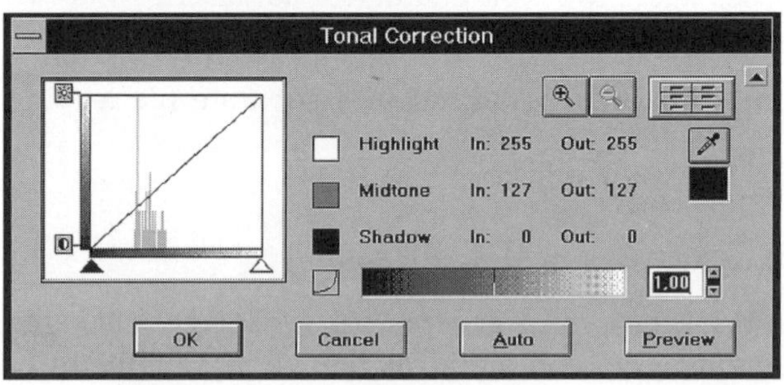

PhotoStyler's *„Tonal Correction"* dialogue box with histogram.

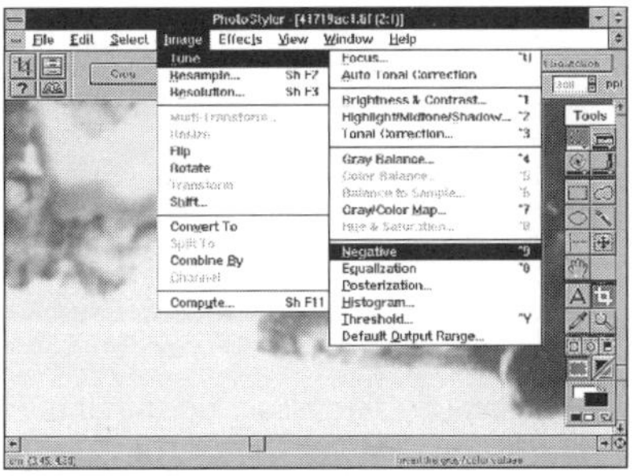

The „*Negative*" command of the „*Tune*" submenu.

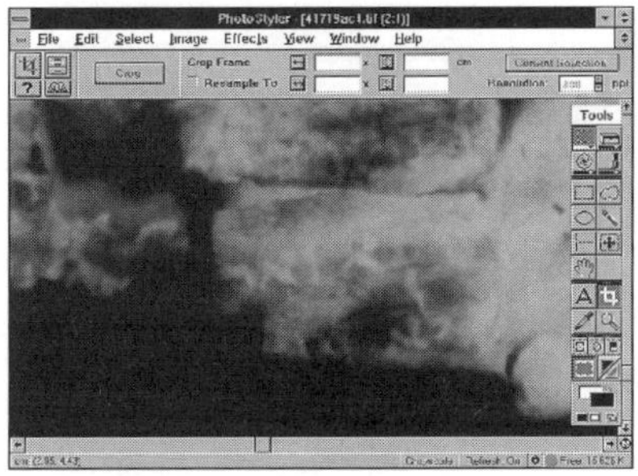

Negative processed with PhotoStyler.

Detail of 4Q180 3. PAM 41719: Courtesy of the IAA

the „*Image*" menu, or press *Ctrl + 1*. A dialogue box with three scroll bars will be displayed on the screen. Place the mouse-pointer on the buttons of the „*Brightness*" and „*Contrast*" scroll bars, hold the left mouse-button pressed and move the mouse: the brightness and contrast will be regulated in accordance to the movements of the buttons. With the „*Gamma*" scroll bar, the regulation of contrast and brightness can be combined with gamma correction.

- To preview the adjustments, click the „*Preview*" button. To fixate the regulation, click the „*OK*" button, and to exit the operation without fixating the results, click the „*Cancel*" button.
- If brightness and contrast are to be regulated for a separated area only, select the area as described for the selection tools before calling the „*Brightness & Contrast*" dialogue box.

! An altered image should be stored in a separate file leaving the original image intact.

Gamma Correction

In contrast to PhotoStyler 1.1, PhotoStyler 2.0 provides gamma correction in combination with the regulation of contrast and brightness, the tonal correction, and the gray/color map.

- To call the „*Tonal Correction*" dialogue box, click the „*Tonal Correction ...*" command in the „*Tune*" submenu of the „*Image*" menu or press *Ctrl + 3*. Move the line of the „*Gamma*" scroll bar in the dialogue box and the image will be altered accordingly: place the mouse-pointer on the scroll bar line, hold the left mouse-button

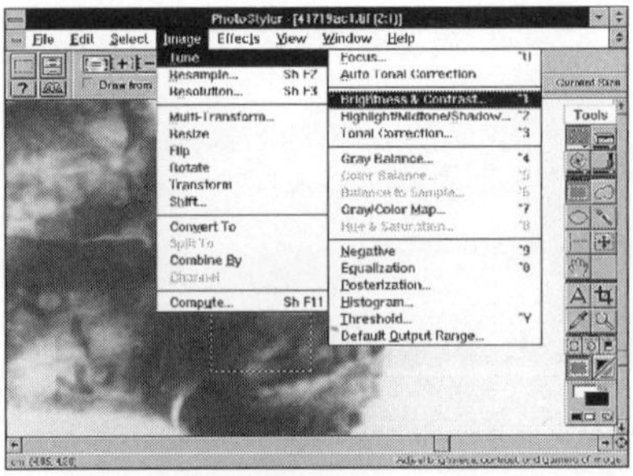

The *„Brightness & Contrast …"* command of the *„Tune"* submenu.

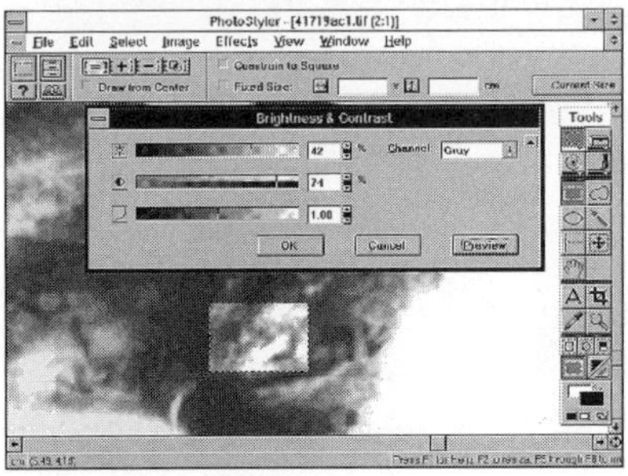

The *„Brightness & Contrast"* dialogue box with enhanced area below (כללה).

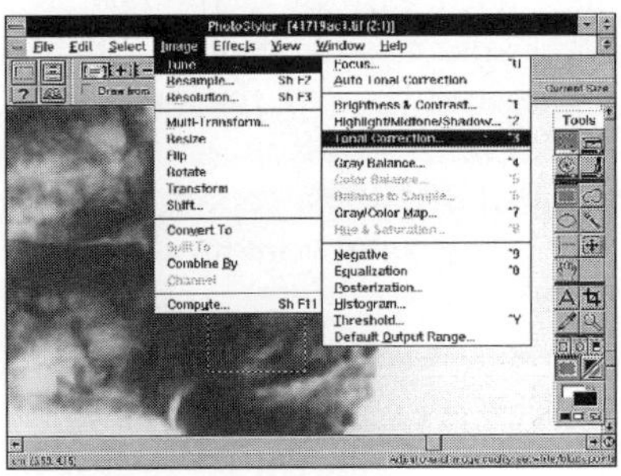

The *„Tonal Correction …"* command of the *„Tune"* submenu.

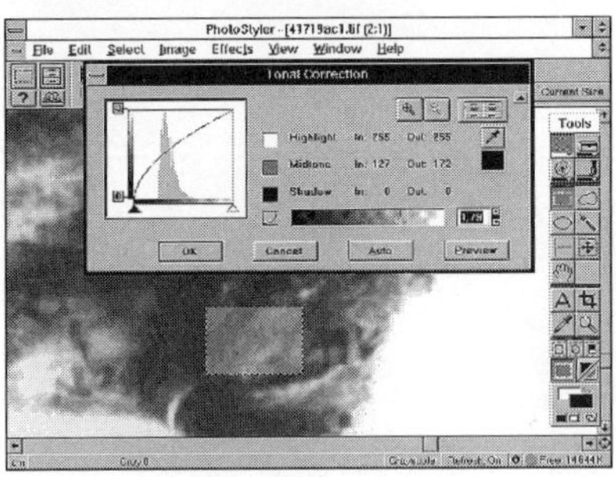

The *„Tonal Correction"* dialogue box with enhanced area below (כללה).

Detail of 4Q180 3. PAM 41719: Courtesy of the IAA

pressed, and move the mouse. Values above 1.00 lighten the image while values below 1.00 darken it.

- Click the „*Preview*" button to preview the alterations and the „*Reset*" command found in the pulldown menu of the „*Filing Cabinet*" button to reset the preview to the original. To fixate alterations, click the „*OK*" button, and to leave the „*Tonal Correction*" without fixating the alteration, click the „*Cancel*" button.
- To enhance only a selected area of the fragment or manuscript, mark it with a selection tool before calling the „*Tonal Correction*."

! An altered image should be stored in a separate file leaving the original image intact.

Gray/Color Map

It is often of great help to assign a new gray-level value to all pixels of a certain gray-level by using the „*Gray/Color Map*."

- This function is called with the „*Gray/Color Map*" ... command of the „*Tune*" submenu of the „*Image*" menu or by pressing *Ctrl + 7*. The then displayed „*Gray/Color Map*" dialogue box provides users with a map which „displays the value of the darkest pixels on the left and the brightest on the right. The mapping curve that runs across the map shows the actual brightness values of the pixels at each point across the map. The horizontal axis of the Gray/Color Map graphs the original gray or color values (input), where zero is black and 255 is white. The vertical axis graphs the new values (output)."[38] The gray-scale ribbons attached to the vertical and horizontal axis of the curve indicate the gray-level represented by a certain point of the curve. Move the mouse-pointer to the curve, hold the left mouse-button pressed, and alter the curve as wanted to reassign gray-levels.
- The „*Filing Cabinet*" button of the „*Gray/Color Map*" dialogue box offers some additionally helpful applications. The „*Piecewise*" command displays handles on the „*Gray/Color Map*" curve. These make working with the curve much easier, but do not achieve results as good as when working without them. Helpful predefined curves can be applied with the commands „*Gamma ...,*" „*Logarithm,*" and „*Negative.*"[39] Use the „*Save ...*" command to save a

[38] Aldus PhotoStyler User Manual, Version 1.1., p. 257

[39] The gamma and the negative curves are also available without the „*Gray/Color Map.*" See the paragraphs „Gamma Correction" and „Equalization."

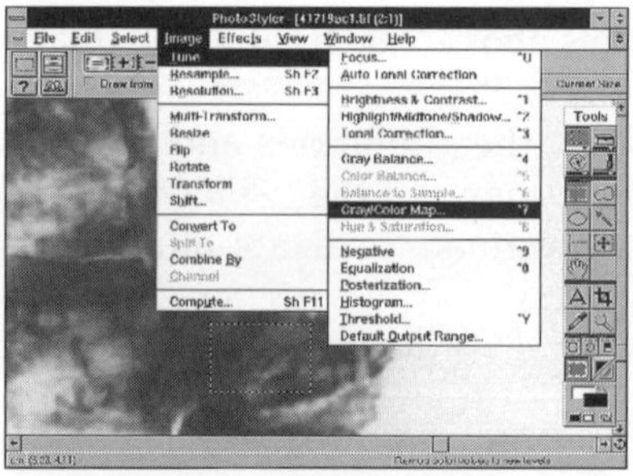

The *„Gray/Color Map . . .“* command of the *„Tune“* submenu.

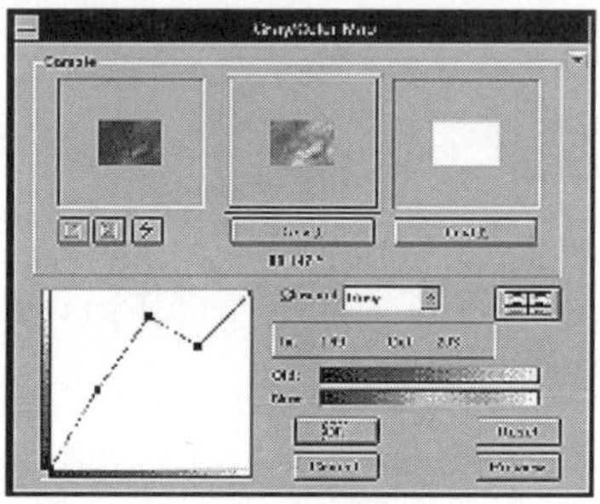

PhotoStyler's *„Gray/Color Map“* dialogue box.

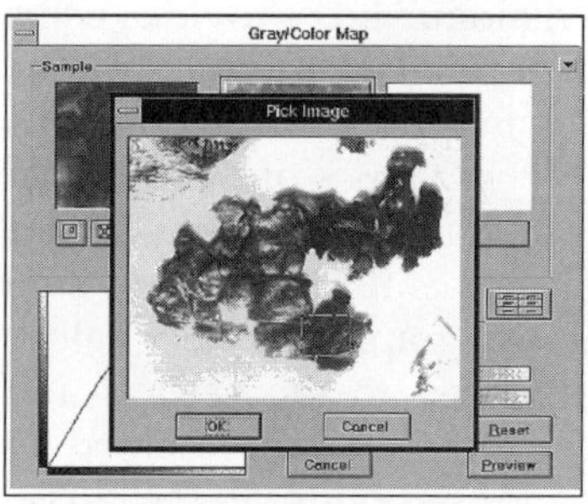

The *„Pick Image“* dialogue box, called from the *„Gray/Color Map“* dialogue box.

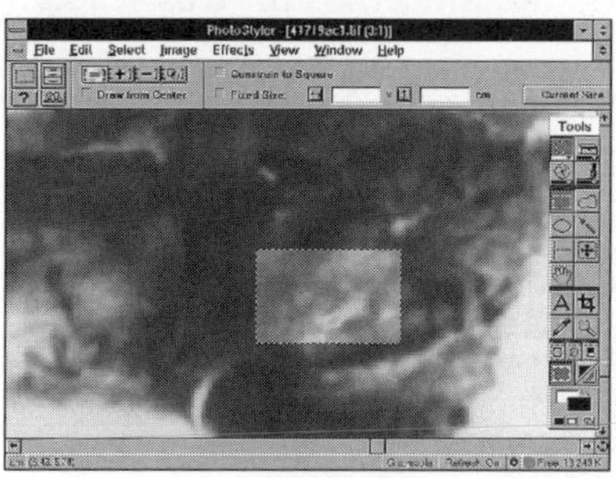

Area enhanced with the *„Gray/Color Map“* (כללה).

Detail of 4Q180 3. PAM 41719: Courtesy of the IAA

current mapping curve for later use, and the *„Load ...“* command to reload it. With the *„Preview“* button, the results of the reassignment can be previewed, and with the *„Reset“* button, the preview can be undone. With the *„OK“* button, results can be fixated and with the *„Cancel“* button, the *„Gray/Color Map“* can be left without fixating.
- To manipulate only a selected area of the current image, mark it as explained for the selection tools before calling the *„Gray/Color Map.“*

! The portion of the image to be displayed in the „Test“ windows of the *„Gray/Color Map“* dialogue box can be defined with the *„Pick“* button.

! An altered image should be stored in a separate file leaving the original image intact.

Equalization

PhotoStyler 2.0 is equipped with several different equalization functions:

- An excellent predefined equalization curve will be executed when the *„Equalization“* command in the *„Tune“* submenu of the *„Image“* menu is clicked or *Ctrl + O* is pressed: mark the area to be reconstructed and click the *„Equalization“* command.
- If a good reconstruction can't be reached by predefined equalization, call the *„Tonal Correction“* dialogue box by clicking the corresponding command of the *„Tune“* submenu of the *„Image“* menu or press *Ctrl + 3*. A histogram of the image selection will be processed and displayed.[40] Moving the small arrows on the lower horizontal axis with the mouse will regulate the input range of the original digital image and the contrast will be increased. Moving the small arrows on the left vertical axis will regulate the output range of the enhanced image and the contrast will be decreased. PhotoStyler 2.0 enables users to adjust the dark, midtone, and bright gray-levels of an image separately. For this, the corresponding commands in the pulldown menu of the *„Filing Cabinet“* button must be used.[41]

[40] The histogram can be enlarged and reduced with the corresponding buttons of the dialogue box.

[41] The *„Pick Color“* function represented by the *„Eyedropper“* button is only for true color images.

PhotoStyler's *„Tonal Correction"* dialogue box.

The *„Reset"* command, displayed after the *„Filing Cabinet"* button is clicked, will restore the manipulated image to its original state. By using the corresponding buttons of the *„Tonal Correction"* dialogue box, adjustments can be previewed, fixated, and canceled.

! The gray-level(s) of the darkened parchment surrounding the former characters can be detected by placing the mouse-pointer on the respective pixels. The gray-level of the pixel the mouse-pointer is pointing at will be displayed on the *„Status Bar"*.

– As usual, selected areas can be enhanced separately if marked before applying any equalization function.

! All of these functions should be used only on selected areas of an image. Using equalization for a whole image won't help you in reconstructing your text because a fragment or a manuscript usually isn't darkened or faded uniformly.

! To reach good results, it is advisable to mark small parts of the darkened or faded areas and work on them individually, especially if large faded or darkened areas of a manuscript are to be reconstructed.

! Using the *„Tonal Correction"* instead of the *„Equalization"* command enables users to combine equalization and gamma correction.

! An altered image should be stored in a separate file leaving the original image intact.

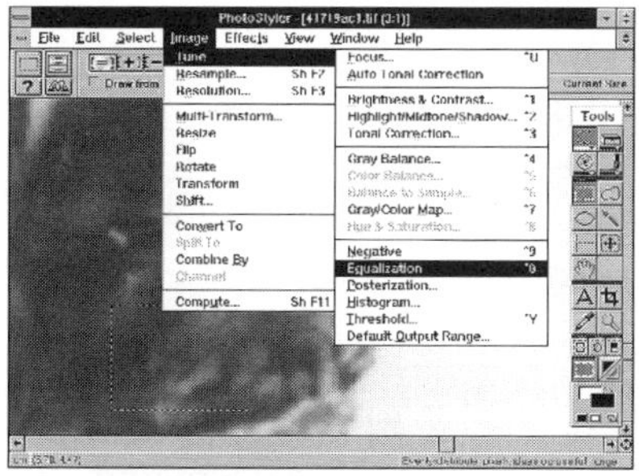

The „*Equalization*" command of the „Tune" submenu.

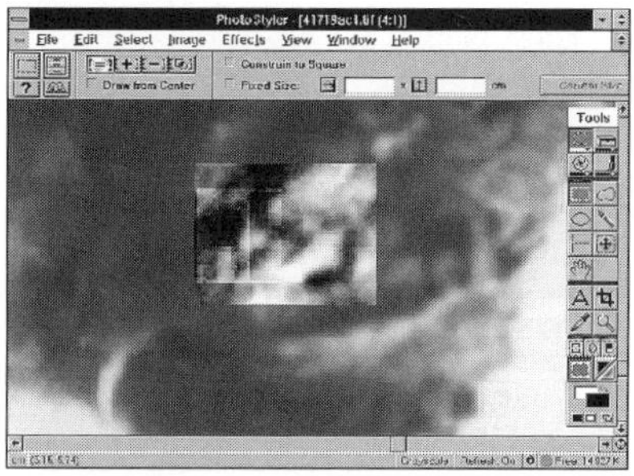

Area enhanced with Equalization (כללה).

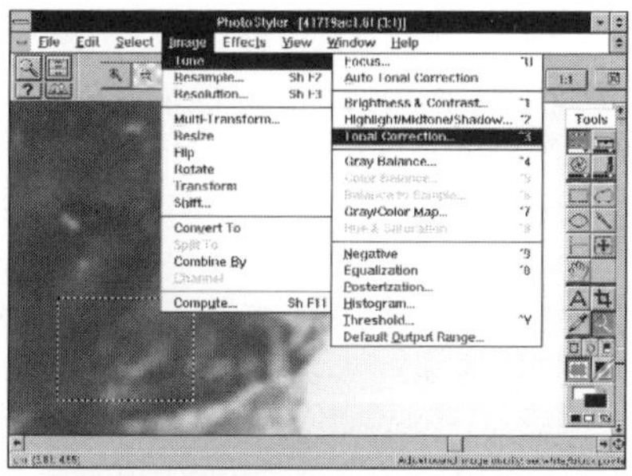

The „*Tonal Correction* ..." command of the „*Tune*" submenu.

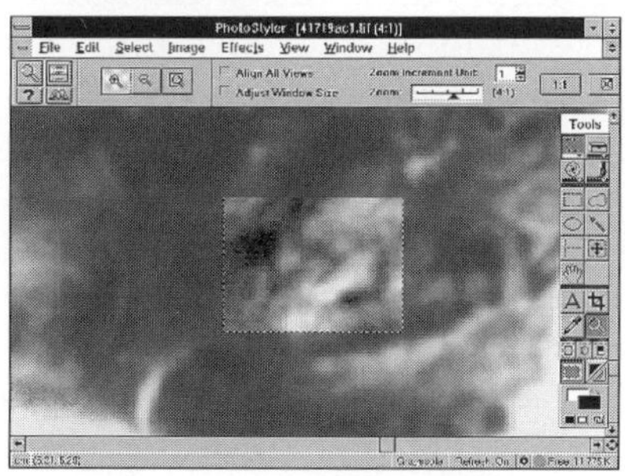

Area enhanced with the „*Tonal Correction*" (כללה).

Detail of 4Q180 3. PAM 41719: Courtesy of the IAA

Shadow/Midtone/Highlight

With *„Shadow/Midtone/Highlight,"* PhotoStyler 2.0 provides users with another helpful application for gray-level adjustment. With this function, one is able to adjust the dark, light, and midtone gray-levels of an image separately.

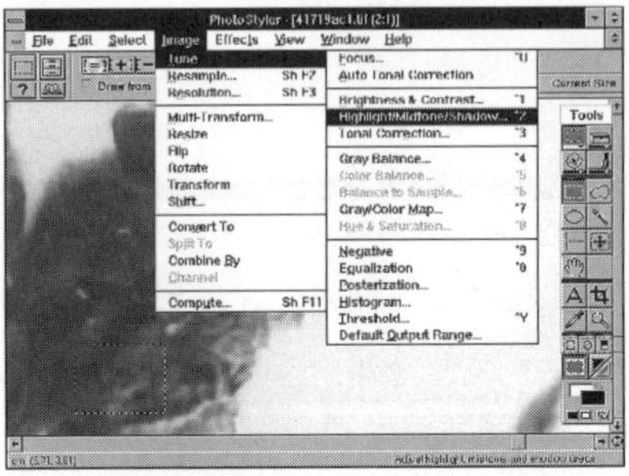

The *„Shadow/Midtone/Highlight ..."* command of the *„Tune"* submenu.

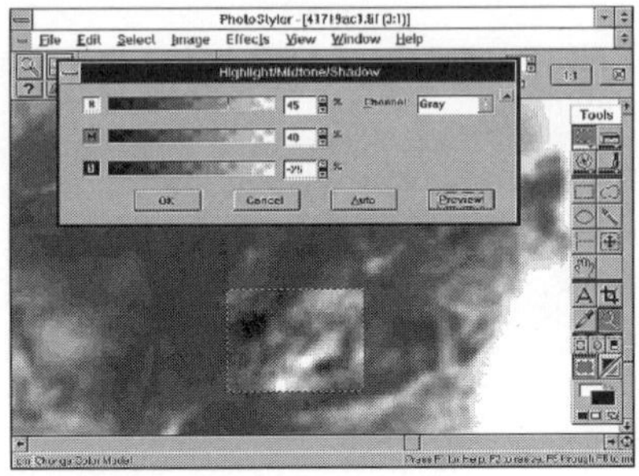

„Shadow/Midtone/Highlight" dialogue box with enhanced area below.

Detail of 4Q180 3. PAM 41719: Courtesy of the IAA

- To call the *„Shadow/Midtone/Highlight"* dialogue box, click the *„Shadow/Midtone/Highlight ..."* command in the *„Tune"* submenu of the *„Image"* menu or press *Ctrl* + 2. In the dialogue box three scroll bars are shown, labeled *„S,"* *„M,"* and *„H."* With these the respective gray-level ranges of the current image can be adjusted: to assign all dark gray-levels to become brighter, place the mouse-pointer on the *„S"* scroll-bar line, hold the left mouse-button pressed, and move the scroll-bar line in the direction of the right-hand side of the scroll bar. To assign all dark gray-levels to become darker, move the scroll-bar line in the direction the left-hand side of the scroll-bar. To manipulate the midtone and light gray-levels of the current image, proceed in the same way with the *„M"* and *„H"* scroll-bars.
- To preview the gray-level adjustments, click the *„Preview"* button of the *„Shadow/Midtone/Highlight"* dialogue box. To fixate them, use the *„OK"* button. To close the dialogue box without fixating adjustments, click the *„Cancel"* button.
- Selected areas can also be adjusted with this function if they are marked before the *„Shadow/Midtone/Highlight"* dialogue box is called.

! An altered image should be stored in a separate file, leaving the original image intact.

3.3.4 Comparison and Joining of Fragments

1. To compare two fragments, first select one of the fragments from the original scanned photo and store it in a separate file. The „*Magic Wand*" tool should be used for this purpose.

   - To configure the wand range, click the „*Magic Wand*" icon and configure the wand range to 30 (for the „*Magic Wand*" tool see the introduction to PhotoStyler 2.0). If this configuration does not work, the gray-level range of the area surrounding the fragment of interest should be analyzed with the mouse-pointer (see above, p. 85), and the color similarity of the wand range should be set according to the range detected.
   - Move the mouse-pointer to the area surrounding the fragment of interest and press the left mouse-button. The white environment surrounding the fragment will be defined as a selected area. To invert the orientation of the selected area from the white environment to the enclosed fragment, click the „*Invert*" button of the toolbox or press *Ctrl* + *I*.[42] Copy the now selected fragment with the help of the „*Cut*" or „*Copy*" command of the „*Edit*" menu to PhotoStyler's private clipboard (see the introduction to PhotoStyler) or press *Ctrl* + *X* or *Ctrl* + *C* respectively.

2. Now the file containing the fragment to be compared must be called, and the selected fragment must be inserted from the private clipboard of PhotoStyler into this file. To do this, use the „*As Selection*" option of the „*Paste*" command found in the „*Edit*" menu or press *Ctrl* + *V*.

3. The transparency of the insert function must be configured: press *Ctrl* + *M* to call PhotoStyler's „*Merge Control.*" To see only the border structure of the inserted fragment, configure the „*Floating Opacity*" box of the „*Merge Control*" dialogue box to the value 1. The border of the inserted fragment will be marked by a blinking marque while the rest of the fragment will be transparent. Place the mouse-pointer on the inserted fragment, hold the left mouse-button pressed and move the mouse: the inserted fragment will

[42] The „*Inverse*" command of the „*Select*" menu can also be used for this purpose.

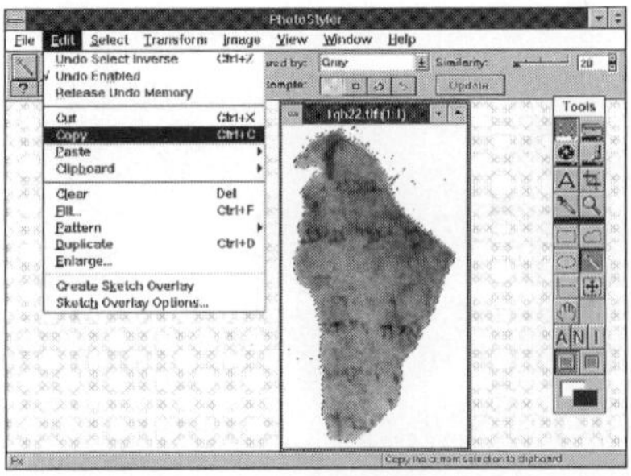

Copying the selected fragment 1QH 22 to the clipboard.

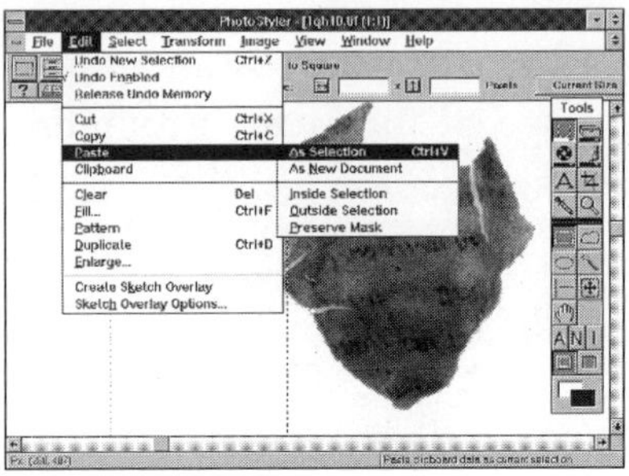

Pasting the fragment 1QH 22 next to the fragment 1QH 18.

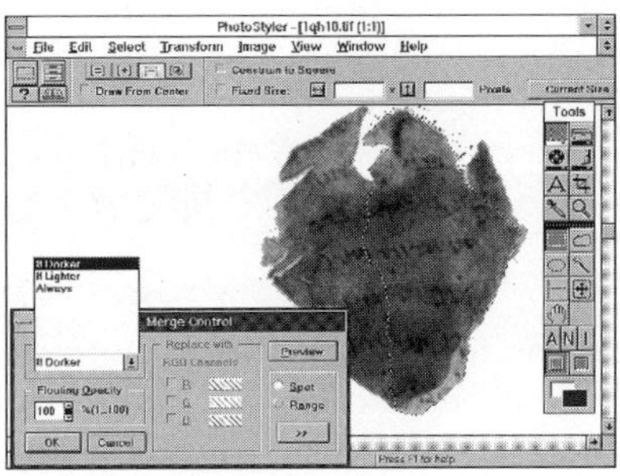

Configuring the transparency of the fragments.

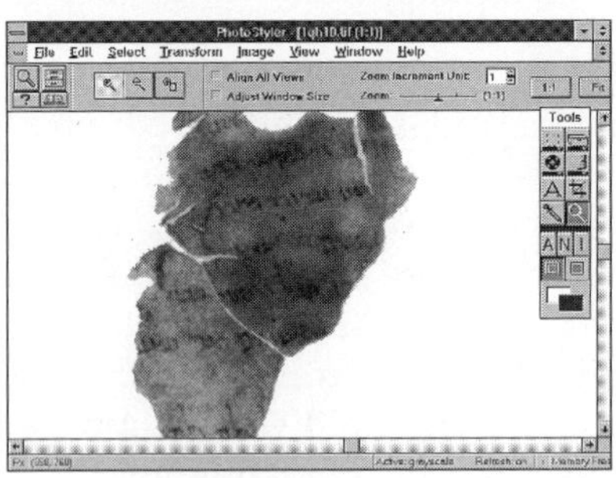

Both fragments joined.

1QH 18 and 22: Courtesy of the Shrine of the Book

follow the movements of the mouse. To change the transparency level of the inserted fragment, again call the „*Merge Control*" dialogue box (press *Ctrl* + *M*) and choose the „*If Darker*" or „*Always*" configuration.

4. Sometimes it is necessary to compare the direction and position of the lines of both fragments. For this purpose configure the „*Merge Control*" with the „*If Darker*" Option and try several values for the „*Floating Opacity*" – use the „*Preview*" button of the „*Merge Control*" dialogue box to preview the tested configurations. You will get a transparent inserted fragment whose dark passages – e. g. its characters – are not transparent.

5. To join the fragments side by side, select them in any way which seems appropriate, copy them to PhotoStyler's private clipboard and then insert them into the file of the fragment to be compared using the „*As Selection*" option of the „*Paste*" command found in the „*Edit*" menu or pressing *Ctrl* + *V* . Once inserted and moved to the right place, the „*None*" button of the „*Select*" toolbox should be clicked to unselect and fixate the inserted fragment (alternatively press *Ctrl* + *N*).[43]

! Sometimes the image into which the selected fragment should be inserted is not large enough. In this case, create a new file and insert all the fragments to be joined or compared into this file. Be sure to keep in mind that graphic files need an enormous amount of the computer's memory. One may easily run out of RAM, even if the PC is equipped with 8 MB or more of RAM.

3.3.5 Mirrorwriting

1. To relocate a mirrorwriting, the mirrorwriting must first be selected out of the original scanned photo and stored as a separate file. For this purpose use the „*Magic Wand*" tool as described above (see Comparison and Joining of Fragments). The selected mirrorwriting should be copied to PhotoStyler's private clipboard with the „*Cut*" or „*Copy*" command of the „*Edit*" menu[44] (alternatively press *Ctrl* + *X* or *Ctrl* + *C*), and saved from this clipboard as a TIFF file.

[43] The „*None*" command of the „*Select*" menu can also be used for this purpose.

[44] The Windows clipboard isn't suitable for the relocation of mirrorwritings. If it is used for this purpose, the selected area is always stored in the form of a rectangle.

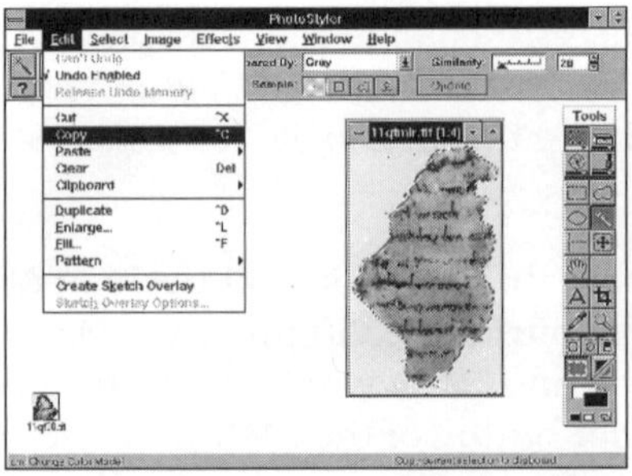

Copying the selected mirrorwriting of 11QTemp XXXVIII to the clipboard.

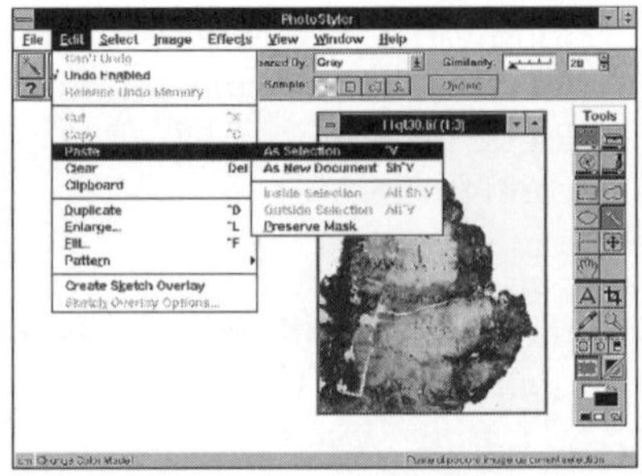

Pasting the mirrorwriting from the clipboard to the file of the home column, 11QTemp XXXVIII.

Courtesy of the Shrine of the Book

2. The file containing the mirrorwriting's home column – i. e. the column from which it has been separated – must then be called to the screen, and the mirrorwriting must be inserted from PhotoStyler's private clipboard into this image. For this, click the „*Paste*" command in the „*Edit*" menu and choose the „*As Selection*" option or press alternatively *Ctrl + V*.

   If the mirrorwriting is no longer stored in Photostyler's private clipboard, call it back to the clipboard. For this, use the „*Load* ..." command in the „*Clipboard*" submenu of the „*Edit*" menu, or click the „*Load* ..." button of PhotoStyler's „*Clipboard Content*" dialogue box, which can be opened with the „*Content* ..." command of the same submenu. In both cases you will be guided by dialogue boxes.

3. After this, the mirrorwriting, which of course preserves the characters in the wrong order, must be „mirrored back": for this, click the „*Horizontal*" command in the „*Flip*" submenu of the „*Image*" menu.[45]

4. The transparency of the insert function must be configured: press *Ctrl + M* to call the „*Merge Control*" dialogue box. For the relocation of mirrorwritings, our experience has shown that it is best to choose the option „*If Darker*" in the „*Use Floating Image*" pulldown menu. Afterwards try several values for the „*Floating Opacity*" to reach the best transparency. Click the „*Preview*" button to preview

[45] For the scaling of the fragment, which will be necessary if the photo of the mirrorwriting and the photo of the column or fragment from which it has been separated are of different scales, see the last paragraph of this section.

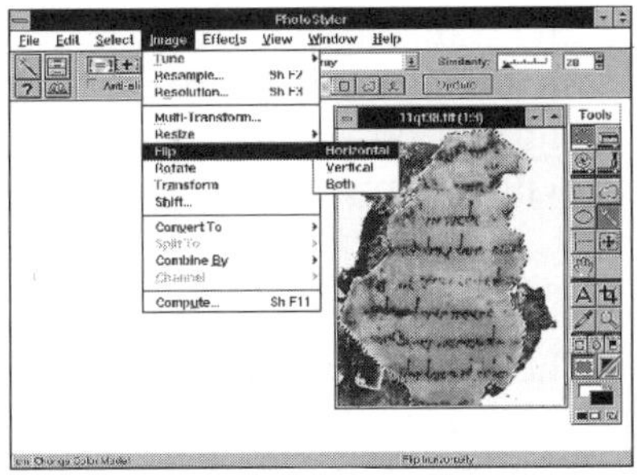

Remirroring the pasted mirrorwriting.

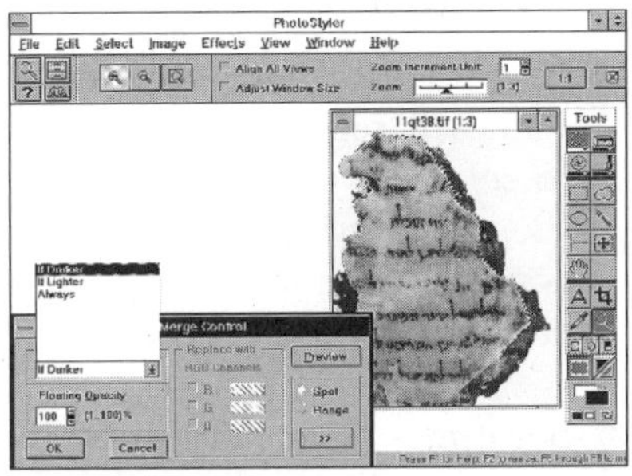

Configuring the transparency of the pasted mirrorwriting.

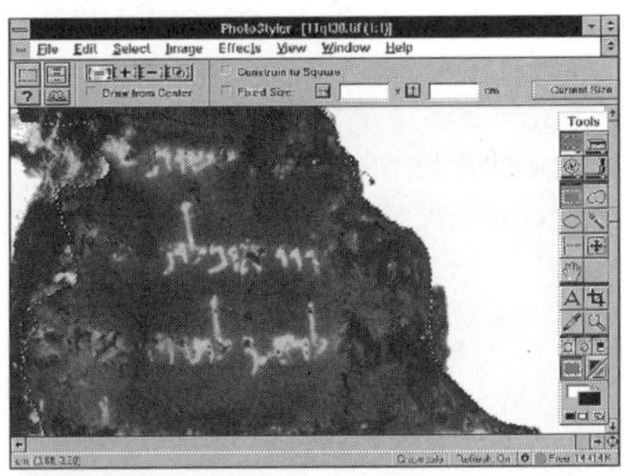

Adjusting the mirrorwriting previously inverted to a negative.

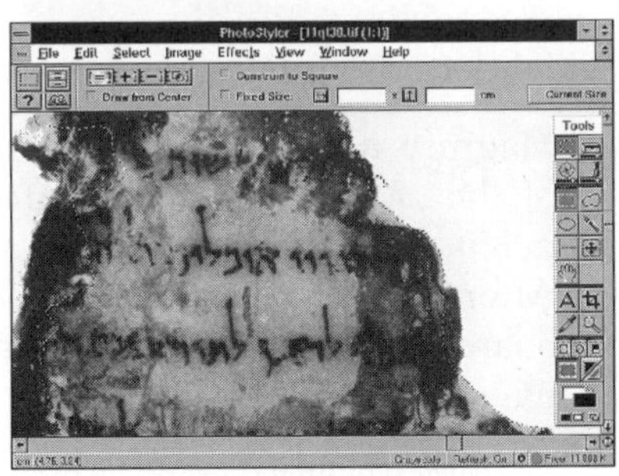

The relocated mirrorwriting.

11QTemp XXXVIII and mirrorwriting: Courtesy of the Shrine of the Book

the transparency and the „*OK*“ button to fixate the configuration. In this way dark areas of the inserted mirrorwriting will be configured non-transparent (i. e. the characters) while its bright areas will become transparent (i. e. the parchment).

5. Now the relocation itself can be done. To move the mirrorwriting on the screen, place the mouse-pointer on the mirrorwriting, hold the left mouse-button pressed, and move the mouse. The mirrorwriting will follow the mouse movements. To fixate the mirrorwriting after successfully relocating it, click the „*None*“ button of the „*Select*“ toolbox or press *Ctrl* + *N*.[46]

! If you try to relocate a large mirrorwriting in a single operation, you will probably run short of RAM. In this case it is advisable to select several small parts out of the mirrorwriting and relocate them individually. For this, use the „*Rectangle Selection*“ tool. This is also advisable when the parchment of the mirrorwriting as well as the parchment of its home column are crumbled.

! Somtimes it is helpful to invert the inserted mirrorwriting to a negative. In this way the characters of the mirrorwriting will be displayed transparent while the surrounding parchment will be displayed black and non-transparent (the inserted mirrorwriting has to be configured previously to transparent). In this way it is possible to see the character fragments of the mirrorwriting's home column through the transparent characters of the mirrorwriting.

3.3.6 Character Fragments

As with PhotoStyler 1.1, there are two different methods of creating and using lettertemplates, depending on the configuration of the „*Merge Control*“ and the selection tool used to select characters from which lettertemplates can be derived.

- Magnify a well preserved character and select it with the help of the „*Magic Wand*“ tool (for the „*Magic Wand*“ tool see above p. 85). As wand range (similarity), several values should be tested. After marking it, copy the character to PhotoStyler's private clipboard with the „*Copy*“ command of the „*Edit*“ menu[47] (alternatively press *Ctrl* + *C*).

[46] The „*None*“ command of the „*Select*“ menu can also be used for this purpose.

[47] For PhotoStyler's private clipboard see above pp. 87–89. The Windows clipboard cannot be used for this operation.

Afterwards go to the character fragments to be identified, mark them with a selection tool, and insert the well preserved character with the „*Paste*" command of the „*Edit*" menu. For this, choose the „*As Selection*" option of the „*Paste*" command (alternatively press *Ctrl + V*).[48]

Press *Ctrl + M* to call the „*Merge Control*" dialogue box. In this dialogue box, the „*Use Floating Image*" pull down menu should be configured with the „*If Lighter*" option. Then click the „*Preview*" button to preview the transparency reached or the „*OK*" button to activate it. If the transparency is not sufficient, try another „*Floating Opacity*" value. In this way a transparent character can be created whose edges are marked by a black and white marque.

This lettertemplate can be moved around on the screen as wanted: place the mouse-pointer on the lettertemplate, hold the left mouse-button pressed, and move the mouse.

– Use the „*Rectangle Selection*" tool to select a well preserved character and copy it – as described above – to the clipboard.[49]

  Then insert it with the „*Paste*" command of the „*Edit*" menu next to the character fragments to be identified. Invert the inserted character with the „*Negative*" command to a negative and enhance its contrast with the „*Equalization*" command (both commands are found in the „*Tune*" submenu of the „*Image*" menu).

  After this, call the „*Merge Control*" dialogue box by pressing *Ctrl + M* and configure the „*Use Floating Image*" pull down menu with the „*If Darker*" option. The result is a transparent character surrounded by an non-transparent dark environment. This lettertemplate can be moved and fixated as usual.

! The lettertemplates can be stored after being copied to the clipboard: for this purpose, use the „*Load ...*" and the „*Save ...*" commands of the „*Clipboard*" submenu of the „*Edit*" menu. In this case inverting to a negative and equalization should be done *before* copying a well preserved character to the clipboard.

! It is recommended to note the exact location from where the lettertemplates have been derived, and, if possible, the scale of the image.

---

48 PhotoStyler will insert the well preserved letter out of the clipboard to any actively selected area of an image. If there is no selected area, the character in the clipboard will be inserted in the upper left corner of the current image.

49 For this operation either the Windows clipboard or PhotoStyler's private clipboard can be used.

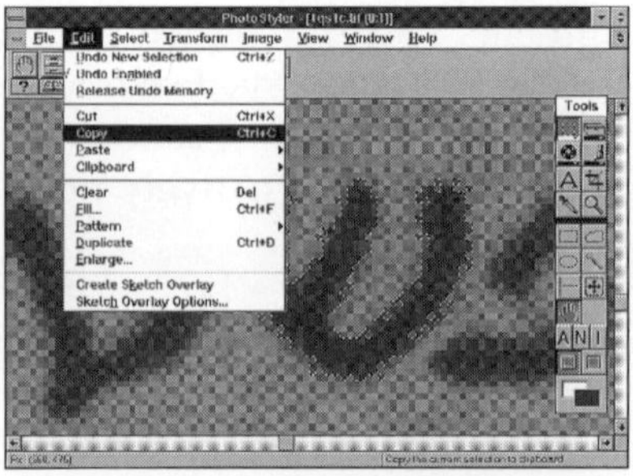

Copying a selected character to the clipboard.

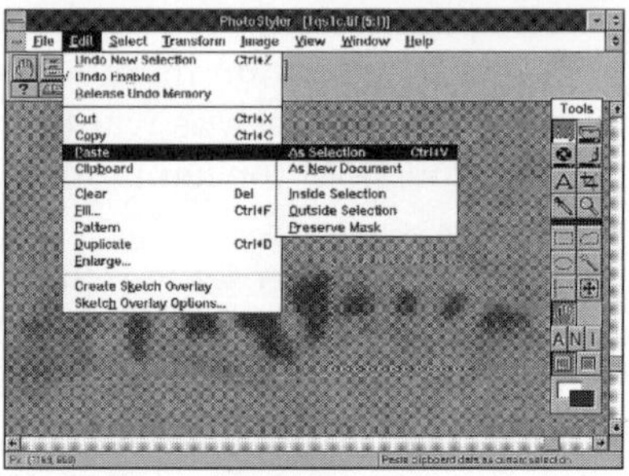

Pasting the character over the character fragments to be identified.

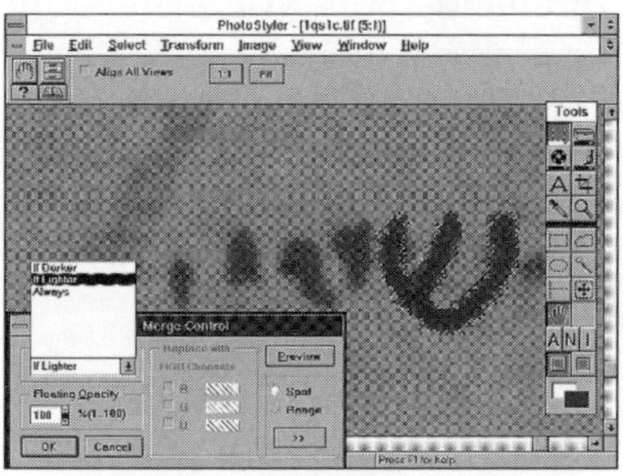

Configuring the transparency of the inserted character.

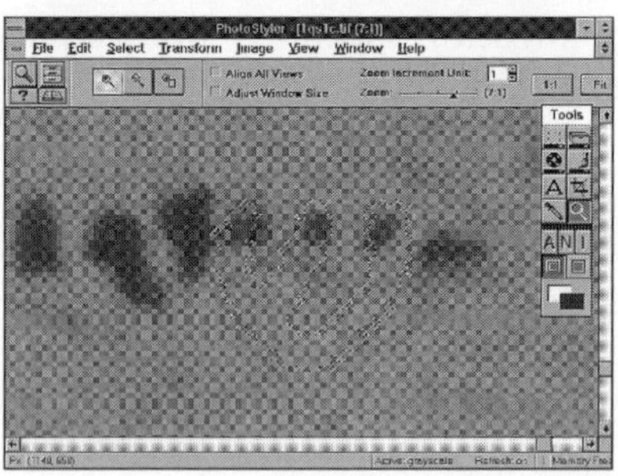

Character fragments identified with the template as the Hebrew letter ש.

1QS I$_{23.25}$: Courtesy of the Shrine of the Book

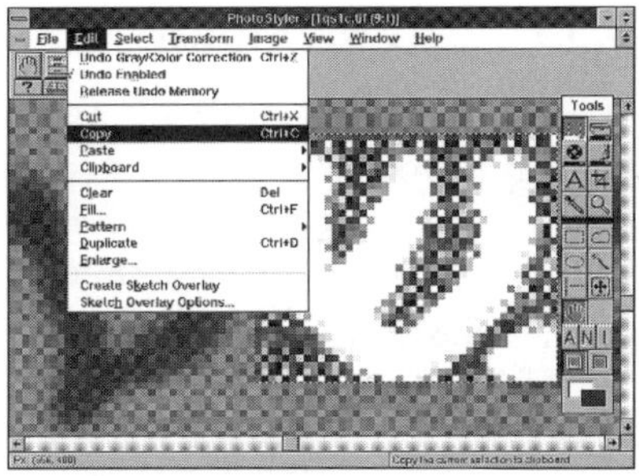

Copying a prepared character to the clipboard.

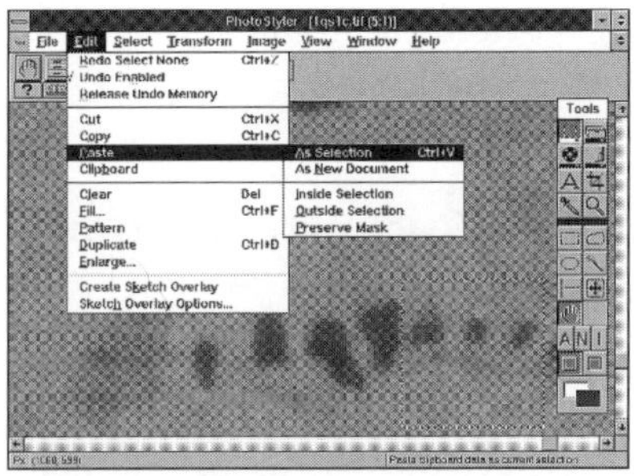

Pasting the character over the character fragments to be identified.

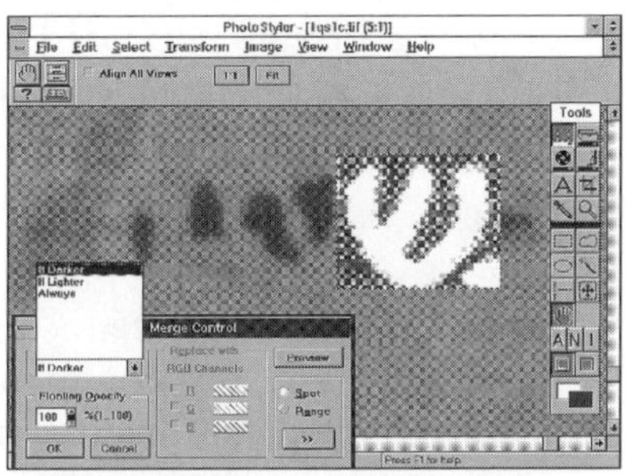

Configuring the transparency of the inserted character.

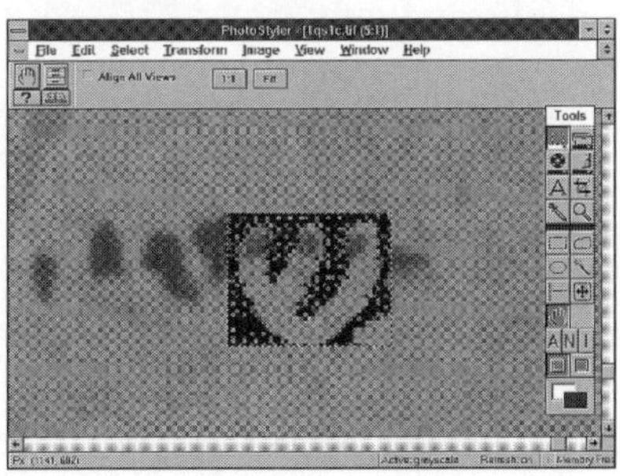

Character fragments identified with the template as the Hebrew letter שׁ.

1QS $\mathrm{I}_{23.25}$: Courtesy of the Shrine of the Book

3.3.7 The Comparison of Characters

If characters of different manuscripts are to be compared (paleography), you can proceed in a similar way, as described for the reconstruction of character fragments. There is only one difference: instead of one text (= image file), two or more must be held open simultaneously.[50] Mark the character of interest, load it into PhotoStyler's private clipboard, and insert it into the image containing the character with which the marked character is to be compared.

! It is recommended to note the exact location from where the lettertemplates have been derived, and if possible, the scale of the image.

3.3.8 Reconstruction of Text Gaps

In a similar way, text gaps[51] can be reconstructed with the original ductus of the scribe of a certain scroll.

1. Select the words or characters to be inserted into a text gap, and copy them with the „*Copy*" command of the „*Edit*" menu to PhotoStyler's private clipboard, or use the keys *Ctrl* + *V*. Then save them to a file using the „*Save* ..." command in the „*Clipboard*" submenu of the „*Edit*" menu.

2. Mark the part of the text gap where the selected word or character shall be placed with the „*Rectangular Selection*" tool and call the stored word or character to PhotoStyler's private clipboard using the „*Load* ..." command of the „*Clipboard*" submenu of the „*Edit*" menu. Then insert it into the selected area by clicking the „*As Selection*" option of the „*Paste*" submenu of the „*Edit*" menu (alternatively press *Ctrl* + *V*).

3. If there are character fragments at the edges of the text gap, try to use lettertemplates as described above.

! It is recommended to note the exact location from where the words and/or characters used for the reconstruction have been derived.

---

[50] For this, call the files successively and click the „*Tile*" command in the „*Window*" menu (or press *Shift* + *F4*) to arrange the files next to each other on the screen.

[51] Text gaps caused by physical damage are often named *lacunae* in the literature on the Dead Sea Scrolls.

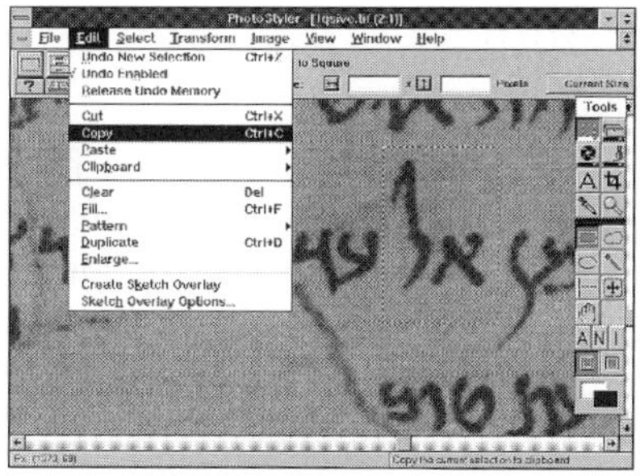

Copying the word אל to the clipboard.

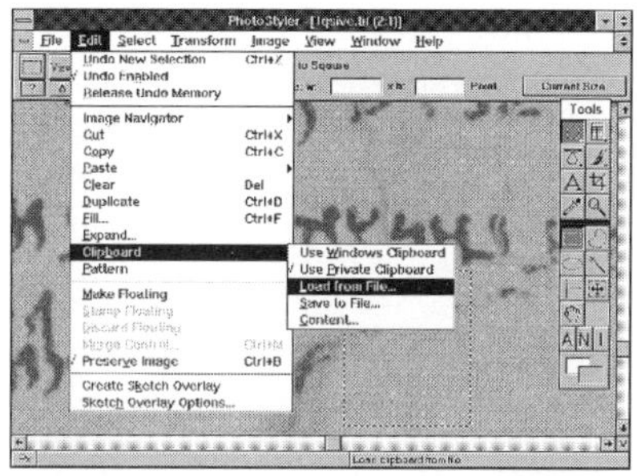

Loading the previously stored word or character into the clipboard.

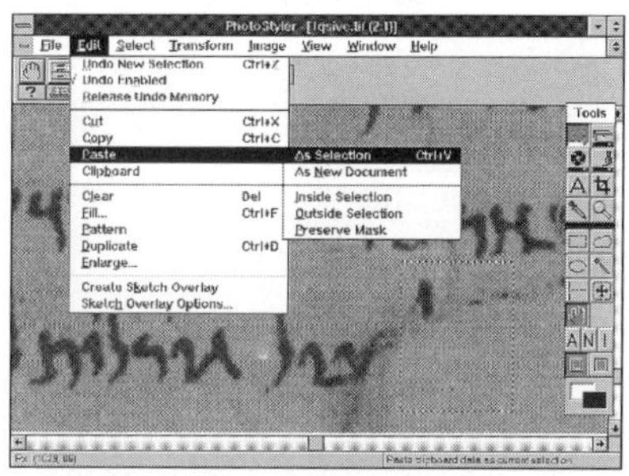

Pasting the word into the text gap.

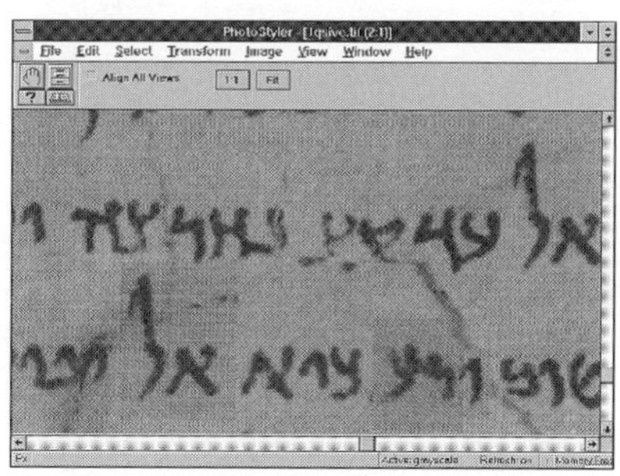

H. Stegemann's reconstruction of 1QS IV_{26} verified. (H. Stegemann, Zu Textbestand und Grundgedanken von 1QS III, 13-IV, 26, RdQ 13, 1988, 95–132, 107 f.)

1QS $IV_{25\,f}$: Courtesy of the Shrine of the Book

Scaling and Rotation

For most of the operations described, it's sometimes necessary to work with images scanned from photos of different scales and inclinations. To deal with these problems, PhotoStyler 2.0 provides users with several different functions for resizing and rotating images, all found in the *„Image"* menu.

- The *„Freely"* command of the *„Resize"* submenu of the *„Image"* menu[52] is helpful in scaling inserted selected areas. After a fragment or character has been inserted into an image of a different scale, click the *„Freely"* command or press *Shift* + *F7*, and the inserted area will be surrounded by a rectangle equipped with handles. If the handles located on the horizontal or vertical lines are pulled with the mouse, the inserted area will be enlarged either horizontally or vertically. The handles located on the corners of the rectangle will enlarge the inserted area in both directions at the same time.

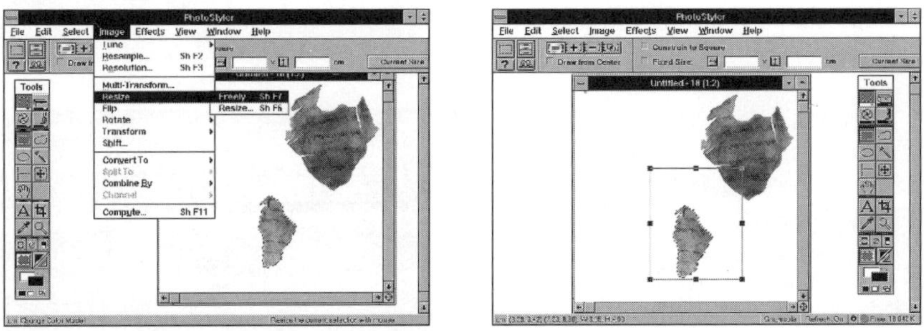

Scaling of a small fragment.

1QH 18 and 22: Courtesy of the Shrine of the Book

  Before resizing, place an object – e. g. a character of the inserted area – above a matching one in the image into which the object is being inserted. If the *„Merge Control"* has been configured to transparent, the size of both characters can be brought to the same scale with the *„Freely"* command.
- Often inserted fragments, mirrorwritings, and characters have an inclination which is different from that of the image into which they are to be inserted. This impairs joining, relocating, or comparing them. To rotate these inserted areas, click the *„Freely"* com-

[52] For the commands *„Resample ..."* and *„Resize ..."* (found in the *„Resize"* submenu of the *„Image"* menu) see PhotoStyler's user guide.

mand in the „*Rotate*" submenu of the „*Image*" menu before fixating the inserted image excerpt. The marque of the inserted excerpt will be equipped with four handles. Place the mouse-pointer on one of these handles, hold the left mouse-button pressed, and move the mouse – the inserted image excerpt will be rotated according to the mouse movements.[53]

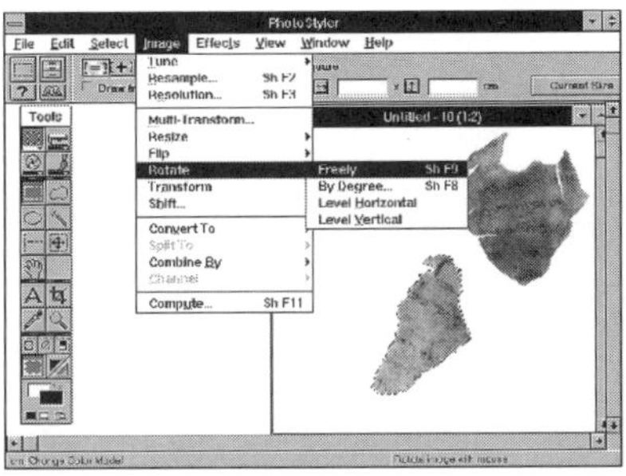

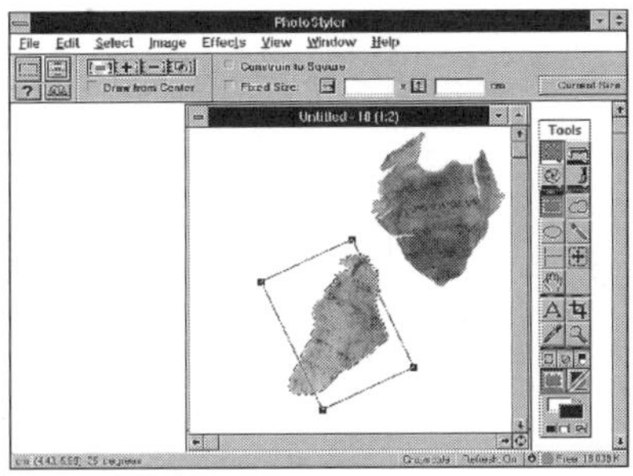

Rotating a fragment.

1QH 18 and 22: Courtesy of the Shrine of the Book

[53] For the commands „*By Degree ...*," „*Level Horizontal*," and „*Level Vertical*" of the „*Rotate*" submenu of the „*Image*" menu, see PhotoStyler's user guide.

3.4 Image Pals Album

This program is to be understood as a small image data base, which can be acquired in addition to PhotoStyler 1.1 and will be part of PhotoStyler 2.0. It enables users to sort images and image excerpts: e. g. the location and kind of a character a lettertemplate has been derived from can be noted in order to get quick access to all lettertemplates of, for instance, the character שׁ of a certain period, text, scribe etc.

If you have acquired some experience with image processing software, there should be no problem in using this program.

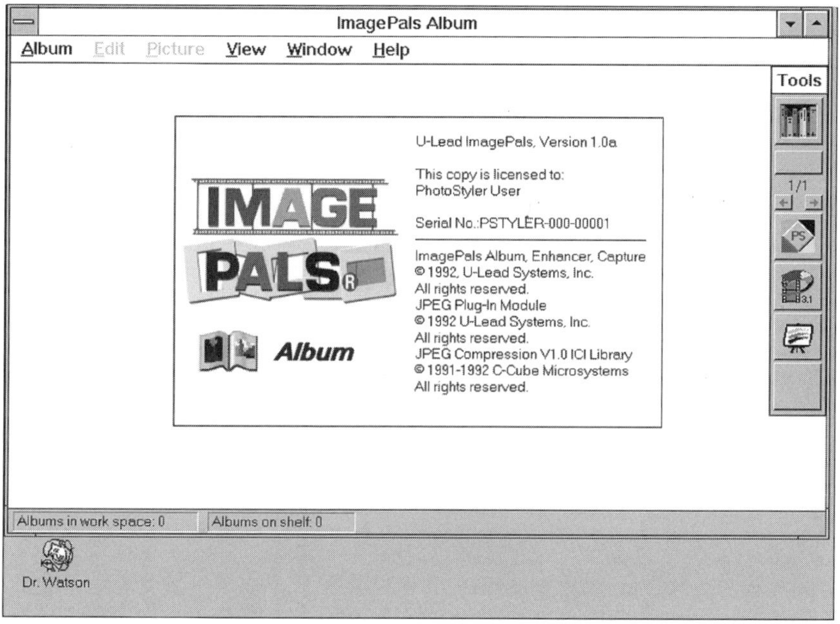

3.5 Picture Publisher 3.1

3.5.1 Introduction and Miscellaneous

Like PhotoStyler, Picture Publisher is a high end image processing package, developed by Micrografx for professional image publication and scanner support. It supports the file formats BMP, GIF, JEPG, PCX, Targa, TIFF, and Kodak's PhotoCD. The program is equipped with drivers for most Scanners and PostScript Printers and also supports the new „*Twain*" scanner standard.

The following commands and tools will only be explained briefly, because they are not specific to CATT, but are needed in some of its operations. For more detailed information see Picture Publisher's user guide.

Commands

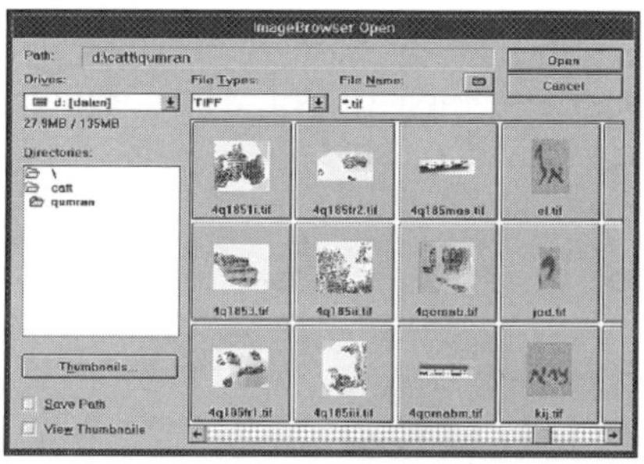

Picture Publishers „*Image Browser Open*" dialogue box with „thumbnails."

Open — To call a file, click the „*Open* ..." command,[54] then „thumbnail" views of all images stored in the current directory will be displayed. To open one of these files, doubleclick its „thumbnail" view.[55]

Recall — As a special feature for calling a file, Picture Publisher offers the „*Recall*" command. Click this command and a list of the last nine files opened with Picture Publisher will be displayed in a submenu. If one of these files is clicked, it will be called to the screen.

New — To create a new file, click the „*New* ..." command and type the measurements and resolution of the file to be

[54] If not mentioned otherwise, all commands explained below are found in the „*File*" menu.

[55] „Thumbnail" views are also used with the „*Save*"' and the „*Save As* ..." commands.

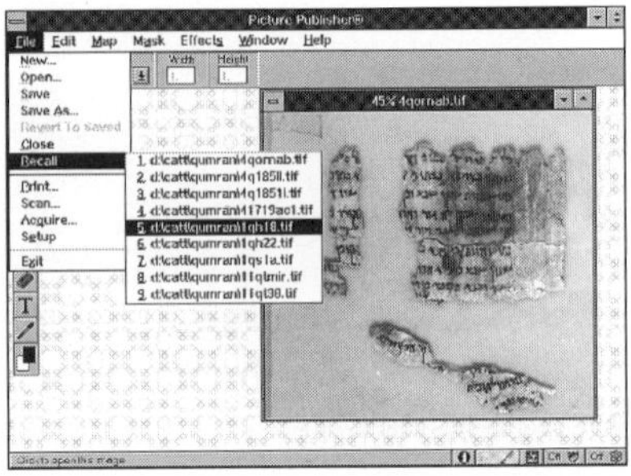

Recalling the file `1qh18.tif` with Picture Publisher.

created in the corresponding fields of the *„New Image"* dialogue box.[56]

! The kind of measurements of the new image (cm, mm, inch, etc.) can be configured in the *„Preferences"* dialogue box, which is called with the *„Preferences ..."* command of the *„Edit"* menu.

! CATT requires a resolution of 300 dpi (= dots per inch).[57] An image of the measurements as shown below will require 1.7 MB of storage space. Make sure that the image file to be created is only as large as necessary.

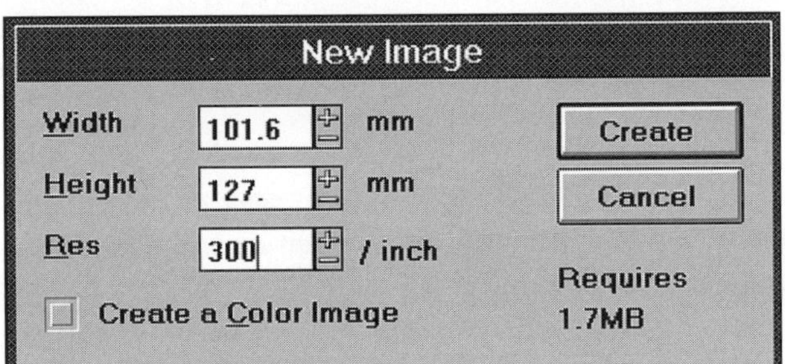

Picture Publishers *„New Image"* dialogue box.

Close

To close a file, click the *„Close"* command or doubleclick the square displayed in the upper left-hand corner of the current image window.

[56] The *„Create a Color Image"* button should be deactivated.

[57] This means that the sides of a square inch have 300 dots, and a full square inch 90 000 dots.

Save — To save reconstructions, click the „*Save*" command. To save a new file, click the „*Save As ...*" command, then you will be guided by dialogue boxes.

! It is advisable to copy the image of the manuscript to be reconstructed to a file with a new name or to save the enhancements to a new file with the help of the „*Save As ...*" command, otherwise the original image will be destroyed.

Restore — To restore an image to the version last saved, click the „*Revert To Save*" command.

Undo — To undo or redo edits,[58] use the first command of the „*Edit*," menu, named „*Undo Edits*" or „*Redo Edits*" respectively. The same effect can be reached by the key combinations *Alt* + *Backspace*, *Ctrl* + *U*, and *Ctrl* + *Z*. Please note that mask operations will not be affected by this command. To undo mask operations, use the „*Revert To Save*" command described above.

Tile — If several images are opened at the same time, they can be displayed next to each other on the screen with the help of the „*Tile Windows*" command of the „*Arrange*" submenu of the „*Window*" menu.

Rulers — The ruler-lines of Picture Publisher are exceptionally well designed. They will be displayed or hidden if the „*Show Rulers*" or „*Hide Rulers*" command of the „*Show/Hide*" submenu of the „*Window*" menu is clicked. The kind of measurements displayed by the ruler-lines is to be configured in the „*Units*" section of the „*Preferences*" dialogue box.[59] The position of the mouse-pointer in the current image is indicated by a small line in the horizontal and the vertical ruler-line.

! The left-hand ruler-line is normally hidden by Picture Publisher's toolbox. To move the toolbox, place the mouse-pointer inside the blank rectangle at the top of the toolbox, hold the left mouse-button pressed, and move the mouse.

58 Edits are understood here as all manipulations of the current image, except mask operations, which won't be affected by the „*Undo*" or „*Redo Edits*" command.

59 The „*Preferences*" dialogue box is to be called by the „*Preferences ...*" command of the „*Edit*" menu.

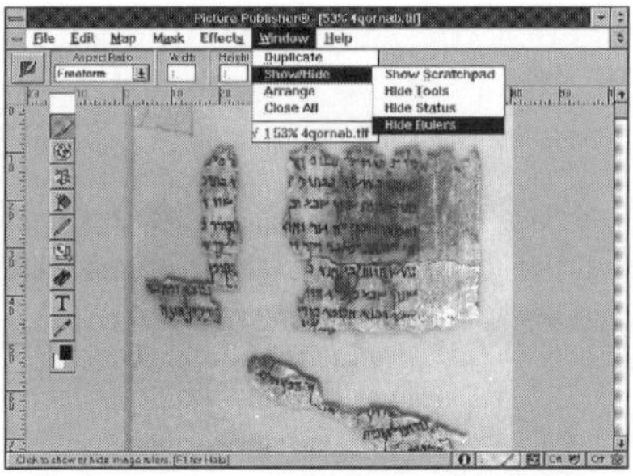

Hiding the ruler lines.
PAM 42265: Courtesy of the IAA

! The measurements indicated by the ruler-lines are not the measurements of the manuscript itself, but of the scanned photo – a photo of a manuscript is normally not scaled 1 : 1 to the manuscript itself.

Exit

To exit Picture Publisher click the „*Exit*“ command of the „*File*“ menu, doubleclick the square displayed in the upper left corner of Picture Publisher's program window, or press *Alt* + *F4*.

Tools and the Programs Layout

Picture Publisher's program window is designed in an extraordinary way. Its toolbox does not display all tools at the same time: tools of same or similar functions are grouped and hidden behind an icon representing the different tools offered, such as all selection tools. All tools similar to each other are displayed in a ribbon similar to a pulldown menu when the corresponding icon is clicked. [60] In addition to the toolbox, Picture Publisher displays some icons on the margin of its program window, e. g. the „*Hand*“ icon is displayed at the lower right-hand corner of the program window.

Several of the tools offered by Picture Publisher can be configured. This can be done in the gray ribbon found below Picture Publisher's menu, the so-called „*Ribbon Area.*“ On the left-hand side of this „*Ribbon Area,*“ a button is found which displays the icon of the currently activated tool. Options and configurations of the tools, once chosen, can be saved by Picture Publisher if this button is clicked (then you will be guided by dialogue boxes). These options and configurations are set with the help of pulldown menus, dialogue boxes, buttons,

[60] In the following, each of the icons symbolizing several tools will be called „*toolbox,*“ e. g. the „*Knife*“ icon, representing the selection tools, will be called „*Selection*“ toolbox.

and bars individually for each tool and displayed in the „Ribbon Area."

The selection tools explained below act in correspondence with the commands of the *„Mask"* menu, therefore these commands will be explained when the selection tools are described. Context sensitive immediate help and information are displayed in the second gray ribbon at the bottom of Picture Publisher's program window.

Picture Publisher provides users with several different selection tools which are all represented by the *„Knife"* icon and are called up by it. If this icon is clicked, the *„Selection"* toolbox will be opened. With the help of these selection tools, the area to be selected can be marked with a blinking marque. Such a marque is called „mask" by Micrografx.

With the *„Rectangular"* and the *„Elliptical Selection"* tool, a rectangular or elliptical area of the current image can be selected. To de-select this area, click the *„Remove Mask"* command of the *„Mask"* menu or press *Ctrl + R*.

With the *„free selection"* tool, masks of any form can be created. In this way, areas of any form can be selected: draw the mask with the mouse around the area of interest holding the left mouse-button pressed while drawing. To de-select the previously selected area, click the *„Remove Mask"* command of the *„Mask"* menu or press *Ctrl + R*.

Like PhotoStyler, Picture Publisher provides users with a *„Magic Wand"* tool, which is named here *„Smart Mask"* tool. It draws a mask automatically by sensing contrasts within the current image and masking along their borders. After the *„Magic Wand"* icon is clicked, the *„Wand Range"* box is seen in the *„Ribbon Area."* In this box, the range of what is to be detected as contrasts must be configured. If a value of 100 % is set, no contrasts will be detected and the entire image will be masked, while, if a value of 15 % is set, anything which differs over 15 % from the gray-level of the indicated pixel is considered by the program as a contrast along which a mask shall be drawn. After the wand range is configured,[61] click the area to be selected, e. g. a character, with the mouse-pointer, now displayed in the form of a magic wand. To

[61] Try several values to get good results.

de-select the area click the „*Remove Mask*" command of the „*Mask*" menu or press *Ctrl* + *R*.

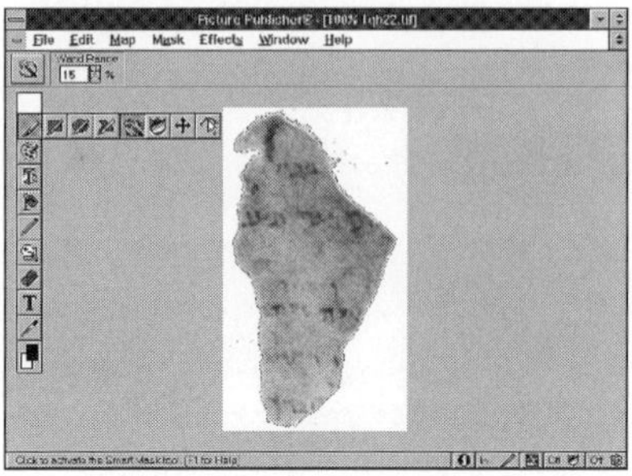

Picture Publisher's „*Selection*" toolbox.
1QH 18: Courtesy of the Shrine of the Book

! For the selection of areas which are themselves well contrasted but surrounded by a background without any contrast, e. g. fragments, it is advisable to click the background near the area of interest with the mouse-pointer, e. g. the white background surrounding most of the fragments of the photos of the Dead Sea Scrolls.

Unlike other image processing programs, Picture Publisher provides users with a „*Mask Transform*" tool instead of a transform menu. Click the „*Transform Tool*" icon and two pulldown menus („*Modify*" and „*Mode*"), two buttons („*Edge*" and „*Quality*"),[62] and a slide bar („*Transparency*")[63] will be displayed in the „*Ribbon Area.*" With the help of these buttons, menus, and slide bars, transparency, size, and inclination of every selected and/or pasted area can be manipulated. How to use these configurations for CATT will be described in the explanation of each operation of CATT.

There are two methods of scrolling the current image.

- Use the scroll bars attached to its side.
- Click the „*Hand*" icon at the lower right-hand corner of Picture Publisher's program window. The mouse-pointer will turn into a hand. Place it inside the image, hold the left mouse-button pressed and move the mouse: the image will follow the mouse movements.

[62] To get good results with CATT, the „*Quality*" button must be activated.

[63] The transparency configurations of Picture Publisher are insufficient for CATT.

To gain information about the current image, click the „*I*" button displayed at the bottom of the program window and the „*Image Information*" dialogue box will be opened.

For the „*Text*" tool see the Picture Publisher user guide.

3.5.2 Magnification

With Picture Publisher, magnification scales are possible which otherwise can be reached only by a microscope. The program provides two separate procedures of magnification. For both procedures click the „*Magnifying Glass*" icon of the toolbox. The mouse-pointer is now displayed in the form of a magnifying glass.

- Move the mouse-pointer to the area of the current image to be magnified and press the left mouse-button several times until a satisfactory magnification is reached.
  To scroll the magnified image on the screen, press the right mouse-button one time. The mouse-pointer will turn into a hand. Hold the left mouse-button pressed and move the mouse – the image will follow your mouse movements. To magnify again, press the right mouse-button a second time – the mouse-pointer will turn back into a magnifying glass.[64]
- As long as the „*Magnifying Glass*" tool is used, the button on the left-hand side of the „*Ribbon Area*" will be equipped with a magnifying glass. When a satisfactory value of magnification is reached, click this button to define the value as the default configuration of the „*Magnifying Glass*" tool for further use.
- The next time the „*Magnifying Glass*" tool is activated, move the mouse-pointer to the area of interest, hold the left mouse-button pressed and draw a rectangle around this area by moving the mouse. The selected area will be zoomed to the value previously configured.
- To reduce the size of the current image (zoom out), set the „*Zoom Out*" option in the „*Function*" pulldown menu of the „*Ribbon Area*" and then proceed as described above.

Picture Publisher provides users with four additional helpful tools for zoom operations, which can be activated in the „*Ribbon Area*" when the „*Magnifying Glass*" icon is clicked:

[64] Otherwise use the horizontal and vertical scroll-bars of the current image window.

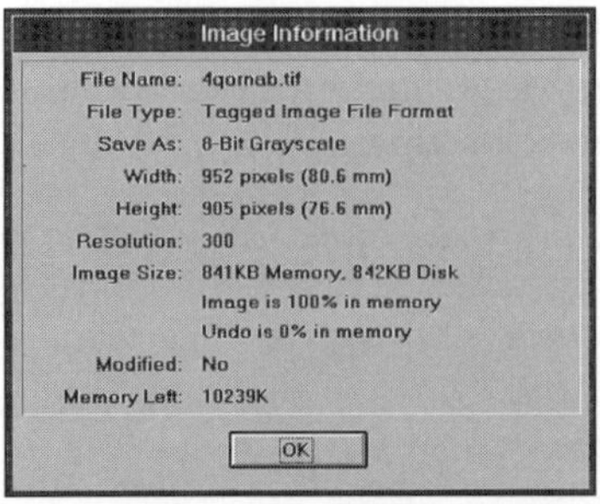

Picture Publisher's „*Image Information*" dialogue box.

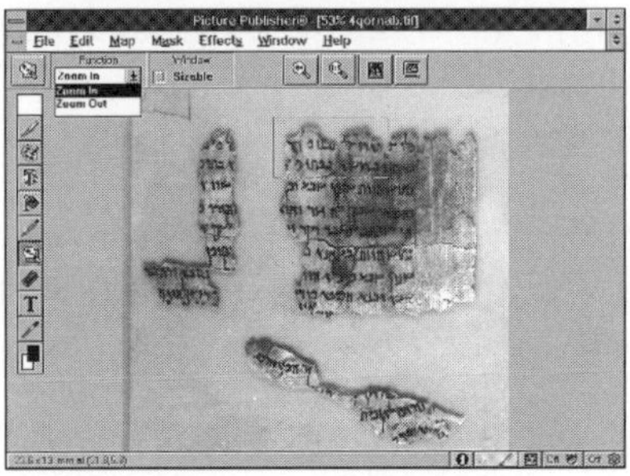

Marking the area to be magnified.

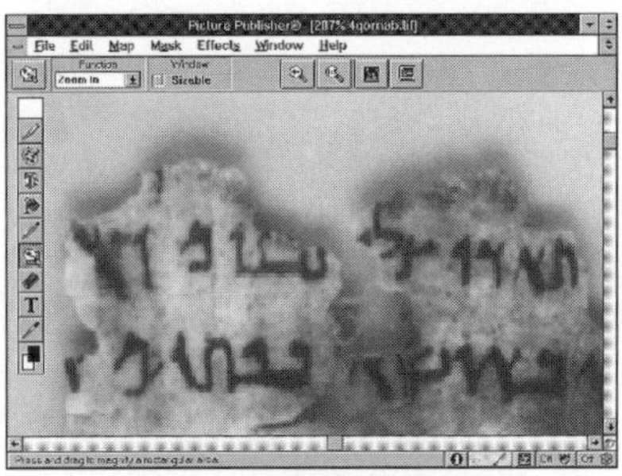

Magnified area.

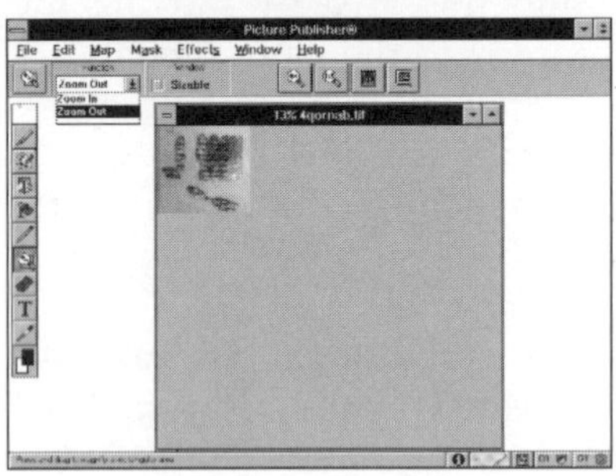

Photograph reduced in size.

4QOrNab PAM 42265: Courtesy of the IAA

When clicked, the *„Previous View“* tool reverts the screen to the previous view displayed – alternatively the *End* key can be pressed at any time in any operation with the same effect, whether the *„Magnifying Glass“* tool is activated or not.

The *„View Actual Size“* tool displays the current image on a scale of 1 : 1.

The *„View Full Image“* tool displays the entire image – alternatively press the *Home* key to get the same result at any time in any operation, whether the *„Magnifying Glass“* tool is activated or not.

The *„View Full Screen“* tool displays the current image as a whole on the full screen without showing Picture Publisher's program window. Press the *Esc* key to return to the program.

3.5.3 Darkened or Faded Texts

Image Analysis by Histograms

As described in the introduction to CATT, histograms are very useful to detect whether or not characters have been preserved in darkened or faded passages of antique manuscripts.

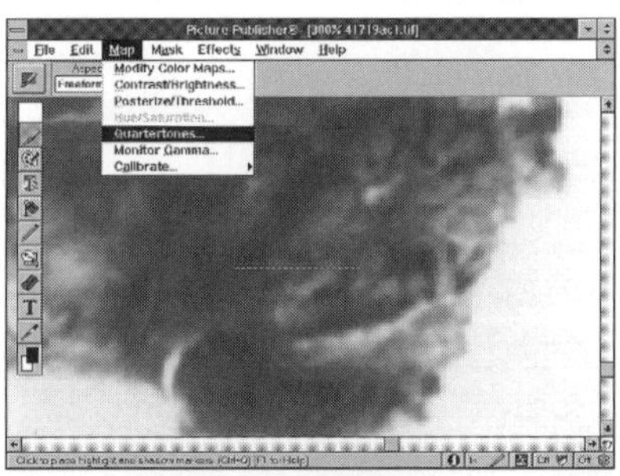

The *„Quartertones“* command of the *„Map“* menu.

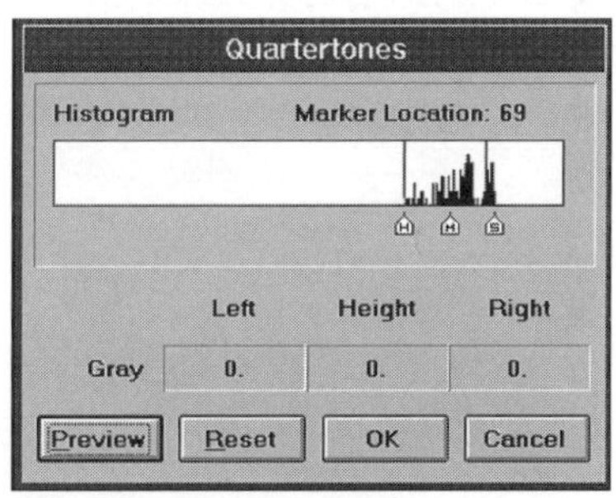

Histogram calculated along the marked line.

Detail of 4Q180 3. PAM 41719: Courtesy of the IAA

- Creating a histogram with Picture Publisher is very simple: mark the area to be analyzed with the rectangular or free-hand selection tool and then click the *„Quartertones“* command in the *„Map“* menu or press *Ctrl* + *Q*. A histogram of the selected area will be processed and then displayed in the *„Quartertones“* dialogue box.

To close this box, click the „*Cancel*" button, and to de-select the selected area, click the „*Remove Mask*" command of the „*Mask*" menu or press *Ctrl + R*.

– In dealing with histograms it is important to remember that a histogram is a graphic representation of the pixel distribution of an image in the form of a curve, ordered according to the respective gray-levels and the amount of pixels. If all pixels are of the same or nearly the same gray-level (the gray-levels from 0 to 255 are represented by the horizontal axis, their amount is represented by the vertical axis), there are no characters preserved. This does not imply that there were never any characters in the analyzed area, but that they have not been preserved. If some pixels of a slightly different value are found, this may indicate that characters are preserved here.

! Good experiences have been made with rectangular selected areas nearly in the shape of a line.

Negative

Creating a negative image with Picture Publisher is also very simple: click the „*Invert*" command of the „*Effects*" menu and the gray-scale of the current image will be inverted to a negative. If a selected area is to be inverted, mark the area of interest before calling the invert function.

The „*Invert*" command of the „*Effects*" menu.

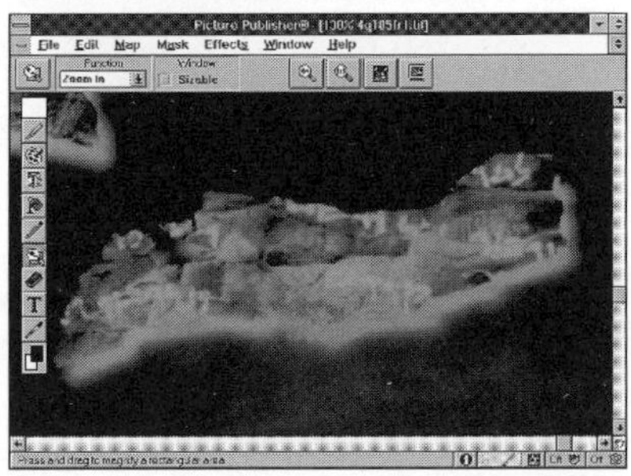

Fragment inverted to a negative.

PAM 43514: Courtesy of the IAA

! An altered image should be stored in a separate file leaving the original image intact.

Regulation of Brightness and Contrast

For the regulation of contrast and brightness, Picture Publisher provides users with an exceptional tool, called *„Contrast/Brightness."*

- To call the *„Contrast/Brightness"* dialogue box, click the *„Contrast/ Brightness …"* command in the *„Map"* menu. In the *„Contrast/ Brightness"* dialogue box, a square provided with two crossed lines is seen. Move the central point of these crossed lines with the mouse-pointer (hold left mouse-button pressed) and the contrast and brightness of the entire image will be regulated. With horizontal movements the brightness of an image will be manipulated, and with vertical movements its contrast.
- To manipulate contrast and brightness of an image separately, use the *„Contrast"* and *„Brightness"* boxes displayed above the square. Click the *„Preview"* button to see the results of your manipulation before making it permanent, and the *„OK"* button to fixate it. If the *„Reset"* button is clicked after the *„Preview"* button, the image will be restored to its original state.
- To regulate contrast and brightness in only a part of the current image, the area of interest must be selected before the *„Contrast/ Brightness"* dialogue box is called.

! The enhancements of contrast and brightness displayed by Picture Publisher on the screen are often better than the real results of the regulation of contrast and brightness seen after the *„Preview"* button is clicked. To save these enhancements, produce a screen shot by pressing the *Print* key of your keyboard – in this way everything that is seen on the screen will be copied to the Windows clipboard (see above p. 28–30).[65]

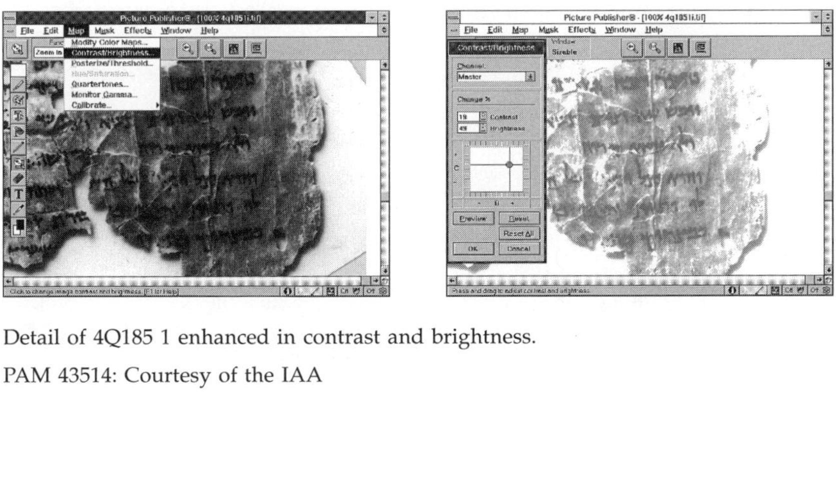

Detail of 4Q185 1 enhanced in contrast and brightness.

PAM 43514: Courtesy of the IAA

! An altered image should be stored in a separate file leaving the original image intact.

Gamma Correction

With Picture Publisher, gamma correction is only available as monitor gamma, which means that the gamma correction will not be saved to a file but only displayed on the screen (see the introduction to this chapter). To call the monitor gamma function, click the „*Monitor Gamma* ...“ command of the „*Map*“ menu or press *Ctrl* + *G*. Drag the slides under the large red, green, and blue color patches to manipulate the image. To get best results, try this operation several times with different monitor gamma values.

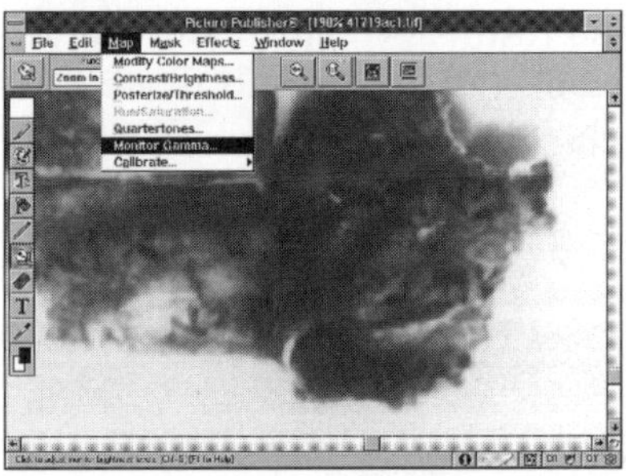

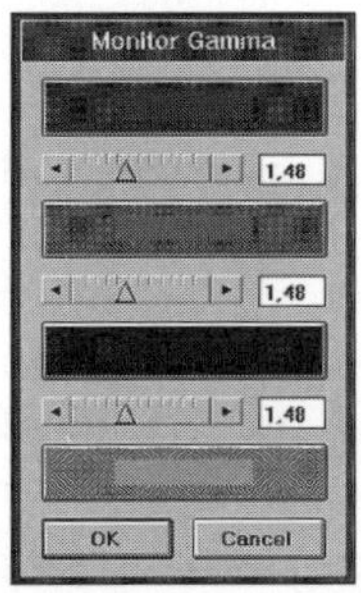

Picture Publisher's „*Monitor Gamma* ...“ command and dialogue box.

Detail of 4Q180 3. PAM 41719: Courtesy of the IAA

! The new monitor gamma configuration will be saved by Picture Publisher in a configuration file. As long as it is not reconfigured, the configuration will be executed with every image called to the screen. Make sure that the monitor gamma value is set back to 1.48 (see the introduction to this chapter).

[65] It is impossible to copy only the content of the current image window, enhanced in contrast and brightness, to the Windows clipboard, because the „*Contrast/Brightness*“ dialogue box functions as an own window. If the *Alt* and the *Print* key are pressed simultaneously only the „*Contrast/Brightness*“ dialogue box will be copied to the Windows clipboard.

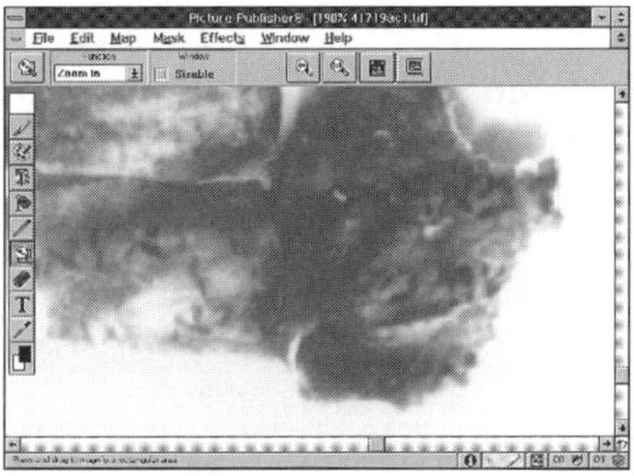

The same detail enhanced with gamma correction (כללה).
PAM 41719: Courtesy of the IAA

! Because Picture Publisher only provides users with monitor gamma, the enhancements reached by the gamma correction cannot be saved to a file. To save them nevertheless, produce a screen shot by pressing the *Print* key of your keyboard – in this way everything that is seen on the screen will be copied to the Windows clipboard (see aboce p. 28–30).[66]

Gray/Color Map

With the help of the *„Modify Color Map"* function, the output density of the primary colors – individually and combined – can be controlled over the full range from highlight to shadow.

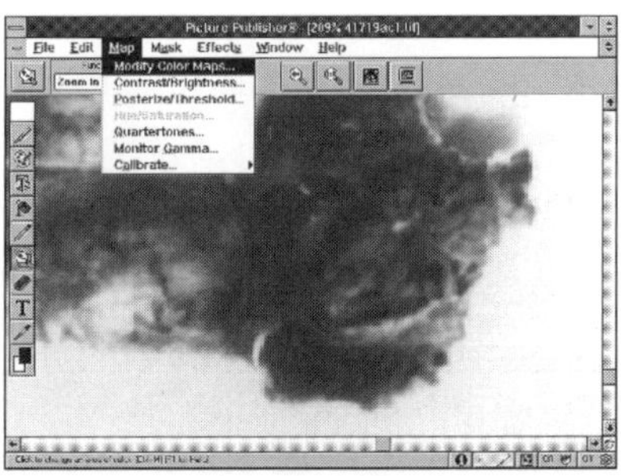

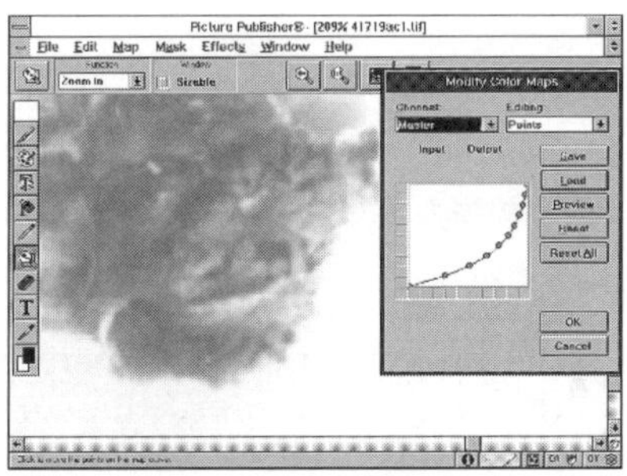

Detail of 4Q180 3 enhanced with the *„Gray/Color Map"* (כללה).

PAM 41719: Courtesy of the IAA

[66] It is impossible to copy only the content of the current image window, enhanced with *„Monitior Gamma"* to the Windows clipboard, because the *„Monitor Gamma"* dialogue box functions as an own window. If the *Alt* and the *Print* key are pressed simultaneously only the *„Monitor Gamma"* dialogue box will be copied to the Windows clipboard.

- To enhance an image with Picture Publisher's color map function, click the *„Modify Color Maps ...“* command of the *„Map“* menu or press *Ctrl* + *M*. The *„Modify Color Maps“* dialogue box will be displayed on the screen. A curve equipped with a number of handles is found in the dialogue box. Any alteration of this curve, by moving the handles with the mouse, will produce a similar alteration of the gray-level of the pixels represented by this part of the curve.
  The horizontal axis of the curve represents the input value while the vertical axis represents the output value, i. e. if the handle of the upper right-hand end of the curve is moved down, all pixels of a certain range of dark gray-levels will be processed to lighter gray-levels.
- With the help of the *„Save“* and the *„Load“* button, any curve previously created can be saved and later recalled. The *„Reset“* button will reset your image to its original gray-scale, which is represented by a ramp with its lowest point at the left-hand side and its highest point at the right-hand side.

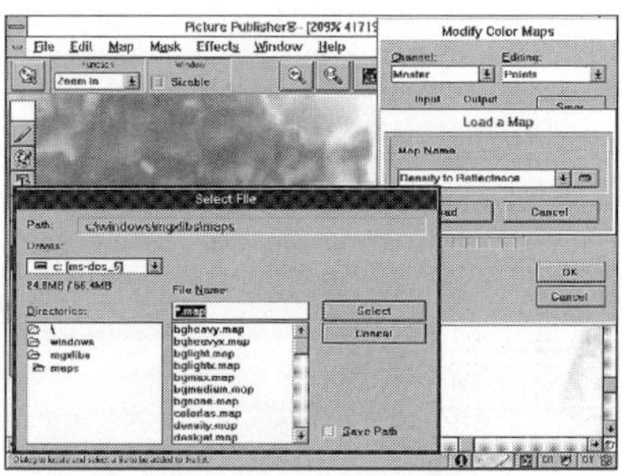

Picture Publisher's *„Select File“* dialogue box.

- In addition to Picture Publisher's capability to create such curves, the program provides many predefined curves, called by clicking the *„Load“* button of the current dialogue box. Another dialogue box, called *„Load a Map“* is then displayed. Click the arrow-button and a pulldown menu will be opened which displays some of these curves. Click the curve of your choice and then the *„Load“* button.[67]
  A large number of additional predefined curves can be called if the *„File“* button displayed next to the *„Arrow“* button is clicked. Click the *„Add“* command of the pop up menu – then you will be

[67] One of the best curves for CATT is named *„Density to Reflectance“*; a negative can be created with the help of the *„Inverted Ramp“* curve.

guided. For the enhancement of darkened or faded manuscripts, it is advisable to test many different curves.

- Selected areas can also be treated with Picture Publisher's „*Modify Color Maps*" function if marked before the „*Modify Color Maps*" dialogue box is called.

! An altered image should be stored in a separate file leaving the original image intact.

Equalization

- To reconstruct darkened or faded parts of a manuscript with the help of Picture Publisher's equalization function, click the „*Quartertones ...*" command of the „*Map*" menu – alternatively press *Ctrl + Q*. The „*Quartertones*" dialogue box is then displayed on the screen.
- At the bottom-line of the histogram displayed in the dialogue box, three markers are shown (H, M, S). If the H-marker is moved with the help of the mouse in the direction of the S-marker, all *h*ighlighted (i. e. bright) pixels of the current image will be made darker. If the S-marker is moved in the direction of the H-marker all dark (*s*hadowed) pixels are made lighter. With the help of the M-marker the neither bright nor dark pixels (*m*idtone) can be manipulated in the same way.
  To enhance darkened or faded areas of a manuscript, often several different configurations of Picture Publisher's equalization function must be tested.

! As with the regulation of brightness and contrast and the „*Modify Color Maps,*" the results of Picture Publisher's „*Equalization*" function displayed on the screen are not identical with the results fixated and saved later to a file. It is advisable to save the much better results displayed before the fixating with the help of a screen shot. Such a screen shot can be reached by pressing the *Print* key – in this way the current view displayed on the screen will be copied by Windows to its clipboard.

! Especially if large faded or darkened parts of a manuscript are to be reconstructed, it is advisable to mark small parts of these darkened or faded areas and work on them individually, to reach best results.

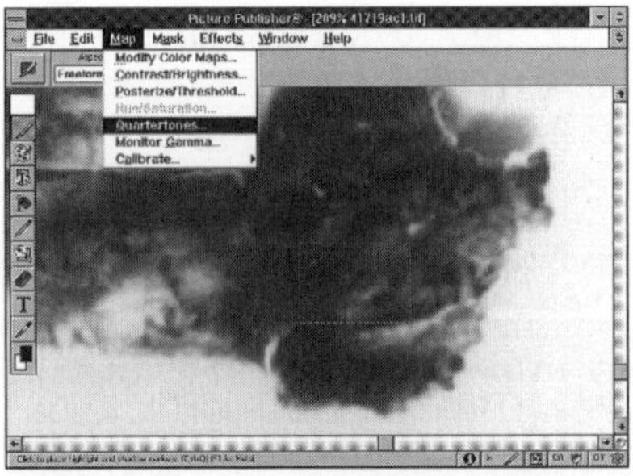

The *„Quatertones ...“* command of the *„Map“* menu.

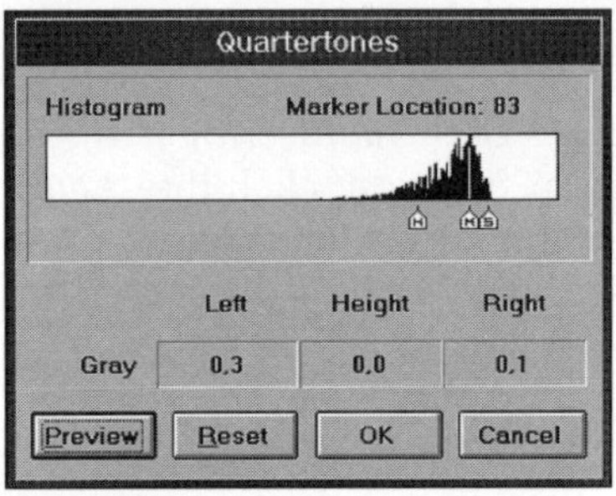

Histogram of the selected area.

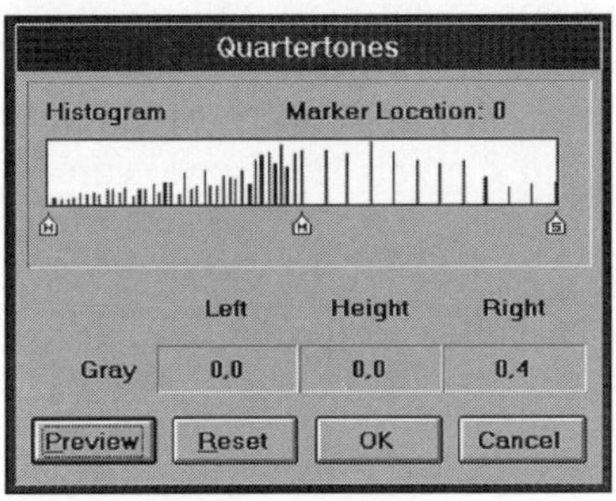

Histogram of the enhanced area.

Area enhanced with equalization.

Detail of 4Q180 3. PAM 41719: Courtesy of the IAA

! An altered image should be stored in a separate file leaving the original image intact.

3.5.4 Comparison and Joining of Fragments

1. To join or compare fragments, it is advisable to first store them separately. Call both files to the screen and display them next to each other with the help of the *„Tile Windows"* command of the *„Arrange"* submenu of the *„Window"* menu. Then click the *„Magic Wand"* icon of the select toolbox and configure the wand range in the *„Ribbon Area"* (try different ranges to select the fragment properly). Click the bright background near the fragment to be selected with the mouse-pointer now displayed in the shape of a magic wand. Copy the resulting masked fragment with the *„Copy"* command of the *„Edit"* menu to the Windows clipboard (alternatively press *Ctrl* + *Ins*).

2. Now activate the window in which the fragment to be compared or joined is displayed with a mouse click, and insert the selected fragment by clicking the *„Paste"* command of the *„Edit"* menu.[68] When inserted, the selected fragment will be surrounded by a rectangular mask equipped with handles. To move the fragment, place the mouse-pointer inside the rectangular mask, hold the left mouse-button pressed and move the fragment with the help of the mouse.

3. To resize an inserted fragment of different scale, click the *„Size/ Scale"* command in the *„Mode"* menu of the *„Ribbon Area,"* and pull the handles on the corners of the rectangle diagonally (hold the left mouse-button pressed and move the mouse).

   To rotate the fragment, click the *„Rotate/Skew"* command in the *„Mode"* pulldown menu of the *„Ribbon Area."* Place the mouse-pointer on one of the corner handles of the rectangular mask and hold the left mouse-button pressed while moving the mouse.[69]

4. To compare the border structers of two or more fragments, choose the *„Mask Only"* option of the *„Modify"* pulldown menu, displayed in the *„Ribbon Area"* when the *„Mask Transform"* tool is activated.

[68] Alternatively use the *„Copy To"* and *„Paste From"* commands of the same menu if the selected fragment should be stored for further use. How to use both commands is explained below pp. 139–139.

[69] If some of these operations will be executed again later, click the *„Mask Transform Tool"* icon and proceed as described above.

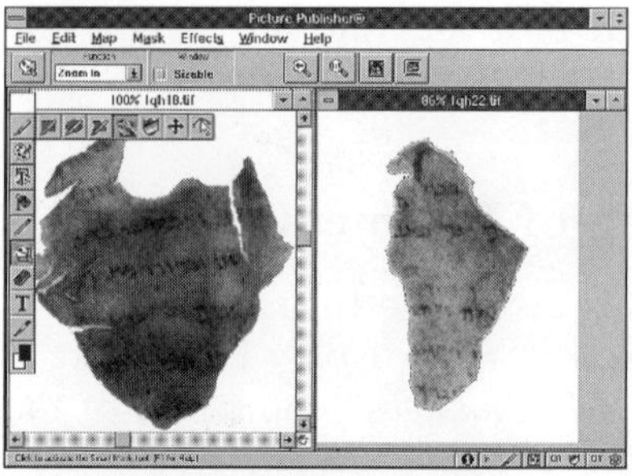

Two fragments to be compared and joined.

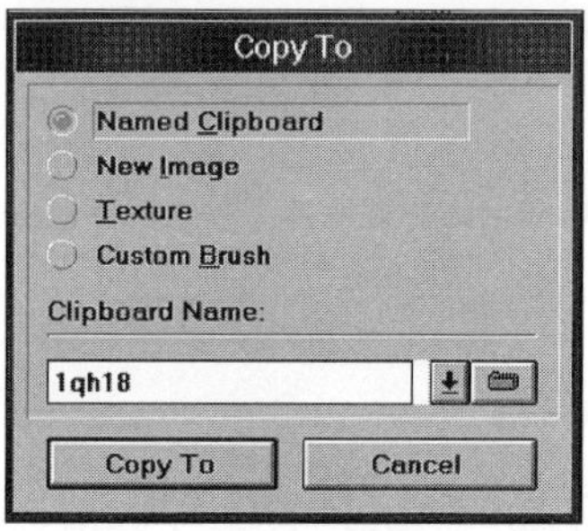

Picture Publisher's „*Copy To*" dialogue box.

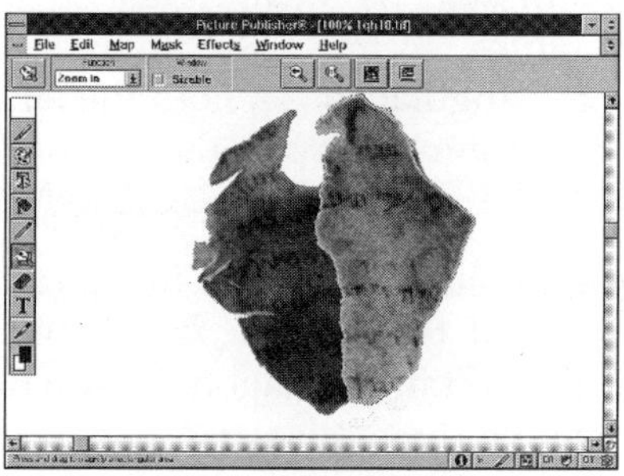

The two fragments compared.

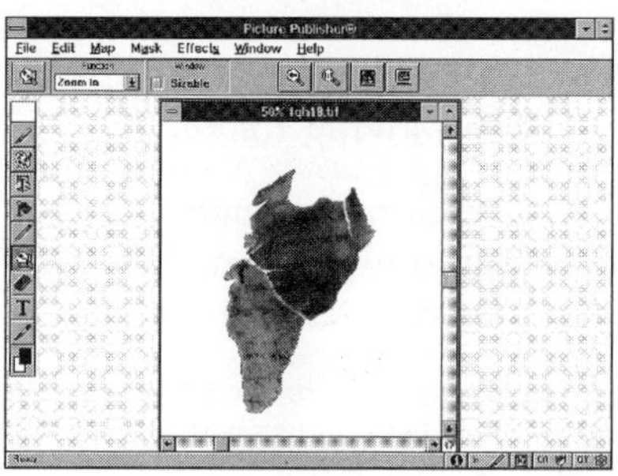

The two fragments joined.

1QH 18 and 22: Courtesy of the Shrine of the Book

To join the inserted fragment to the side of a fragment, click the *„Remove Mask"* command of the *„Mask"* menu or press *Ctrl + R*.

5. If only the comparison of border structers of selected fragments is of interest, select the fragments with the *„Magic Wand"* tool and save the resulting mask with the *„Save Mask"* command of the *„Mask"* menu. Afterwards activate the image in which the fragment to be compared is found and call the previously saved mask of the fragment of interest with the *„Load Mask"* command of the *„Mask"* menu, and proceed as described above.

! Picture Publisher's transparency configuration is insufficient for CATT – the lines of underlying fragments can't be made visible while moving inserted image excerpts above them to compare border structures.

! It is advisable to note the exact locations and identifications of the fragments from which the masks have been derived, as well as the scale of the images in which the selected fragments have been inserted.

3.5.5 Mirrorwriting

Because the transparency configuration provided by Picture Publisher for gray-scale images is insufficient for CATT, mirrorwritings cannot be relocated.

3.5.6 Character Fragments

1. To select the character the lettertemplate is to be derived from, magnify it to screen size. Then click the *„Magic Wand"* tool and set the wand range in the *„Ribbon Area"* to fifteen percent.[70] Click the character to be templated with the mouse-pointer, now displayed in the shape of a magic wand. A mask in the form of the borderline of the clicked character will be processed. Save the mask with the *„Save Mask"* command of the *„Mask"* menu (after the command is clicked, you will be guided).[71]

---

[70] Normally a wand range of fifteen percent works well for this operation, but with some manuscripts other ranges may be necessary. In this case try several different values.

[71] If the character fragments to be identified are in the current image, remove the mask (Ctrl + R), otherwise call the image containing the character fragments.

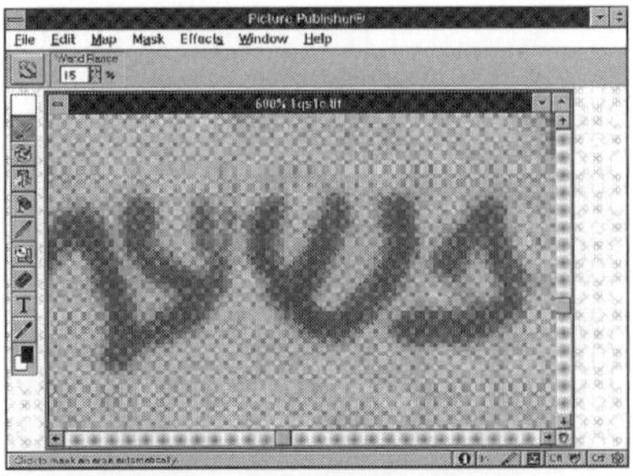

Character selected.

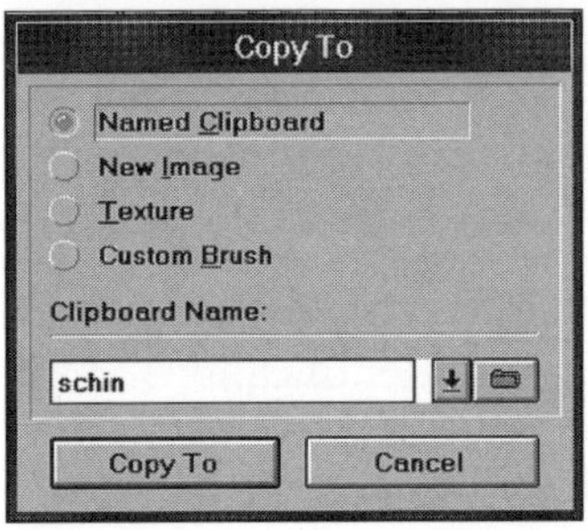

Picture Publisher's „*Copy To*" dialogue box.

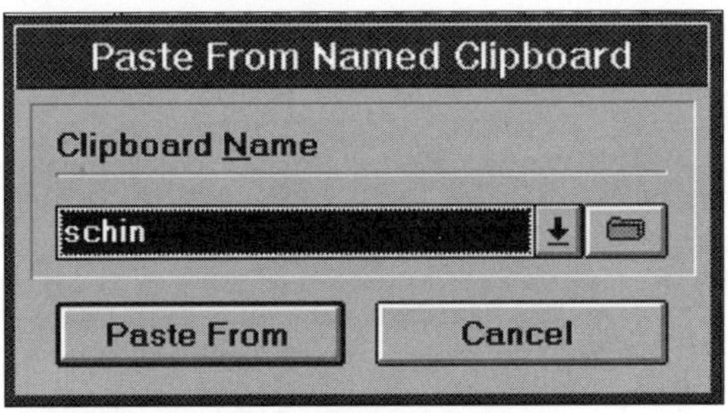

Picture Publisher's „*Paste From Named Clipboard*" dialogue box.

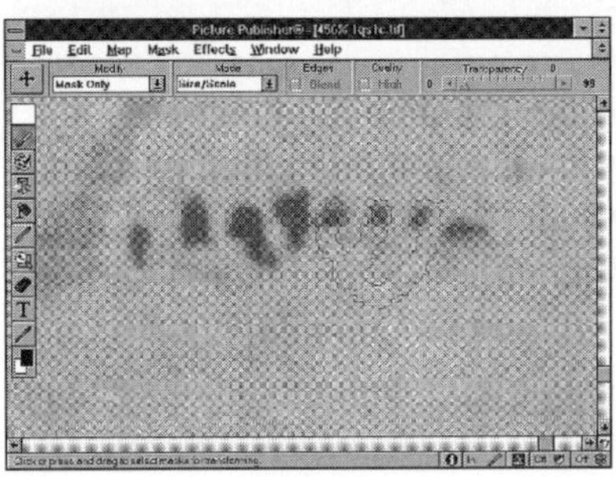

Character fragments identified with the lettertemplate as the Hebrew letter שׁ.

1QS $I_{25\,f}$: Courtesy of the Shrine of the Book

2. Call the file containing the character fragment to be reconstructed and magnify this character fragment to screen size. Then call the mask to be used as a lettertemplate with the *„Load Mask"* command of the *„Mask"* menu and activate the *„Mask Transform"* tool.[72] Place the mouse-pointer inside the rectangle surrounding the lettertemplate and move it above the character fragment to be identified (hold the left mouse-button pressed and move the mouse).

! Make sure that the *„Mask Only"* option is set in the *„Modify"* menu of the *„Ribbon Area"* (this menu is displayed as long as the *„Mask Transform"* tool is active).

! Note the exact location of the image from which the lettertemplate has been derived as well as its scale etc.

3.5.7 The Comparison of Characters

For the comparison of characters, proceed as described in the preceding section.

3.5.8 The Reconstruction of Text Gaps

With Picture Publisher, the reconstruction of text gaps is very simple:

1. In a first operation characters and words necessary for the reconstruction of a text gap should be selected and saved. With single characters, the *„Magic Wand"* tool should be used as described in the introduction to Picture Publisher, and for whole words, the *„Rectangular Selection"* tool.

2. After a word or character is masked, click the *„Copy To ..."* command of the *„Edit"* menu, and the *„Copy To"* dialogue box will be displayed. Choose the *„Named Clipboard"* option and type the name of the file the selected word or character should be copied to in the *„Clipboard Name"* box. Afterwards, click the *„Copy To"* button or press *Enter*. The selected character or word will be stored

[72] If you work with images of different scale, move the lettertemplate to a well preserved matching character in the current image and enlarge it as described for the comparison and joining of fragments while comparing it with the underlying character.

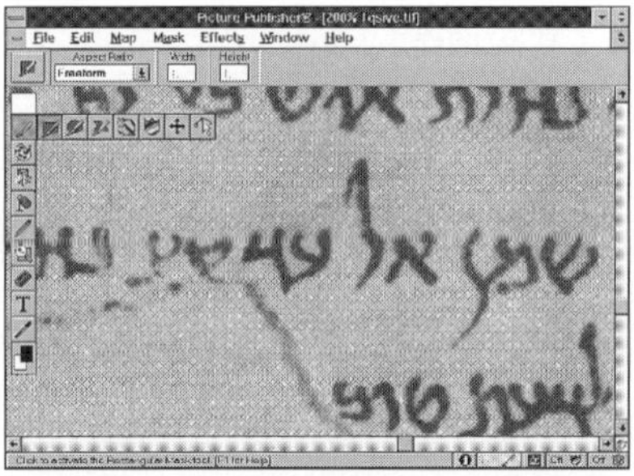

The word אל selected.

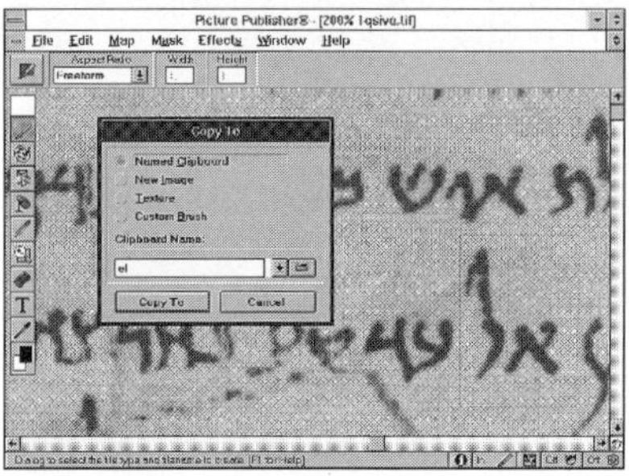

The selected word copied to a named clipboard file.

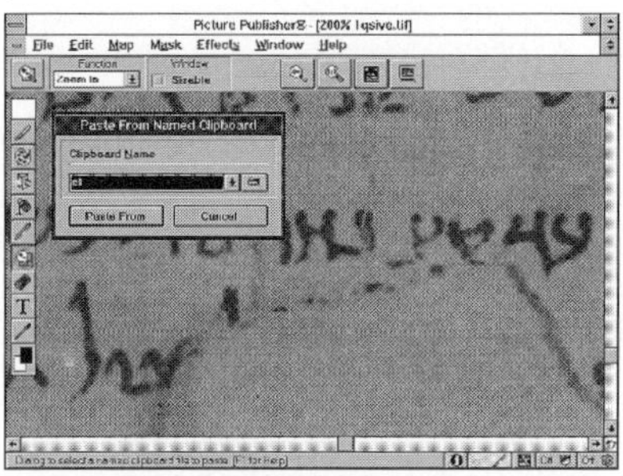

The named clipboard file selected.

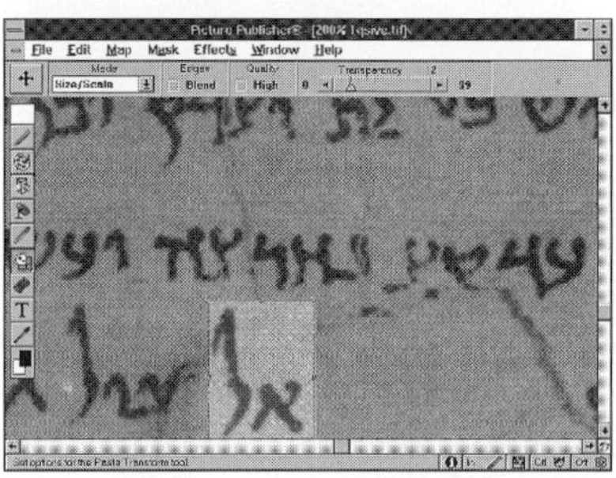

The word אל copied from the named clipboard file to the text gap.

1QS IV$_{25\,f}$: Courtesy of the Shrine of the Book

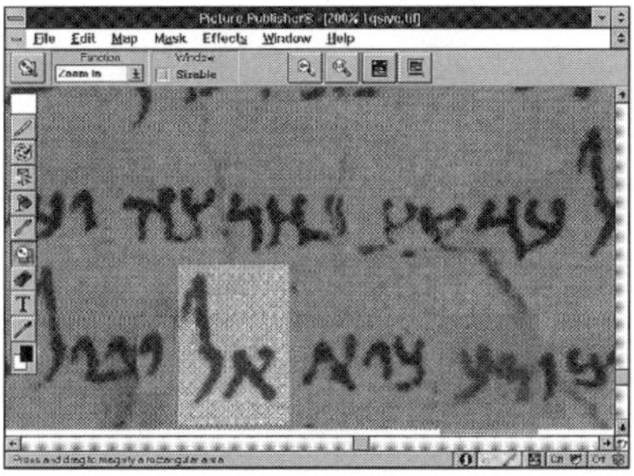

H. Stegemann's reconstruction of 1QS IV_{26} verified. (H. Stegemann, Zu Textbestand und Grundgedanken von 1QS III, 13-IV, 26, RdQ 13, 1988, 95–132, 107 f.)

in Picture Publisher's „Clipbits" directory as a TIFF-file with a corresponding mask-file (MSK).[73]

3. Call the file containing the text gap to be reconstructed. To insert the selected characters or words previously stored, click the *„Paste From ..."* command of the *„Edit"* menu. The *„Paste From Named Clipboard"* dialogue box will be displayed. Look in the *„Clipboard Name"* pulldown menu for the character or word to be inserted and click it. Then click the *„Paste To"* button or press *Enter* and move the inserted character or word to the text gap to be reconstructed. To fixate the inserted character or word, click the *„Remove Mask"* command of the *„Mask"* menu or press *Ctrl + R*.

4. To undo all reconstructions, click the *„Undo Edits"* command of the *„Edit"* menu or press *Alt + Backspace*, *Ctrl + U*, or *Ctrl + Z*. If you are working with images of different scale, resize the inserted characters or words as described in the following section.

! Make notes of the exact location from where the selected characters and words have been derived as well as of the scale of these images etc.

Scaling and Rotation

To scale or rotate inserted image excerpts, the *„Mask Transform"* tool is to be used:

– To scale an inserted fragment or character, click the *„Size/Scale"* command in the *„Mode"* pulldown menu of the *„Ribbon Area."* Click the inserted image excerpt: it will be surrounded by a rectangle equipped with handles. Place the mouse-pointer on one of

73 For the deletion and renaming of these files, see Picture Publisher's user guide, 2-40.

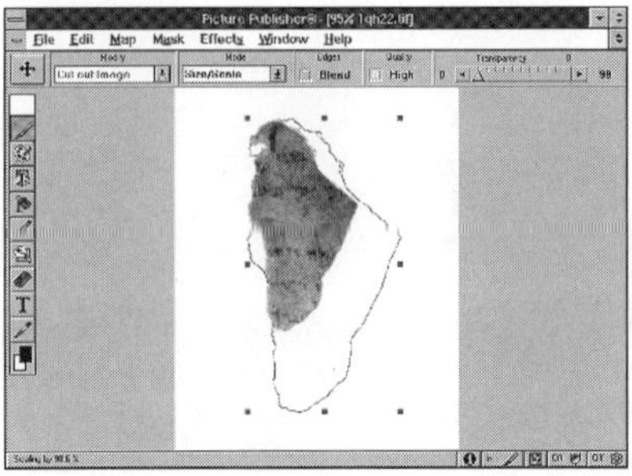

Fragment scaled.
1QH 22: Courtesy of the Shrine of the Book

the handles attached to the corners of the rectangle and pull diagonally (hold the left mouse-button pressed while moving the mouse): the fragment will be resized vertically and horizontally at the same time.

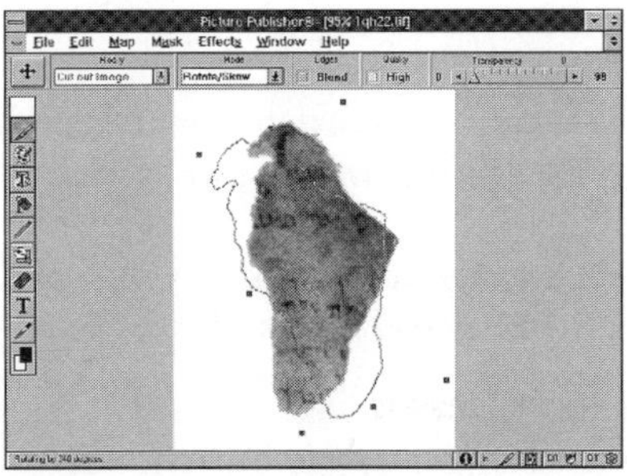

Fragment rotated.
1QH 22: Courtesy of the Shrine of the Book

– To rotate the fragment, click the „*Rotate/Skew*“ option given in the „*Mode*“ pulldown menu of the „*Ribbon Area.*“ Place the mouse-pointer on one of the corner handles of the rectangular mask and hold the left mouse-button pressed while moving the mouse.[74]

[74] If some of these operations will be executed again later, click the „*Mask Transform Tool*“ icon and proceed as described above.

Chapter 4

Miscellaneous

4.1 File Compression

As already explained above, graphic files need an enourmos amount of storage space. Often there is not enough space for them either on the hard disk(s) or a floppy disk. To store them nevertheless, these files can be compressed, i. e. temporarily reduced in size. Four different procedures exist for file compression.

1. Programs especially designed for file compression can be used, such as PKZIP or LHARC. Normally these programs are available as shareware for reasonable prices. But when using files packed with these programs, the files must always be decompressed before working on them with an image processor.
   If compressed files are copied onto a floppy disk and sent to another person, the program for decompression must always be sent along with them, in order that the addressee is able to decompress them.
2. Specialized hardware units can be used for compression. Normally these are expensive additional boards available for the PC. This means that the compressed file can only be read by your own computer or one with the same compression board – in all other cases you must store and send the files uncompressed on a floppy disk.
3. Some image file formats have an inherent, effective file compression scheme (such as GIF) or an additional option for compression exists for them (such as the LZW compression for TIFF).
   With all these types of compression no data will be lost. The compression is done by algorithms which have been developed especially for file compression.
4. The JPEG (Joint Photographic Experts Group) or JPG file format represents another method of file compression especially developed for image files. It offers compression up to a ratio of 100 : 1.

Unlike LZW compression offered by TIFF images, JPEG compression is a „lossey“ compression scheme. This means that some of the original data is discarded: when decompressed, this lost information has to regenerated.

! Use this format only when you want to store a finished reconstruction. Do not use it for work in progress. Each time you save a file in the JPEG format a part of the original image information is lost, i. e. a part of the manuscript to be reconstructed. This means the image of the manuscript you are working with will deteriorate slightly.
The image file shown on p. 145 measures 10.8 × 7.46 cm. and has a resolution of 220 dpi. In the TIFF file format it needs 650,174 Byte, in the EPS file format it needs 1,227,953 Byte, and in the JPEG file format 3,376 Byte of storage space.

4.2 File Conversion

Sometimes publishing houses or research institutions may ask for results of your work stored in a file format not supported by your image processor, or you may get scans in such a format. In both cases file converting programs can be of help. This software is specialized in the conversion of files among different graphic file formats.

Two programs may be named here: HiJaak is a professional file converter which provides users with many additional functions. The Graphic Workshop is available as shareware for a very reasonable price, but is not equipped as well with additional functions.

- Sometimes image files can be altered when converted from one file format to another. Especially the conversion to the EPS file format causes many problems: often the size of the converted image is altered.
- If a large number of files are to be converted to the same file format, this can be done in a single operation with a file format converter, while doing it with your image processor file by file would require a good deal of time.

4.3 Further Editing

For the publication of the results of your work, it may be necessary to equip the reconstructed images of a manuscript with markers, lines,

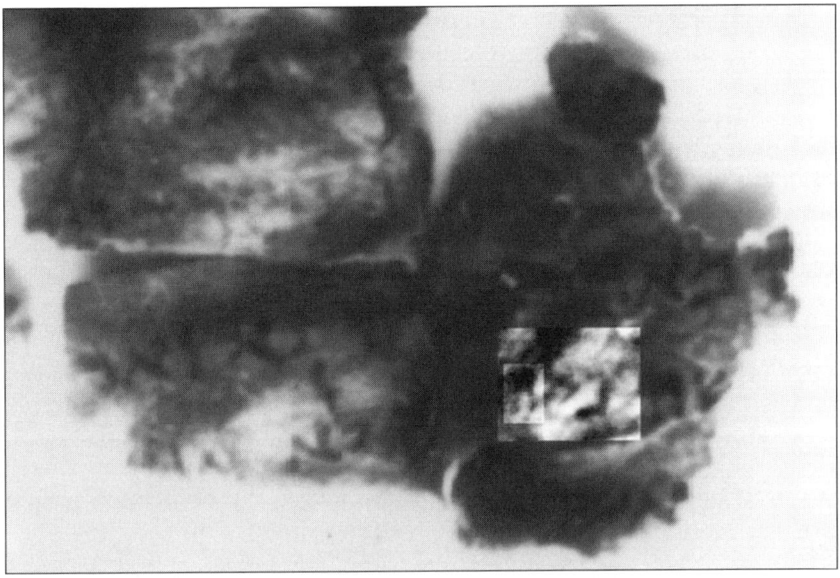

Detail of 4Q180 3 stored in the TIFF file format and reconstructed afterwards.

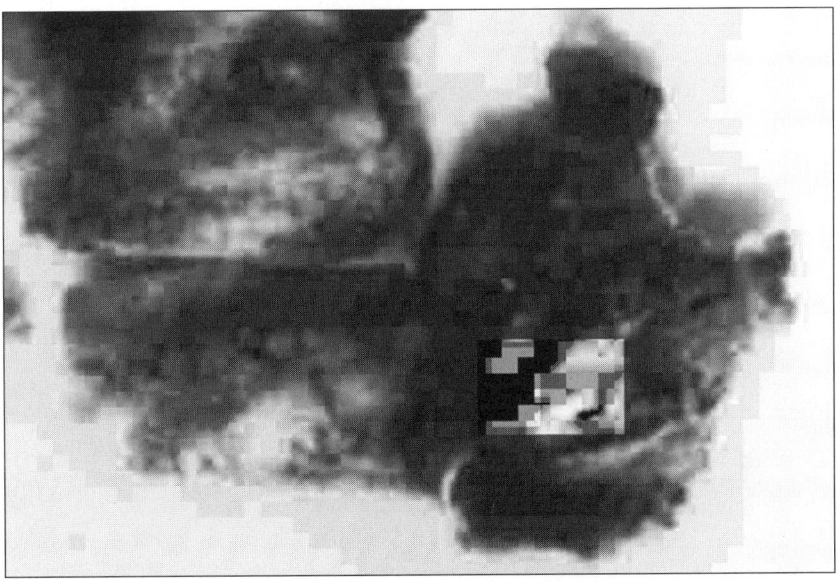

The same detail stored with the highest possible compression rate several times in the JPEG file format and afterwards „reconstructed."

PAM 41719: Courtesy of the IAA

numbers, and/or characters in order to mark a reconstruction, count the lines of a manuscript, etc. For this purpose, the drawing and writing functions of the image editing program you are working with can be used. But this will result in low quality for publication: Letters and lines produced with the writing and/or drawing functions of an image editing program normally have broken edges, because these functions work pixel-oriented. They do not „overwrite"the image with lines and characters, but change the graylevel of the pixels which are covered by lines and/or characters to black. This means that a character which is inserted in an image file with the resolution of 150 dpi will only be printed with this resolution, which is of course far too low for printing.[1]

It is therefore advisable to use specialized vector-oriented graphic programs for this purpose, such as CorelDraw! or Aldus FreeHand. They will „overwrite"the image with characters and lines: in this way characters and lines inserted in an image can be printed with a high resolution, while the image itself is printed with 150 dpi.

4.4 Presenting the Results

If a lecture is to be held on the results of your work on damaged manuscripts with the CATT method, it would naturally be of great advantage to present them to the audience. This can be done in different ways.

1. Outprints can be produced with a 600 dpi PostScript laser printer, such as the HP IV^{M}.
2. Slides can be exposed with a machine designed for reproducing digitalized images on slide film.
3. Overhead folios can be printed or exposed.
4. A „slide show"can be produced by a presentation program and displayed with the computer.

Every method has its advantages and disadvantages:

1. With the 600 dpi laser printer, images can be produced which are of a quality only slightly better than that of photos normally

[1] Images are printed with low resolutions because in printing gray levels are produced with black points of different size. Many large points at one part of an image will produce a black area, while smaller points will leave small areas between the points blank and in this way produce a gray area. Points of different size are reached in printing by building up one image-point out of several points produced by the Linotype. For this reason the printed resolution of an image can at the moment not be above 220 dpi.

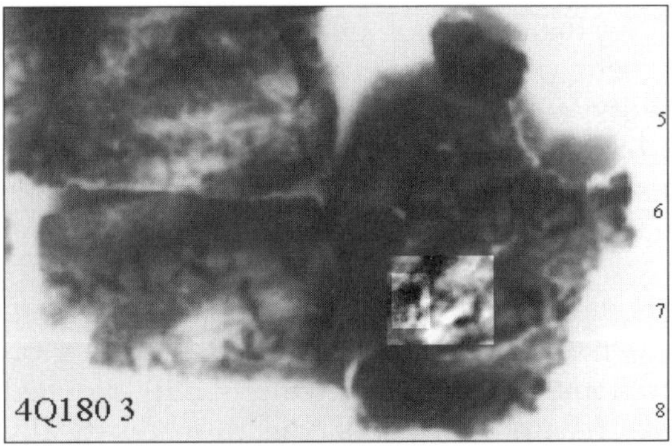

Detail of 4Q180 3. Numbers inserted by PhotoStyler 1.1.

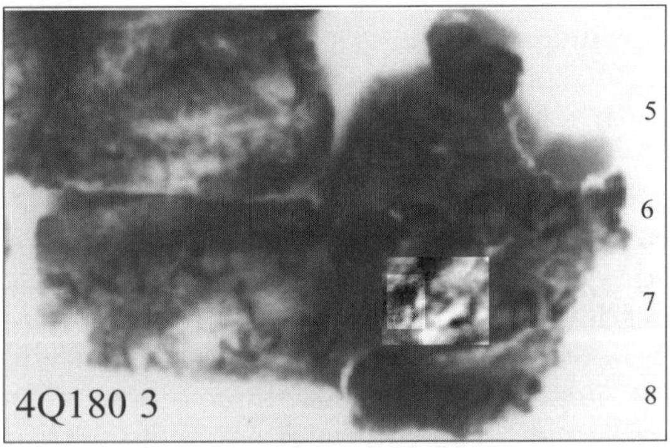

Detail of 4Q180 3. Numbers inserted by FreeHand 3.1.

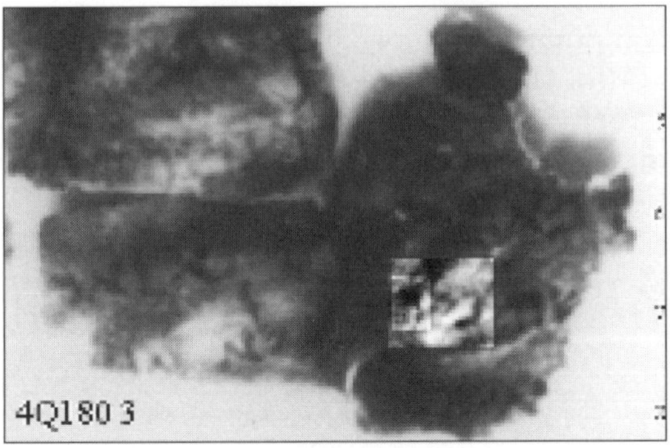

The first plate on this page reduced to a resolution of 70 dpi.

PAM 41719: Courtesy of the IAA

found in a newspaper. But the resolution of printed images which can be reached with these machines is not good enough for printing images of high quality. 600 dpi equals an image raster of ca. 70 lines per inch (lpi) or 28 lines per centimeter. If an image is to be printed with a resolution of 155 lpi and 256 graylevels, this must be done on a Linotype machine with a minimum resolution of 2540 dpi.

2. Producing slides with a slide developing machine is very expensive. Prices differ between $20 and $80 per slide depending on the price level of your home country – but the quality reached is of course very good (the price per slide can drop drastically if more than one slide is developed in a single order). The only technical device you will need during the lecture is a normal slide projector.
3. Overhead folios can be printed with a laser printer, but then again the quality of the outprint will be very low. If the folios are produced with an exposing machine, the quality of the folio will be good but expensive.
4. Slide shows can be produced and displayed with the computer. For this purpose specialized presentation programs such as Aldus Persuasion can be used. With them you will be able to produce excellent and convincing demonstrations, which can be developed as slides or displayed by a computer. The exposition on slides will again be very expensive. For a presentation with a computer, an appropriate machine is needed, i. e. a computer equipped with at least a 486 DX 50 processor, 8 MB RAM, a SVGA local bus board, and a large screen (20 inch in diameter minimum).

! If you decide to use a computer for the presentation, get in contact with the computer expert of the university where your lecture is to be held some weeks beforehand. Be aware that there may be many problems in compatability and in the configuration of the computers used.

Appendix

Publishing the Results

by Timothy Doherty

Apart from research, one of the foremost concerns of a scientist in any field is presenting the results of his or her work to the scientific community for scrutiny and future use. This is usually done through publication in a scientific journal or monograph. The use of photographic material – although relatively rare in theological publications –, presents few problems other than raising costs: one just sends a print or – more recently – a slide to the publishers and they take care of all the rest.

This method is no longer directly possible with the results of image manipulations done with CATT. Once scanned (digitalized) and changed with the methods described in the proceeding chapters of this book, the image no longer exists on a film negative or a slide and can therefore not be exposed on photographic paper and screened for printing using conventional equipment. But publishing your data may be very important, especially to convince sceptical colleagues of your results and consequent readings of hitherto ambiguous or undecipherable passages.

At present there are three methods we would suggest for getting your images into a printable form: 1.) your publisher can work with graphical image files (tiffs, etc.); 2.) you can have a slide made; 3.) you can provide the publisher with offset film material as needed.

Before we proceed to a detailed description of these possibilities, we want to offer one word of caution:

! *Never, under any circumstances* should you send the publisher a print from a laser printer for publication, be it 300 dpi, 600 dpi or whatever. The results in printing will be atrocious and may end up in discrediting your work. *Never* let any publisher or DTP-operator talk you into doing so; these are usually individuals who are uninformed of the possibilties of achieving excellent quality, as with all the pictures in the proceeding chapters of this book. Use laser prints only to inform the publishers as to the general size and shape of the images – tell them *not* to use them for printing! (See the examples on p. 155.)

1. Sending in an Image File

Surely the easiest and most elegant way for you to publish your images is to have a publisher who knows what to do with a digital image file. All you have to do is to file the final stage of your work – or whatever you choose – on a diskette and to send it to the publishers.

Experience shows however that presently most publishers don't even know what an image file is and certainly don't know what to do with one. The large publishing houses well known to theologians and philologists are no exception. In fact, most publishers react very strangely when told that the images one wants to publish exist only as bits and bytes in the computer and not physically on film. Their remarks and recommendations are often equally as strange. Remember, don't send them a laser print for publication, even if they tell you to (see the caution paragraph above and the examples on p. 155).

The CATT user is therefore usually left on his or her own to solve the problems. The following sections offer two workable solutions.

2. Making a Slide

A new technology makes it possible to have a normal film slide (dia positive) made from an image file. To find a company in you area which can do this, contact a typesetting firm, a lithograph company, a graphic design studio, or a DTP-studio in your city and ask them where this can be done. Make sure you tell them you want a slide developed and not an offset film. You may have to call a few firms or even a firm in the next larger city to get the required information. The slides can usually be made in a few days time and can be sent as is to the publishers.

A pleasant side effect of making slides is that you can have them exposed on normal photo paper for your personal use and you can use the slides for lectures. A possible drawback is that making slides is often a bit expensive, although prices vary and may sink drastically per slide when multiple slides are made in a single order.

3. Making an Offset Film

The most complicated and unpleasant way to prepare your images for printing is to directly have the final offset film made which will be used at the printers. This will most certainly involve many telephone calls with and letters to the editor at your publishers, who will probably not understand what you want or why it's necessary. This should be considered as a last ditch effort when your publisher has no idea what a digital image file is and you can't have a slide made.

It should be stated here that the chances of something going wrong along the way are not minimal, especially if you have no professional experience in offset printing.

Three facts must be established before you can actually have the film made: 1.) the exact size the picture will have in the publication; 2.) the type of film to be used; 3.) the screen frequency. Getting the necessary information is the only real problem. Once you have the information, the rest is relatively easy. The authors of this book have been through all this a number of times and can describe some of the pitfalls which may occur.

The first step is to contact your publisher and find out which editor is responsible for your book or journal. This does not mean the scientific coordinator named as „editor" in the publication, but the actual employee at the publishing house.

As a rule, editors deal mainly with authors and the contents of books and don't have much to do with the actual physical production and consequently don't know very much about it. Aside from the fact that the editor will certainly be very surprised by your questions, he or she will probably have to refer you to the production manager responsible for your publication. Even the production manager may have to ask the printers for details and will probably be very suspicious as to why you want to know all this, etc. You will surely repeatedly be asked, why you can't just send in a glossy print or negative, and you will have to repeatedly impress on them that your image exists only in the computer. All of this may take some time.

! If the editor just gives you the information offhand, make sure he or she really *knows* what he or she says and doesn't just *think* it – bad experiences have made us careful.

The Size

The size your image will have in the publication should be the one question your editor will be able to answer without refering to his or her colleagues. But this is often decided on shortly before printing, when the typesetting and proofing is finished and the layout (makeup) is being done. With a little coaxing, you may get a photo plate for yourself and get the size information earlier.

The Type of Film

The actual type of film the printers will need is not really the question at hand – graphic arts film will be used. The real question is how the image should be exposed on the film. There are two criteria which can in turn be combined, giving four possibilities. The two criteria are 1.) whether the image should be a positive or a negative and 2.) whether the film coating should be on the „front" side of the film („readable") or on the „back" side of the film („unreadable," „mirrored").

The most common form is *positive-unreadable*, but this can vary, depending on how the printers handle the plates. If the positive/negative aspect is wrong, the printers will usually be able to transfer it to what they need, but if the coating is on the wrong „side" of the film, you image can be badly blurred.

The Screen Frequency

Images are not printed as a series of gray levels, as you see on your computer screen. The image is reduced to a pattern of variably sized black dots with a constant distance between their centers. This distance is called the „screen frequency." If you are not familiar with this technique, examine some black and white photographs in a normal newspaper and in a good magazine with a magnifying glass. You will see that the centers of the dots in the newspaper picture are farther apart than those of the magazine picture. The screen frequency of the newspaper picture is probably about 80 lpi (= 30 lpc) and the magazine picture about 120 lpi (= 48 lpc). The screen frequency the printers need depends mainly on the quality of the paper used, but also on the type of printing plate and machine.

Using the optimal screen frequency is very important. If the frequency is too coarse, you will forfeit valuable quality and detail (see the example on p. 156). If the frequency is too fine, small dots may „break away," i. e. they will not be printed, and larger dots may clot, rendering your image unusable (see the example on p. 156). The screen frequency you will need will probably be between 120 lpi and 150 lpi. 130 lpi is most probable for normal paper (as in this book), and 150 lpi for high quality glossy art paper.

! Don't confuse *dpi* (dots per inch) with *lpi* (lines per inch). *Dpi* is the *resolution* of your image, i. e. the amount of pixels (picture elements) used to make up the image in the image file itself. *Lpi* is the dimension used for the *screen frequency* when putting the image on film by the Linotype machine and should only be set by the DTP-operator. *Dpi* and *lpi* do not have any direct correlation as far as this book is concerned.

To make everything theoretically easier, you can use the checklist on page 157. Send a photocopy to your publishers after having spoken with them.

Making the Film

Once you have all the necessary information, you have to use the *sizing* command of your image processing software to bring your image to the correct size.

! When changing the size, only experts should attempt to change the resolution (dpi). Images usually only need about 210 dpi when being put on film, but changing the resolution may have adverse effects which cannot be explained in detail here. Don't forget: *dpi* has nothing to do with *lpi* (see above).

The next step is similar to what we described above for having a slide made. You have to find a DTP-studio and tell them what you need. Tell them you want to give them a digital image film (tiff, pcx, etc.) and need an offset film with the specifications given to you by the publishers. Make sure the DTP-operators don't try to make any

„corrections“ in the image (calibrations, etc.) and that they really use the screen frequency you specify.

! Don't let the DTP-operators try to persuade you to let them use the highest resolution possible (150–160 lpi): this will be wonderful on the film, but may be unprintable (see the proceeding section).

Once you have the film, be careful with it: don't let it get bent or scratched.

If you have any problems with the methods described in this appendix, feel free to write to the authors of this book for assistance.

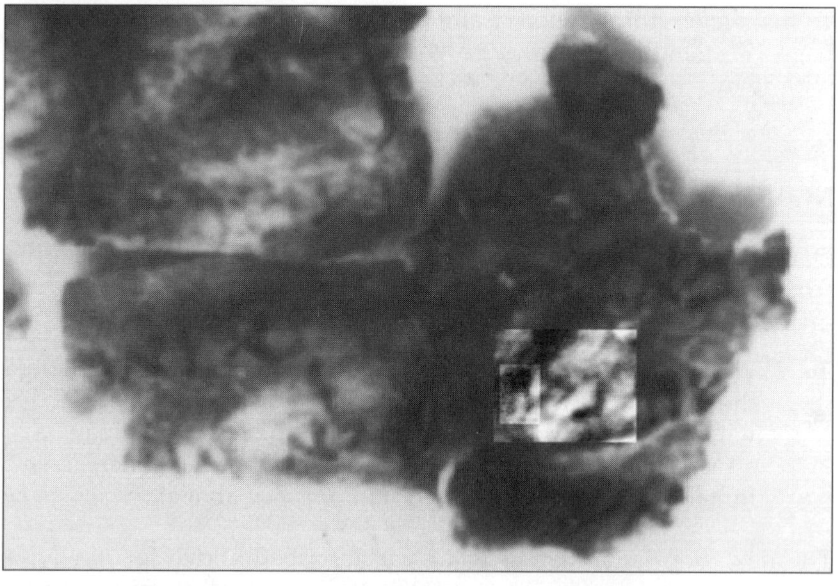

This image will be used on the following pages to demonstrate what may happen to your image if the instructions given above for printing are not followed. This is how the image should look.

PAM 41719: Courtesy of the IAA

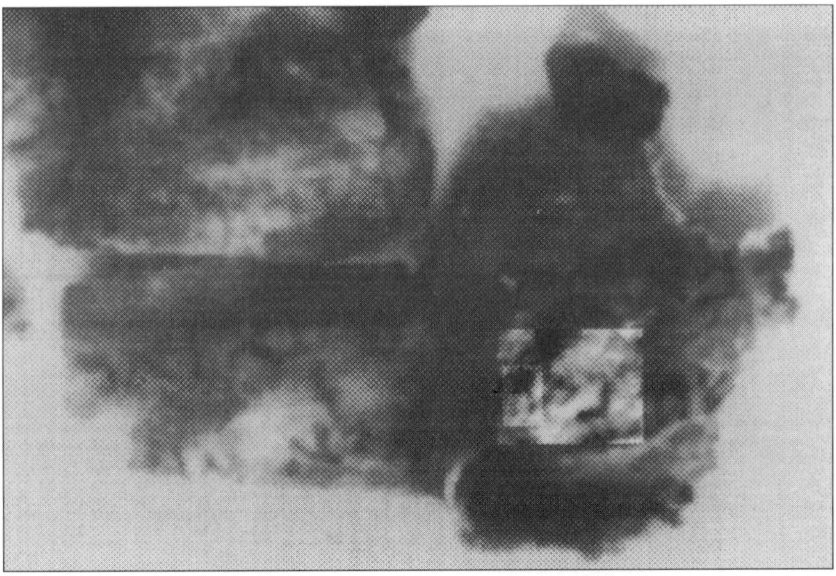

Two examples of how your image will probably appear in print if you send the publishers prints from a laser printer.

PAM 41719: Courtesy of the IAA

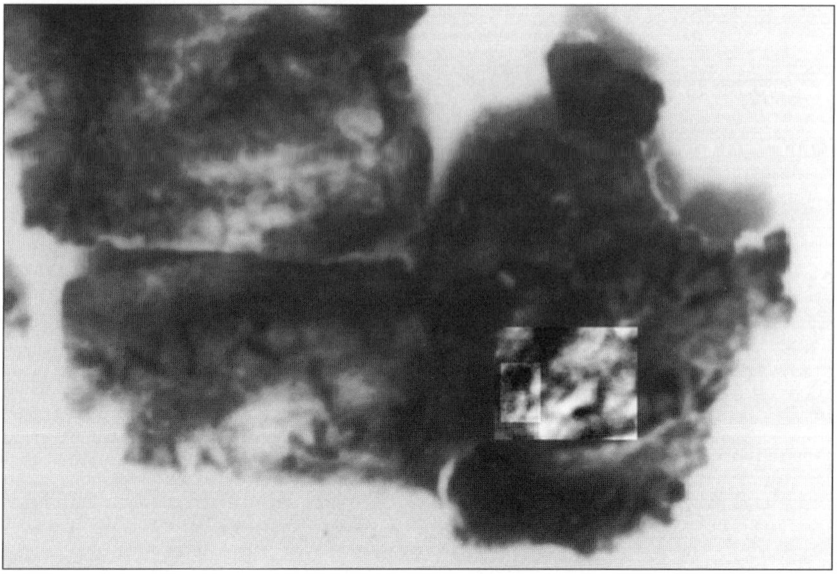

Example of an image with a screen frequency too high (fine) for the paper.

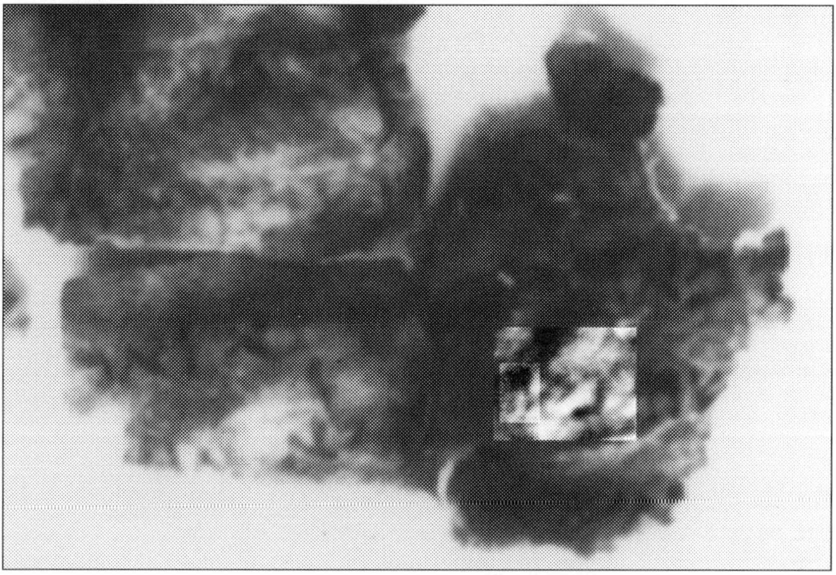

Example of an image with a screen frequency lower (coarser) than necessary for printing.

PAM 41719: Courtesy of the IAA

To the publishers:

Dear Sirs,

The pictures I plan to publish in your publication cannot be delivered to you as normal photographs since they only exist as digitilized computer graphics files. As we have disussed, I will send you an offset film for the printers. Please provide me with the following information from your production department or your printers:

1.) picture size (width × height)

1. ________ × ________ 2. ________ × ________

3. ________ × ________ 4. ________ × ________

5. ________ × ________ 6. ________ × ________

7. ________ × ________ 8. ________ × ________

9. ________ × ________ 10. ________ × ________

2.) film exposure

☐ positive ☐ negative

☐ readable ☐ unreadable/mirrored

3.) screen frequency

________ lpi (line per inch)

or

________ lpc (metric – line per centimeter)

Index of selected items